Where do I go from here?

Where do I go from here?

GEORGE BEST
AND
GRAEME WRIGHT

Queen Anne Press
Macdonald & Co
London and Sydney

First published in 1981 by Queen Anne Press, a division of
Macdonald & Co (Publishers) Ltd, Holywell House,
Worship Street, London EC2A 2EN

ISBN 0362 00556 7

Photoset by Cylinder Typesetting Ltd, London

Printed in Great Britain by Hazell, Watson & Viney, Aylesbury, Bucks

Acknowledgments

The authors thank the following for permission to quote: Adrian Henri and Jonathan Cape Ltd for the poem 'Red Card' from the anthology *From the Loveless Motel*; Geoffrey Green and Hodder and Stoughton for extracts from *There's Only One United*; Denis Law and Queen Anne Press for an extract from *Denis Law. An Autobiography*; Arthur Hopcroft and Collins for extracts from *The Football Man*; Souvenir Press for an extract from *The International Football Book, No. 2*; Sir Matt Busby and Weidenfeld and Nicolson for an extract from *Soccer at the Top*; *The Times* for the match reports of Benfica v Manchester United (1966 and 1968) and Real Madrid v Manchester United (1968) by Geoffrey Green; the *Daily Mirror* for the report of Chelsea v Manchester United (1964) by Ken Jones; *The Observer* for the report of West Ham United v Manchester United (1967) by Bob Ferrier; the *Irish News*, Belfast for the report of Northern Ireland v Scotland (1967); *The Guardian* for the report of Manchester United v Leeds United (1970) by Eric Todd; the *Los Angeles Times* for the report of LA Aztecs v NY Cosmos (1977) by Shav Glick.

Grateful thanks are also due to the *Manchester Evening News*, David Meek, and the North American Soccer League for their willing cooperation.

Dedicated to the memory of my mother,
and to the future of my son Calum.
With special thanks to my wife Angela
for her love and understanding.

Right from the off,
straight into your penalty area
a quick one-two and it was all over
bar the shouting. Easy
Easy sang the terraces.
Half-time: I've given you a hundred per cent
and more. Two down, and I've got it all
to do again.

At the end of the day
the lap of honour. Your ribbons
round the Cup. I am
sick as a parrot. I am
over the moon you tell the cameras,
the waiting millions.
Back home I walk
alone.

ADRIAN HENRI, *Red Card*

Introduction

Manchester United 4, Benfica 1; 29 May 1968

Seven magic minutes that gave Manchester United the Cup

from Geoffrey Green, Football Correspondent

At last Manchester United have climbed their Everest and after 11 years of trial and effort their dreams have come true. Last night they became the first English club to win the European Cup when they beat Benfica, of Lisbon, the holders of '61 and '62, and so followed the break-through achieved last year by Celtic against Internazionale-Milan.

So the crown sits on the heads of the first English club to enter this competition, seeing its wide horizons and the possibility of it on a world scale. And having now won, with a dramatic burst of seven minutes in the first half of extra-time, they have helped to beat back the Latin domination that for so long had taken Continental football by the throat.

Next Manchester United will challenge Estudiantes, of Argentina, for the World Club Championship next season, a season that will see both United and City of Manchester treading the paths of Europe. What rivalry that will engender in the year to come.

There have been many occasions of Wembley to remember, but few, apart perhaps from the final of the World Cup itself and the Stanley Matthews epic of 1953, to equal last night. Out of nothing eventually there grew a dramatic climax. The first half was episodic and a busy dullness as a spate of ruthless tackling by the Portuguese defence and a symphony of whistling by the Italian referee broke the match into a thousand pieces.

A waiter might well have dropped a tray of glasses, such was the clatter, the crash and the bang of it all, with football secondary and both teams clearly out of humour with each other and with officialdom. Yet this merely proved to be the crucible. Out of the fire and the cruelty there finally lived something to remember.

It came to a boil in extra-time as Manchester United, once heading for victory but robbed of their prize 10 minutes from the end of normal time,

Match report reproduced from *The Times* by permission.

suddenly found a fresh wind that took them home in full sail. In a magical spell of seven minutes Best, Kidd and then Charlton struck like cobras to add to the goal which Charlton had first glanced in with his head to give them the lead soon after the change of ends of the first half.

In those moments the world shifted on its axis and became a place for men with steady limbs and firm hearts. Life frequently ends things with a whimper rather than a bang. When for so long it had been a whimper now we actually did end with an explosion.

For so long there were butterflies at the pit of the myriad stomachs and suddenly it was all over. The barber shop critic, that powerful thinker, who said that United would win in extra-time, was indeed proved to the hilt and I shall willingly submit to a shave from his razor.

When the untidy, often ugly, baggage of that opening half had been brushed out of the way the match at last began to find its stature as the blue shirts of Manchester United finally found rhythm, pattern and purpose.

Earlier Sadler, put clean through by Kidd, had shot past the Benfica post to miss a dolly. At this level it was equivalent to dropping Sobers in the slips. One cannot afford to do that and it seemed that United could yet pay the price, for Eusebio was constantly prowling like a caged, hungry animal, threatening danger, which he showed after only 10 minutes from the kick-off when he almost splintered Stepney's crossbar with a thunderbolt from 20 yards.

Yet when Dunne and Sadler worked a movement down the left and over came Sadler's cross for Charlton, rising on spring heels, to glide the ball home off his thinning head, it seemed that United were heading for their long awaited glory.

It should have been theirs, too, without the need of extra-time had not Sadler again given Henrique the chance to save an open goal with his feet after Best had mesmerised and opened the defence with a dazzling dribble and a shot which the goalkeeper could only partially parry.

Then there was Best himself, dancing clear of everyone and trying to dribble past the goalkeeper with a delicate touch only to be robbed at the last inch. So when all this had come and gone and United had failed to drive in their nails, there came the crux of the battle. With 10 minutes left the giant Torres rose like some Eiffel Tower to a diagonal cross to the right and head the ball square for Graça to crack in the equalizer.

How United survived those last 10 minutes of normal time only Stepney, under the crossbar, may be able to tell. But I doubt if even he knew much about two saves – both of instant reflex action which somehow or other kept out scorching shots from Eusebio in the last three minutes before the whistle as Eusebio went through the United defence like a knife through butter. In my book United owe Stepney a debt this night for those two remarkable parries when all seemed lost.

So out of a gathering darkness, as Benfica seemed to gather new strength and a new poise, United rose. Once more as in Spain in their return leg with Real Madrid they fell back on their morale and unconquerable spirit.

Again it made giants of men who seemed to have given their last ounce of strength as they searched for the final yard to the summit. The scene before the beginning of extra-time resembled some battlefield as the players of both sides fell back upon the velvet surface of Wembley seemingly exhausted, their limbs taut with cramp and their last fibres of strength apparently gone.

But suddenly there came the miracle. Within seven minutes of the beginning of extra-time United found their Camelot. First Kidd nodded backwards a long clearance from Stepney from one end; at the other suddenly the dark-haired Best had wriggled his way like some will-o'-the-wisp past two tackles, drawn the goalkeeper in close to him as does the matador draw in the bull.

With a delicate, elusive swerve Best was past Henrique and he drove in the knife coldly and clinically. Almost at once Charlton's corner from the left was headed by Kidd to bring a brilliant save from Henrique, but the young Manchester man was alert to his duty. On his nineteenth birthday he rose like a salmon once more at the second attempt to nod in the rebound.

That was 3-1 and hardly had the cheering died than Kidd and Charlton worked another smooth movement down the right. Over came Kidd's cross and Charlton, somehow, with a wonderful, glancing flick, turned the ball into the far top corner for 4-1.

That was it and as the teams changed over once more for the second bit of that extra-time Wembley once more resembled a battlefield as the players were given their last ministrations. It was over, apart from one more remarkable save by Stepney, left-handed, low down at point-blank range from Eusebio. No wonder at the end Matt Busby said: 'I am the proudest man in England tonight.'

So an emotional night reached its climax. The struggle itself was crystallized with a duel at one end between the giant Torres and the black panther Eusebio against Foulkes and Stiles. The fact that neither, in the end, scored left the United men as the victors, though somehow I would have dearly wished a goal from Eusebio before the end as a tribute to his marvellous power and poetic movement.

At the other end it was the elusive Best, being chopped, harried and bruised from start to finish as he tried to bring his artistry to full flower. But soon, trying to dominate his ruthless opponents, he began to play with a kind of fury which overstretched itself as he attempted to beat the hordes of Benfica off his own bat.

Perhaps the greatest eye-opener of the struggle was Aston at outside-left. Without any flowery touches, time after time he cut the right flank of the Portuguese defence open by sheer, uncomplicated speed. It was simple enough. He merely pushed the ball past Adolfo and showed his heels to the Portuguese. Long before the end the packed stadium was chanting his name. Certainly this will be a night for him to remember among the many others.

At the back Dunne was also masterly, as he covered every stray opening that presented itself at the rear of the faithful Foulkes and the abrasive Stiles, who had a face-to-face duel with Eusebio.

Crerand, too, was calmly masterful as he ranged the central areas at the side of Charlton. But I suppose in the end this could be said to have been Charlton's night. With two goals off his own bat it was he who went at last to collect the giant European trophy as the stadium rocked with joyful noise.

Behind him, weary, but happy, straggled his side and when the moment for the lap of honour arrived, Charlton himself was too tired to carry the giant Cup around the stadium. He handed it over to his lieutenants and slowly trotted at the rear, no doubt thinking of all the years that had gone to make up this moment of glory.

So ended a dramatic night, when the banners waved and turned this great stadium at Wembley into a scene of carnival.

Manchester United: Stepney; Brennan, Dunne; Crerand, Foulkes, Stiles; Best, Kidd, Charlton, Sadler, Aston.
Benfica: Henrique; Adolfo, Humberto, Jacinto, Cruz; Graça, Coluna, Augusto; Torres, Eusebio, Simoes.

Life rarely works out the way you plan it. I was going to score a hat-trick that night and take Wembley by storm. I had it all worked out. Instead, 'chopped, harried and bruised', I had to settle for a single goal. But what an important goal! There are still times when I close my eyes and see the ball going towards the goal and I'm sure it's going wide. Even watching video re-runs of the game I have my doubts. But go in it did and from that treasured moment the European Cup was ours. Afterwards there would be that long, tired, happy climb up those Wembley steps to collect the Cup and our winners' medals, the lap of honour, the interviews and the celebration party at the Savoy Hotel. But for me that goal was the European Cup final. I recall little else.

Then, sitting amidst the pandemonium of the dressing-room where tears flowed as freely as the champagne, came the anti-climax. I felt it after every game; always had. It was as if I'd had my stage taken away and been deprived of my audience – for all that tonight's performance had been extended and there was a standing ovation at the end of the act. Now I could only sit and wait for the high. Not the kind that comes from stuffing something up your nose or into a vein. A self-stimulated high that comes to many artists after a performance. For me, so in love with football, it was enough to have been out there playing to spark the fire. And the more important the occasion, the greater the high.

But this night was different. The adrenalin slowed and I could feel myself no longer part of the laughter and the tears. I was there but I didn't belong. All around me were men and women for whom this was the greatest night of their lives; the climax of all the years of planning, tragedy, disappointment and determination. It should have been that for me. Instead, although I was not to know it at the time, it was the beginning of the end.

Chapter 1

A damp Friday afternoon in February. Cars crawl and people hurry through the Edinburgh mist, the lights along Princes Street draw shoppers to the warmth of stores, buses fill with people going home, going somewhere. Me, I stand at my hotel window looking out; gazing at the figures far below. Simply filling time with forty-eight hours to kill before Sunday's Cup game against Ayr United. Looking out of the window or watching television, not for the programmes but for the company of the voices. The painter or the writer might profit from the time spent studying people in the street. Other people are what they work with. I just wanted to be out there among them; to be one of them.

It could never be; not in Britain. The moment I walked through the hotel door it was like running the gauntlet. A pen and piece of paper would be thrust into my hand; some stranger would want to talk; another to shake my hand; others to smile, stare, insult, wave. How could I join those people in the bus queues when I'd spent my adult life crossing to the other side of the street to avoid them? So I stayed in my room until, as the night drew in, the telephone brought the invitations, the drinks and the company that was preferable to the solitude. Everybody, it seemed, was happy to drink with George Best, and who was I to disappoint them? It didn't take too many drinks to become the Georgie Best they wanted to drink with.

The other George Best wouldn't have interested them much. There aren't too many people willing to spend their afternoons in an overheated hotel room watching second-class racing with yesterday's superstar. I don't know that I found it so easy myself. I wanted to lead a normal life, not merely exist. My life had consisted of doing something to the full or not doing it at all. Tomorrow was the next day: when the match reports were read, or the hangover came on, or the girl got dressed and went home to bed. Today was the day I played the game to please the millions – and how they loved it! Tomorrow was for the nine-to-five man who sweated one third of his day away for his wife and kids and read about Georgie Best, superstar, to relieve the boredom. He didn't want to read about some lonely mixed-up Irishman who couldn't come to terms with what he wanted from life. That might have been too much like his own life and he didn't need reminding of that. What was it they said when Wyatt Earp, an old man thinking about dying, began to tell of Tombstone and the gunfight at the OK Corral; how it really was? 'To hell with the truth; print the legend.' That's how it had been over more than a decade for Georgie Best. People wanted to read about the legend.

Or did they? The newspapers rarely gave them the chance to forget the old stories; as I was soon to discover yet again. And once more I would learn to my cost that you should never trust the media. What they have they use to their own advantage. Like the Scandinavian magazine I'd been doing a story with earlier in the week. Usual thing; a reporter and a photographer; the photographer clicking his way through a couple of rolls of film while I try to concentrate on the same boring routine of questions and answers. This particular day, though, things had gone wrong from the start. The reporter had made a muddle of the arrangements, and when we finally met up I was having a few, quiet, after-training lagers with several of the Hibs lads in a bar near the North British, my temporary home. Nothing heavy; just taking it easy, talking and taking the mickey out of everyone and everything the way most players do. But this reporter; he's starting to get restless because I'm feeling loose and not in such a hurry as he is. Maybe I should have been. He was paying for the story. But it was early, and I had a whole afternoon and evening in front of me with nothing definite to do. I saw no reason to hurry. In the end, he got so unpleasant that I gave him back his cheque and told him to stuff the interview. I didn't want to do it.

They soon got their own back, though. Friday night in the hotel bar eased into Saturday; Saturday became Saturday night. And on Saturday night, following the rugby international between Scotland and France, there was one almighty party going on in the North British. Players, fans, Frenchmen, Scots; it was bedlam, but it was better than sitting in my room on my own. The drinks were coming fast and furious. Someone introduced me to Jean-Pierre Rives, the French captain, and we talked and drank; or rather I did the drinking. He'd had enough. The main difference, though, was that he'd played his game and I still had mine to play the next day. Except that I didn't. When Tom Hart, the Hibs chairman, came by for me on Sunday I was out like a light; sleeping off a week's misery and as many days' drinking. It had happened before; I'd been on a three-day binge in Manchester earlier in the season and missed Hibs' game at Morton. On that occasion they'd been terrific and tried to cover up for me, despite the fact that the moment I made my peace I was back in the car and heading down to Manchester again. This time I'd gone too far once too many times. I was told to pack my bags and get back to London. Hibs, struggling in the Scottish Premier Division, no longer needed me. Why pay two and a half thousand pounds a game to a drunk? I was out, and on Sunday afternoon, while Hibs beat Ayr 2-0 in the fourth round of the Scottish Cup, I flew back to London to an angry, uncertain, but understanding wife.

On Monday the press had a field day: they put our flat in Putney under siege from the early hours, camped on the stairs, drank the neighbours' milk, and rang the doorbell incessantly until the door was opened and some words, however few, were spoken. Grown men sprawled in their cars for hours in case we left the flat. And somewhere, in Stockholm, Copenhagen or wherever he was, that photographer went through his rolls of film and found a shot of George Best, looking as if he's falling asleep in the middle of a really mad drinking session. You need only get the angle right, make sure the glasses on the table are in shot, crop the picture a bit if necessary, and you can flog it around the world. World exclusive pictures of George Best on the binge that ended his career with Hibernian. And conveniently forget to say the photo was taken in advance of the event. Who cares?

Seemingly a great number of people cared about George Best, judging from the letters, cards and telegrams that follow my more publicised misdemeanours. That Monday, the messages were approaching a hundred by the end of the day. Religious organisations with the right intentions and the wrong solutions; my Dad in Belfast, naturally deeply concerned; former footballers with their answers to their own drink problems; fans saying 'you're still the greatest'; Fulham offering training facilities if I wanted them. And among them all a telegram saying 'We think we can help you', unsigned but giving a London phone number. There was something about it; the way it came during the first real lull in the day as Angela and I were sitting there, not going over and over why I'd made a mess of everything again but enjoying a moment of peace and togetherness without the phone ringing or the press banging on the door. Even the dog was all barked out.

Angela opened the envelope, and for the first time that day her voice had some lift in it.

'What do you think?' she asked after reading it aloud.

I looked at her, non-committal. She looked so eager and at the same time desperate. There'd been other times like this; times she'd sworn she'd taken enough; and each time she'd given me another chance.

'Oh, come on, Bestie', she cried. 'I'm going to call them. At least see who they are.'

'They' were an organisation called Conservation of Manpower; run by a very helpful, sympathetic guy called Boris Serebro in St Swithin's Lane in the heart of the City. Angela made an appointment and the next day we went along. No hassle. It was almost too easy; as if fate had provided the perfect answer. Except, of course, it wouldn't be easy because solving my problem was ultimately in my own hands. The Conservation of Manpower could only help. They could provide Antibuse pills to make my system react against alcohol; they could give me regular oxygen treatment to alleviate the pressure that built up in my head and set off the depressions that led to the drinking bouts; and they listened whenever Angela or I needed to talk to them.

In some ways, they were as important to Angela as they were to me. Once I'd come to terms with taking the pills every day – I usually have to be pushed into taking even vitamins or aspirin – then at least I knew I couldn't drink. And I thought this would give Angela the opportunity to unwind. Instead, as I began to have more confidence in the treatment, she grew more and more miserable and depressed. When I mentioned this at the clinic one day, Boris Serebro smiled softly and nodded in agreement.

'We've seen it happen so many times', he explained. 'The wife has to hold all the tension inside her over the years, just to keep life going as normally as possible. The fear and the hurt all become part of her life. You think you're on the way to stopping drinking and you expect Angela to lose those barriers she's had to build up to protect herself. It may take her as long as it takes you. It depends whether or not you abuse her trust in you. But bring her in; get her to come and talk to me one day. It'll help her to know why she feels the way she does.'

It was only then that I began to realise just how deeply I was hurting her by these sudden drinking bouts that would, virtually without warning, completely disrupt our life. Her health was suffering far more than mine had ever done. Indeed, as I learnt later, her own doctor in America could tell when I was drinking heavily from how ill she looked. Even in the months to come there would be days of apprehension when she knew I'd gone out without first taking the Antibuse pill. I suppose it was thoughtless and inconsiderate; but there would be days when I'd want to go without the pills. Not so that I could go off and drink, but because I wanted to beat this thing on my own. I needed help, I knew that, but pride, pig-headedness or determination made me want to achieve it without being totally dependent on something. It was a risk; rather like beating two defenders and taking the ball up to a third instead of passing to a team-mate. There was a chance of success, a challenge, and if it came off the satisfaction would be all the greater.

The clinic had something else going for it, too. Next door was one of the best cake and pastry shops I've ever seen, and when it comes to cream cakes I consider myself something of a connoisseur. Right from the days as a kid in Manchester when I was madly in love with a girl called Maria. We used to babysit for relations of hers who owned a bakery and cake shop and lived above it. I think that's what started me off; on the cream cakes as well. Romantic evenings in front of the telly became mini-training runs up and down the stairs gathering and gorging cream cakes. It must have done wonders for her spots – and her figure – but I don't remember that. I was fifteen and so much in love. The age when you're in and out of love every week: a girl on the bus (I was into bus queues in those days) or the blonde in the typing pool at the Manchester Ship Canal Company where I worked when I first joined United. They were all older than me of course; older women and vastly experienced; probably all of eighteen or nineteen. Not that I ever talked to them. Not that I talked to many people in those days. My accent was so broad that everything I said had to be repeated three or four times before I was understood. I found it easier to say nothing.

Talking to the doctor at the clinic, however, set me to thinking again about writing a book; setting out my story as I saw it. Everyone else had had their say, it seemed. I'd tried before, several times in the past few years. I even had a publisher. But the writing didn't come as easily as I'd thought. Having signed my name to countless newspaper articles hadn't helped, I suppose. Talking to someone who converts the spoken word to written word is not the same as sitting

18

there yourself, pen in hand, trying to fill the space between the blue lines. I'd known times when my head was full of ideas which I'd jot down on a pad. They'd be useful once I got going, but the first problem was making a start. I'd rarely written letters; even when I was living in England and Angela was in the States I'd always phoned. Several times a day more often than not. I tried talking into a tape, but it ended up more Angela talking to me with Dallas, our Alsatian, growling in the background. Even when I did get going I found I tended to digress a lot.

By the following week I had another good reason for wanting to start work on a book. Tom Hart was willing to take me back at Hibs provided I kept up with the treatment and, with Angela, lived in Edinburgh for the rest of the season. They'd help us find a flat. It was a wonderful, generous offer; a chance to get fully fit, train regularly, and play. But it also meant being in a new city with most afternoons free – and afternoons can be dangerous. Working on a book would occupy my time, and it would also enable me to look back over my life – at the good and bad times – and perhaps discover what, if anything, was making me go off on these destructive binges.

So it was that the beginning of March 1980 saw the return of Georgie Best to Easter Road. There wasn't the same blast of publicity that followed my departure, but that didn't particularly trouble anyone. And to ease the pressure a little, Hibs provided me with an alias and moved me temporarily to the other end of Edinburgh's Princes Street, into the Caledonian Hotel. Angela and I became Mr and Mrs Smith, which wasn't always easy to remember. There was one night – Angela was filming in Manchester – when the desk rang through to say that Mrs Smith was on the phone, only for me to reply that I knew no Mrs Smith and to say I wasn't in. Anyway, as I moved about the hotel everyone seemed genuinely glad I was back. I still had to run the autograph gauntlet, but that was little price to pay for a second chance. And I was determined no-one at Hibs would regret giving it to me. One thing I'd come to realise. It didn't matter from which end of Princes Street I was looking, the views were similar. Except that from the Caledonian end it was sober so long as I kept taking the pills.

Chapter 2

Chelsea's record wrecked – even 'Doc' admits George was Best

by Ken Jones

At the end they stood and acclaimed him. They gave him their hearts because he had won them with every bewitching swerve, every flick of his magic feet. It was that way at Stamford Bridge last night. A night that belonged to a bundle of brilliance called George Best.

Not yet nineteen, only a year in the Football League, Best plays for Ireland against England in Belfast on Saturday. And the boy from Belfast showed 60,769 fans at Stamford Bridge why he seems destined to become one of the great wingers of our time.

Chelsea manager Tommy Docherty swallowed the bitter pill of the season's first defeat and described Best with one word . . . 'Fantastic'.

England fullback Ken Shellito, who played Best with calm despite the torture, raced to him at the end to acclaim his skill. Barry Bridges and John Hollins waited to clap eager hands on Best's back.

Head down on his chest, the little Irishman shambled into the tunnel. It was over. But who will forget it? Best's brilliance, his devastating application of touchline skill, revived memories of Stan Matthews and Garrincha. It was the top icing to a top quality United performance.

Their sometimes brittle skill blossomed into full power as they held Chelsea's ferocious start and then hit them with everything at their command. They tight-marked Chelsea schemer Terry Venables and forced him deeper and deeper until the only pass he could make was the long ball that was eaten up by Billy Foulkes and Nobby Stiles. They cut the heart out of Chelsea's momentum by marking the men who [in previous matches] had been moving so devastatingly into dangerous positions.

In the thirty-second minute Best had United in front with a goal that was more a credit to his own determination than to what looked a bad mistake by McCreadie. Chelsea were caught flat-footed coming out for a corner.

Match report reproduced by courtesy of the *Daily Mirror*.

Denis Law headed on a Pat Crerand pass, and as McCreadie tried to turn it back to Bonetti, Best nipped in to cut the ball home.

United survived thundering Chelsea pressure early in the second half . . . then Bobby Charlton hit the bar with a header and centre-forward Herd missed a sitter from six yards.

It looked as though stamina might have settled it then. But United got the goal they wanted and it was a goal made again by the brilliance of Best. He dummied clear of a tackle, chipped the ball into the goalmouth, and Law leapt to head home as the ball came off Bonetti's fingers.

Chelsea: Bonetti; Shellito, McCreadie; Hollins, Hinton, Harris; Murray, Tambling, Bridges, Venables, Houseman.
Manchester United: P. Dunne; Brennan, A. Dunne; Crerand, Foulkes, Stiles; Connelly, Charlton, Herd, Law, Best.

The more I wonder when it all began, the more I keep coming back to that game. Not so much the game, perhaps, but the morning after. Waking up to find my name plastered over every London newspaper. I'd had notices before, but there was something about this game. It had aroused so much interest. I suppose as much as anything it was the contrast between the two sides: Matt Busby's cultured performers giving a glittering demonstration of his philosophy of attacking football; Tommy Docherty's exciting young lions, the new glamour side taking the League Championship by storm with their blend of skill and hard running. Names like Bonetti, Barry Bridges, Terry Venables, Bobby Tambling and Ron Harris were on every West Londoner's lips. Yet we went to Stamford Bridge one Wednesday night, took them apart brilliantly, and ended the season as League champions on goal average from Leeds with Chelsea third. At home we beat the Londoners 4-0, and indeed the only League match we lost at Old Trafford that season was 0-1 to Leeds in December.

Perhaps, too, I remember that particular match because I was able to savour it on my own: have breakfast in my hotel room, spread out all the papers, and relive those moments when everything I tried seemed to come off. I was eighteen; acclaimed by the national press. And that was when it hit me. For the first time I realised what could happen and what was going to happen. I was part of a team that had magic. I wasn't stupid. Shy perhaps, and quiet. But my mind was quick, and I was street-wise. Growing up on a council estate in Belfast soon teaches you that. This team was going to be special and

I would become special with it. I could feel it. I couldn't express what I felt in words, not then, and even if I'd wanted to there was no-one to talk to. Dave Sadler, my room-mate, and the others were already on their way back to Manchester. I was still in London because I was flying home to Belfast later in the day for the Northern Ireland game on Saturday against England.

I poured myself another cup of tea and walked over to the window. We were staying in the President, just off Russell Square, and directly opposite my room there's a small hotel and some apartments: windows to look in and watch the people. In one of them I spot these two blonde girls, and I'm sure they are looking at me. I'm feeling so good that morning that I'm brave enough to chance a wave; and sure enough one of them waves back. I could hardly believe it. I gave her a smile and she and her friend laughed. So I looked about the room, found the biggest piece of paper there – a blotter off the desk – and, having written down the room number in large figures, held it up to the window. The phone rang before I'd replaced the blotter! The girl was Swedish, in London with her friend for a week on holiday. Great, I said. I'm just having some breakfast. Why don't you come over and have some with me? She laughed – didn't giggle – and said she would.

I couldn't believe it. If anyone had said to me, plan your two perfect days, I wouldn't have thought of anything better. Beating one of the best sides in England; my play praised in all the papers; and now this beautiful Swedish girl apparently coming up to my room. I still didn't know if she was serious, but she was. And the fact that she didn't know who I was, in the light of experiences to come, makes the memory all that nicer. Mind you, when she began looking at the strategically placed newspapers lying all over the bed she soon realised.

Before that game, life – I think – was fairly normal for a young lad at a famous football club. Except, of course, that I was already a regular in the first team, whereas most of the lads I'd come to know since first joining United at fifteen were playing for the Reserves in the Central League or the A and B teams in the Lancashire League. Yet being at the top so soon made little immediate difference to my life. Money has never worried me and I can't recall, during my years at Old Trafford, ever going up and asking for a rise. I was just so happy to play. Nor did I find First Division football difficult. That's still my most vivid memory of my first team début against West Bromwich in 1963, only a year before that memorable Chelsea game.

How easy it was. I was able to go out there and do the same things I'd been doing since I was a kid. It all came so naturally to me. Whenever I got the ball I played it instinctively, just as I'd always done, so I never had time to worry about trying this or trying that.

Marking me they had Graham Williams, a Welsh international left-back with a reputation as a hard but fair defender, and after I'd taken a knock on the ankle in the first half the Boss switched me to the left wing in the second. I was to play many more times against Graham over the years, and I remember meeting him at some function a few years after he'd retired. He came up and said he wanted to look at me face to face. All he'd ever seen of me was my backside and the number on my shirt. Not a hundred per cent true, but a nice compliment from a likeable and talented fellow pro.

After the West Brom game it was back to the Reserves and even the Junior sides with my mates until Christmas. I was at home in Belfast on holiday when a telegram arrived telling me to report to Old Trafford urgently. That period around Christmas and New Year was often a bad time for injuries – not enough recovery time between games – and I thought they needed me to play in the Reserves. In fact, I was so sure that I had the cheek to insist they fly me back to Belfast afterwards so I'd have more time with my family.

My father was more confident.

'They'd only send you a telegram if they wanted you for the first team', he said, with that working-class instinct that automatically acknowledges the importance of a telegram.

'No way', I told him. 'I'll be lucky to get a game for the Reserves.'

So we took a little bet on it and my father won. After being thrashed 6-1 at Burnley on Boxing Day, United dropped both their wingers – Shay Brennan and Albert Quixall – and brought in Willie Anderson and myself for the return match at Old Trafford two days later. This time it was our turn for the goals. We won 5-1 and I scored my first League goal. That was a terrific thrill, just as it was going home to find my name in the local papers and my parents so quietly proud and pleased for me. After that I was a first team regular, and teams like Spurs, West Ham, Everton, and Liverpool would provide wonderful flowing matches in which I could happily exploit and develop my skills. The Spurs matches I remember with much affection. Even though that great side of the late fifties and early sixties was breaking up, they still had a terrific reputation for playing attacking football, and when the two of us met the atmosphere was tremendous. Two teams expressing themselves by attacking and entertaining. There was no crowd violence at those games either. The fans were too contented; bubbling with appreciation at what they were being offered on the field.

Looking back on them, these were some of the happiest days of my life. I was doing what I'd crossed the water to do: play football for one of the greatest clubs in the world. And now that I'd signed professional forms – in 1963, on my seventeenth birthday – I no longer had the hassle over outside employment which had bugged me ever since my arrival at Old Trafford. In those days, the Scottish and Irish Football Associations insisted that any youngster going to an English club before he was seventeen must sign as an amateur, work in an outside job and train part-time only. This was to stop the flow of talented kids from Scotland and Northern Ireland, but to me it was an anathema. It meant I couldn't train full-time with the other apprentices, and it only helped increase the feeling of insecurity which drove me more and more into my self-containment during those first uncertain months.

I'd already been turned down by Glentoran because I was too small, and when I first went across to Old Trafford I could never see why this important English club should have any interest in some five feet tall weakling who'd been rejected by a Belfast club. The apprentices looked so fit, and so big. Eric McMordie, with whom I'd travelled for the trial, was just like me, a skinny little Belfast kid with a flat broad accent, and when we looked at the lads we were going to train and play with, we were convinced there was no way we would make it. What we forgot, of course, was that between fifteen and seventeen you start growing taller and filling out, and the club made sure you were given the right food. But we were both homesick and naive: we hadn't even known the Lancashire cricket ground was called Old Trafford and had looked at the taxi driver as if he was crazy when he asked 'Which Old Trafford?' at the station. That night, in our digs at a Mrs Fullaway's in Chorlton, all we could think about was going home. Eric especially; he missed his family; he hated Manchester; and I felt if he went back, I wasn't going to stay there on my own.

The next morning, when Joe Armstrong, United's chief scout, came by for us, Eric told him we wanted to go home on the next boat. The look on Joe's face was worth remembering. He just couldn't believe it. Eric had been on United's books since he was thirteen, and now he was telling them he didn't want to stay even for a trial. Joe looked at me, and I kind of nodded. I didn't have Eric's cheek: it took me all my time to look at Joe.

The club were good about it, though, and that same day we caught the night ferry home to Belfast. When my mother came to the door the next morning she nearly had a heart attack. She was sure I'd been up to mischief in the short time I was away and that they'd sent me home. No-one could believe I'd simply packed my bag and come home; turned down the opportunity every kid in the country dreamed of. But my father understood, and he played it cool. Didn't try to push me into going back straight away but gave me time to think how stupid I might have been. Without my knowing it he spoke to the club and was assured by Mr Busby that United would still like me over there. Then, when he saw how much I regretted not making the most of my chances, he said he'd had a phone call from Mr Busby and that Manchester United wanted me to go back. It was great psychology, but of course I didn't think of that then. I jumped at the news and the following day I was back at Mrs Fullaway's, which was to be my home for all but a brief part of my Manchester days. Eric wasn't so lucky. He got one hell of a hiding from his father, and no second chance. Later, however, he signed for Middlesbrough, and we had numerous happy experiences and escapades playing together for Northern Ireland.

Those first weeks at Old Trafford were made hell by doubts; only on the pitch did I stop worrying, because then I could justify my presence by my skills. Not that I had any confidence that my skills were greater than those of others on trial. Every day we'd train, play some five-a-side, join in games with the amateurs and apprentices, and meet our heroes – the first-team players. Being Irish, the high-light was meeting players like Harry Gregg and Jimmy Nicholson. Harry Gregg was already an Irish folk hero, a survivor of the Munich air disaster: that gave him a special aura, even if it didn't stop me sending him the wrong way twice in a five-a-side match at The Cliff training ground. That was me, though. Off the field I didn't know what to say to him; on the field he was just another footballer to turn it on against.

But many times I walked away from that training ground wondering if it was for the last time. Maybe it was because no-one seemed to take much notice of me. I remember feeling out of it because I had to catch a bus to Old Trafford, whereas some of the other boys were within walking distance. There were probably just as many travelling by bus but I didn't notice them. And as I would learn later, no-one thought it necessary to reassure me of my place there because they thought I took it for granted I'd be offered forms. But no: even as the first week became two, and two moved on to three, I was always expecting the sympathetic hand on my shoulder and those end-of-the-world words, 'I'm sorry, George'. So many other kids, players I thought looked better than me, had come and gone, just disappeared. You'd turn up one morning, someone wouldn't be there, and you'd overhear one of the other lads saying 'He's gone home. They sent him home.' A lot of the time you never had the chance to say goodbye.

Even among the lads who stayed on there was so much talent that I used to wonder how I could make it to the top. Just in my position alone – I was playing at inside-forward – there were people like Eamonn Dunphy, Barry Fry, Barry Grayson, Sammy McMillan, Phil Chisnall and Dave Latham all vying for a place. I used to think that if I had to sit around and wait in line I was never going to get a game. Obviously that isn't the way it works. A lot of promising youngsters seem to reach a certain point where they blossom quickly or stagnate. Then, too, others are late developers. But if you have the talent you come through, as I discovered that week in September 1963 when I couldn't find my name on the team-sheets for the Reserves or the Junior sides. For a moment I thought I'd been dropped, and I don't know what it was that made me look at the first team sheet. But there I was, not as a player but as a reserve for the match at Old Trafford against West Brom. What I didn't know was that Ian Moir, who was listed to play on the right wing, had a groin strain and that the Boss thought I was ready for a run at the top. The only reason they didn't tell me on the Friday was to save me lying awake all night with nerves. They needn't have bothered. That's something I've never been troubled by. But I was in a daze when the Boss took me aside at lunch – we used to go to a local golf club for our pre-home match meals – and told me I was playing. I remained in that daze until we left for the ground.

Actually playing for the first time at Old Trafford remains to this day impossible to explain. But I'll always remember that tremendous feeling of running down the tunnel and out on to the pitch. As you emerge from the tunnel the crowd directly opposite are the first to spot the players, and that's when it starts. This enormous roar. As you come out on to the pitch it's almost as if some giant hand is turning up the volume control: the noise just gets louder and louder until it seems to reach an ear-shattering climax. I'd experienced nothing like it in my life. It was the first time the hairs on the back of my neck ever stood to attention. Even later in my career, playing at Liverpool or Benfica's Estadio da Luz or in front of 130,000 at Real Madrid's Bernabeu Stadium, nothing quite compared with that first time at Old Trafford. It will be there until I die. Once the game was under way I was oblivious of the noise, though I think subconsciously you're affected by the swell of crowd sounds. Didn't Dick Francis think it might have been the wave of applause that caused Devon Loch to sprawl and fall when he was well clear on the run-in in the 1956 Grand National? But however well you can shut out the noise, you can't escape an awareness of the atmosphere, especially somewhere like Old Trafford. There's a special feeling at that place, even if you're standing on the empty terraces in the middle of summer with the goalposts gone, the grass growing long, and the only sound the banging of workmen's hammers echoing around the stands.

*   *   *

The 1963-64 season, in addition to giving me my first team début and my first cap for Northern Ireland – a 3-2 win over Wales in Swansea – gave me a taste of that special feeling which comes from winning a trophy: in this instance the FA Youth Cup. When this competition began in the early 1950s, Manchester United took possession of it rather in the same way that Real Madrid monopolised the European Cup. United, with those youngsters who were to become immortalised as the Busby Babes, won it five seasons on the trot from 1953 to 1957. Then there was that post-Munich period of rebuilding at Old Trafford, and it was 1963 before it looked as if the club could boast a youth team faintly comparable to the greats of the 1950s.

I went into the youth team at sixteen, playing a few games after they'd been knocked out of the 1962-63 Youth Cup. That was during my so-called 'amateur' days before I was allowed to sign as a professional at seventeen: when I was theoretically working during the day and training on Tuesday and Thursday nights. Nor was I the only kid upset by this petty piece of bureaucracy. One of my closest friends in the early days was John Fitzpatrick, who'd come down from Aberdeen, and he was similarly affected. Perhaps that's why we became such good friends.

My first job was as a clerk at the Manchester Ship Canal Company. I was a glorified tea-boy really, and I had nothing to look forward to but another two years of spending my days there while the other lads trained every morning at the club and spent their afternoons playing pool, going tenpin bowling, and drinking tea and Cokes in a Salford cafe. Running errands for enslaved nine-to-five workers was not why I'd gone to Manchester. I might just as well have been at home in Belfast with my family, working my time as an apprentice compositor in a local newspaper office. Every chance I got I complained, and every time I complained the club explained the situation and how it just wasn't possible for me – or John – to stay at the club without an outside job. To appease me a bit they tried to work a deal whereby I'd have to work only four, maybe three, days a week and so would have more time for training. It wasn't strictly according to the rules, but I was learning early that rules are bent by necessity. Manchester United, it seemed, thought it necessary to keep me happy.

They even found me a new job, shifting loads of wood in a wood-work factory. That lasted from eight o'clock to lunchtime of the first day: lugging around lumps of wood all day was definitely not my scene. Back to the Ship Canal Company, but another department. That lasted until I had a row with one of the bosses and we were back to square one again. In the end they found us both a job in an electrical firm with a tolerant boss who didn't seem to mind how much time off we had for training. Then again, he was hooked on Manchester United, so I suppose we made it worth his while over the next few years.

Afternoons after training were spent mostly with the other lads, making sure everything from the toilets to Bobby Charlton's boots was spotless. In the evening it was out after tea to the bowling alley or the snooker hall; home by ten-thirty, which is when most of the landladies had instructions to have their lads home. At fifteen and sixteen I suppose we were just like a lot of kids at that age. Except for the football we were going through all the same stages: first girl-friends, looking forward to our first car, first beer, not much money. My weekly wage packet then was £4 1s 9d, and three pounds of that went home to Belfast. There wasn't much to spend the rest on anyway: snooker, bowling. You made a Coke last all night.

28

It was at that time I met Maria: she with the cream-cake cousins. She was friendly with Mrs Fullaway's son Steve, with whom I'd hang out sometimes when I wasn't with the lads from Old Trafford. He was a year or so older than me, so maybe Maria was older too. I can't remember; except that I used to fancy her like mad but didn't have the courage to say anything to her. That Belfast accent again! So I decided the best thing to do was write her a note – I'd always been good at English at school – and pass it to her when I had a chance. Which came one evening when the three of us were walking back to her house; or rather, Steve was walking her home and I tagged along to slip her this note. Only it all backfired because a couple of days later Steve came into our room and handed me the note I'd written. How he'd come by it I don't know, but I was so embarrassed. He, fortunately, thought it was all one big laugh and couldn't have cared less. Furthermore I started going out with Maria, so it ended up all right.

Or did it? On her afternoons off we used to go to her house and take advantage of her mother being out at work. Then one day her mother came home early while we were still upstairs. Talk about panic! Frantic whispers about what we were going to do. How was I going to get out of the house undetected? In the end we worked out the obvious solution. Maria would go down into the kitchen to keep her mother occupied while I sneaked down the stairs and out of the front door. All we forgot was that the front lawn was overlooked by the kitchen and Maria's mother had a lovely picture of tomorrow's hero in full furtive flight. I hope she had a good laugh at my expense. For my part I was learning early that the path of true love is fraught with pitfalls.

Before too long I was to discover it is also the path to trouble and heartache. Her name was Kay, and I fell for her at the bowling alley; sitting looking at her for three or four hours when I should have been at home in bed. My own! All I was doing was trying to pluck up courage to go across and talk to her. Eventually she came over and started talking to me. Turned out she was 'sort of related' to June Ritchie, the film star, and for the first time since I'd arrived in Manchester I was late home. It must have been all of eleven-thirty, and Mrs Fullaway didn't half give me a ticking off; especially when I told her I'd been watching *Come Dancing*! I gave her a big smile and promised it wouldn't happen again, but of course it did. This was true love; the great passion of my life; and if it meant staying out till midnight I was going to. After all, I was getting on for seventeen; old enough to have my own key, so I thought. Mrs Fullaway thought differently and let time take its proper course. She was right, too. I went home to Ireland to see my parents one week, and when I came back I discovered the love of my life had run off to marry another. I was shattered and quite disillusioned with girls for the time being. I returned to my first love, football, with renewed ardour.

It was the right time to, as well, because being in the youth team really made us feel we were part of the Manchester United family. We were made to feel special, and even though we all knew they were spinning us a line, we kind of believed it when they told us to 'forget the first team. They're not as important as you.' And in a way it's true, because if you have good youngsters coming through the future of the club is secure. For the Youth Cup games we were given the same treatment as the first team players: the pre-match meal at a smart hotel if we were away or at the golf club if we were at home, and then driven in the team coach to the ground. No turning up for the game an hour before the kick-off trying to remember where you last put your boots.

One year we travelled over to Switzerland for an annual youth tournament in Zurich and then played a few matches around the country. Although you didn't realise it, everything was geared to preparing you for a career in football: with Manchester United if you were good enough; and if not, perhaps with another club. But to us, then, it was all part of the excitement of growing up. Going abroad was new and there were plenty of good laughs getting up to all the mischievous things kids do. Going to strip clubs, getting wide-eyed and legless on a few glasses of beer, taking it in turn to carry each other back to the hotel and get to bed without disturbing the trainer. Nothing was serious except the football, and we couldn't get enough of that.

Weekdays were great, because we often wouldn't have a game and could go to the First Division matches at Old Trafford. On Saturdays, after our own game finished, we'd try to get back to Old Trafford to catch the last minutes, a scramble of lads dashing from the coach and rushing up to the back of the stand. The real highlight, though, was the visit of European clubs: to see in action such players as Gento, di Stefano and Puskas. Not just in the game, either, but in the warm-up beforehand. British players have always tended to spend this time bashing the ball as hard as possible at the goalkeeper.

These players spent their time entertaining the crowd – while at the same time tuning up their ball control – with tricks I'd never seen attempted before. Some of the things, performed with right foot and left, stuck in my mind even more than the game, and I recalled what my father used to tell me about Len Shackleton, the Clown Prince. These people were artists and entertainers as well as footballers and that is how I came to think of myself: as an entertainer. Someone who would make people laugh and go away from the game happy with what they'd seen.

Football, to my impressionable young mind, was seen to be fun, and I determined to express that in the way I played. As long as there were players of similar talent around me, such an attitude was fine. But in later years I had to realise that, when I was not playing well, this style of play actually handicapped my team. By then, however, it was too late to change my game overnight to suit new demands. My formative years had been conditioned to developing a free-wheeling self-expression of my talents: the word had come down from the Boss not to 'tinker with the boy's style. Let him develop his own way, naturally. He's something special.'[1]

*   *   *

Once I won a regular place in the first team I began to move away slowly but surely from the lads with whom I'd spent most of my Manchester days and nights. Yet it was this inevitable drift which made winning the Youth Cup in 1964 even more enjoyable than playing First Division football. It was perhaps my last chance to play with my pals; with the lads of my own age against others of the same age-group.

To win the Cup we beat Swindon in what, for me, was quite a week. It began on the Saturday at Old Trafford with a 3-1 win over Nottingham Forest to maintain our challenge against Liverpool for the League Championship. On the Monday night I scored our goal when we drew 1-1 at Swindon in the first leg of the Youth Cup final, and sandwiched between that and the second leg at Old Trafford on Thursday was my second game for Northern Ireland; on Wednesday night when we beat Uruguay 3-0. Then it was back to Manchester on Thursday morning to round off a hectic, exciting six days by setting

[1] *There's Only One United*. Geoffrey Green. Hodder and Stoughton, London. 1978.

up a couple of goals from rebounds for Dave Sadler, my room-mate at Mrs Fullaway's, who scored a hat-trick in our 4-1 win over Swindon. John Aston got the other goal. To see the delight on the faces of the coaching staff you'd have thought we'd won the FA Cup itself.

For me, more memorable were our two games in the semi-finals against Manchester City, because even at this level the prospect of the two Manchester clubs in conflict really got the city going. The previous season United had just escaped relegation to the Second Division but City had actually gone down. So it was all pretty heavy stuff. Our game had become that season's 'local derby' and the knives were out. There was all the pre-match build-up, and Mike Doyle, a self-confessed Manchester United hater, was shouting off about what City were going to do to us.

There was a crowd of something like 25,000 at Old Trafford for the first leg – a few First Division teams would settle for that – and we made fairly sure of the tie by beating them 4-1. But it was a closer game than the score suggested, for we weren't three goals better than them on the night. More that everything went right for us and not for them. They were confident they'd get the better of us in the return at Maine Road, even if the odds were against their pulling back our three-goal lead to square the tie. Come the night, though, we went there and beat them again, 4-3. That really was a thrill, because before we met they were so sure at Maine Road that they had a better youth team than we had at Old Trafford.

Making victory even more sweet was the fact that Mike Doyle, on his home ground, had scored an own goal. He and I had been chasing a through ball from John Fitzpatrick, and as we both slid in at the same time he knocked it into his own goal. The next day, in one of the local papers, there was this lovely photograph of him lying on the ground, the ball in the back of the net, and me leaning against the goalpost laughing at him. It made the whole thing for me. It was tremendous. All our boys loved it. I did manage to score myself later on and Dave hit a couple, while for City Glyn Pardoe, with two, and Bobby McAlinden were the goalscorers.

The sad thing is that some of those lads have been all too easily forgotten[1]. And for some of them, the Youth Cup was their only

---

[1] The Manchester United team which won the FA Youth Cup in 1963-64:
Jimmy Rimmer; Alan Duff, Bobby Noble; Peter McBride, Dave Farrar,
John Fitzpatrick; Willie Anderson, George Best, David Sadler, Albert Kinsey,
John Aston.

important trophy in football. Of those who played in the final, Dave Sadler and John Aston were in the side that won the European Cup; Dave played four times for England, John once for the Under 23 side. Jimmy Rimmer won one cap, while he was at Arsenal. Bobby Noble, who captained us, was a terrific prospect; an England youth international. There seemed no way he wouldn't go to the top. Denis Law, like myself, thought Bobby would have taken over from Ray Wilson eventually and been England's left-back for many years. 'He had a little bit of a chip on his shoulder, and was inclined to be a bit naughty. He liked to let players know he was there, and he had no respect for anyone's reputation.'[1] But shortly after he made the first team, in November 1967, he was badly injured in a car accident and that was the end of his career.

John Fitzpatrick suffered a terrible knee injury when it looked as if he was establishing himself in the first team. Willie Anderson and Albert Kinsey moved on. Eddie Harrop, Alan Duff, Dave Farrar and Peter McBride one by one drifted away from Old Trafford. Yet we were a fine team that season. Furthermore, seventeen years on, we were the last Manchester United team to win the Youth Cup, and we made a lot of people happy doing it. We also surprised a few.

[1] *Denis Law. An Autobiography*. Queen Anne Press, London. 1979.

Chapter 3

Benfica 1, Manchester United 5; 9 March 1966

Benfica tamed after seven successful years

from our Association Football Correspondent

Manchester United tonight destroyed the white flower of Benfica, in their Luz Stadium [in Lisbon], in a thrilling outburst of attacking football. 'Luz' is Portuguese for light, but Benfica – European Cup finalists four times in the past five seasons and winners of the trophy twice – were consigned to darkness. Manchester are in the European Cup semi-final round for the third time since 1957.

They reached that stage with the most inspired, inspiring, and controlled performance I have seen from any British side abroad in the past 20 years – matched, perhaps, only by England's 4-0 win over Italy in Turin in 1948. Had I not seen it, I would not have believed it.

This night of magic, then, saw Manchester, in the presence of 75,000, wipe out almost goal by goal the memory of their sorry show in this city two years ago, when they lost 0-5 to Sporting Lisbon in the European Cup-Winners' Cup. That can be forgotten, because it was shoddy. Tonight never will be forgotten. It will live on in the minds of everyone who saw this masterly exposition of mobility and skill, a performance which tamed Benfica for the first time at home in any European Cup tie over the past seven years.

With Madrid and Milan, Lisbon has become one of the power houses of the continental club game. Above their stately stadium stands a gigantic eagle. For so many seasons now it has been a predatory bird, but its feathers were painfully ruffled tonight.

Benfica passed quietly into the Lisbon night, heavily mourned by their followers. They passed with laboured, feverish movements, relying too much on Eusebio, the cunning dark leopard, who for once was caged by Stiles, his stealthy tracker around the edges of the Manchester penalty area. And because Eusebio could not fully express himself, and Torres could not dominate in the air, Benfica found themselves confined, and their only majesty at the last was that of tragedy.

Match report reproduced from *The Times* by permission.

The Manchester opening conditioned all that followed. In the first quarter of an hour Best, twice, and Connelly had charmed the ball past Costa Pereira in brilliantly coordinated movements to take their 3-2 advantage of Old Trafford to the unbelievable position of 6-2. All was done in a twinkling, almost, before the Portuguese had opened their eyes. Best, with his long dark mop of hair, is known in these parts as 'The Beatle'. Now he was the best of all, as he set a new, almost unexplored, beat. The rest caught the mood, and their refined actions flowered, unbelievably courtly and delicate – yet deadly.

Best seemed quite suddenly to be in love with the ball, and the whole side followed his lead. Before our astonished eyes came the disintegration of a great Benfica side. And Benfica are just that. But football digs into the spirit and as Manchester were inspired, Benfica were demoralized. The powerful Portuguese force lost their hearts, their minds, and their skilful presence.

At the kick-off, and for the first few moments, Eusebio and company began with a deceitful air of infallibility. But soon United were striking gold, the Portuguese beat around the Manchester goalmouth like a trapped bird, and long before half-time – 2-6 down on aggregate – time began to glide away from them.

Manchester lived up to their word. They came to attack – not to defend. Mr Busby, the manager, has raised a standard which all should follow, and he did so with a side that has the skill to attack, but did so with concentration and power. Their football was marvellously fluid, the ball being stroked along the pitch, long or short, making space and time for themselves as they bemused the opposition. They might have been musicians extemporizing in some modern jazz idiom.

Manchester soon struck. In the sixth minute Charlton was checked. Dunne curved a free-kick into the penalty area, and Best, rising on spring heels, headed beautifully past everybody. After 12 minutes Charlton passed back to Gregg. The goalkeeper cleared straight down the middle of the field, Herd headed downwards and backwards, and there was Best, gliding like a dark ghost past three men, to break clear and slide the ball home – a beautiful goal. Hardly had that made sense than a quick, triangular movement between Charlton, Law, and Connelly ended with Connelly beating Costa Pereira at close range.

There the score remained until half-time, with Manchester surviving a series of free-kicks by Eusebio, bent and dipped from the edge of the penalty area as the Italian referee punished the smallest action by Manchester. Seven minutes after the interval the crowd came to life again as Benfica began a bombardment and Pinto lashed a shot just wide. Then Benfica got one foot back into the match as Brennan, under pressure from Eusebio, lobbed the ball backwards over the head of his advancing goalkeeper.

Came more massed attacks from Benfica as the crowd roared and Eusebio tried to break free, supported by the lively Simoes with Pinto the midfield link. But Manchester held on calmly, Foulkes covering the tall head of Torres. Then Manchester broke free again, and in the final minutes a quick build-up saw Law's cutting pass put Crerand in for a fourth goal, and in the dying minutes Charlton, a hero in midfield, burst free himself and passed three men to deliver the *coup de grâce*.

Benfica: Costa Pereira; Cavem, Germano; Cruz, Pinto, Coluna; Augusto Silva, Eusebio, Torres, José Augusto, Simoes.
Manchester United: Gregg; Brennan, Dunne; Crerand, Foulkes, Stiles; Best, Law, Charlton, Herd, Connelly.

Sir Matt Busby later said that the way we played in this game had given him one of the greatest moments in his life. But was it, as Geoffrey Green, *The Times* football correspondent, wrote, a 'most controlled performance'? Inspired and inspiring, yes; but controlled? Only in as much as anything off the cuff could be so. That night in Lisbon we were controlled only by the limitations of our individual and collective talents; not by any blackboard diagrams or pre-match planning. The Boss's instructions that we play it tight for the first twenty minutes, to see how the game was going, were blown in the wind within the first ten minutes. But if he minded we never heard.

This was the game when Paddy Crerand broke a mirror in the dressing-room while we were kept waiting for twenty minutes as Eusebio was presented with his European Footballer of the Year trophy. Maybe I thought those were the twenty minutes the Boss was talking about! The mirror incident wasn't bad temper or anything sinister: just a bit of bad luck on Paddy's part while some of them were fooling around with a ball to calm their nerves. But it upset a few of the players, footballers as a rule being genuinely superstitious when it comes to pre-match behaviour. Paddy had the last laugh, though. When we came in at half-time, three goals up, he called out 'Anyone got another mirror?' We could afford to laugh then.

Why I played the way I did that night is one of those inexplicable things. Genius, and I believe that on the football field I had it, is something you simply can't begin to explain. I've been interviewed by American journalists to whom analysis is of the greatest importance. Why do you kick the ball with the inside of the foot some times and other times with the outside? Why did you go past that defender on his left side? Why and how? It all seems so important to them, whereas to me it's natural. Football is a simple game. Why complicate it with analysis? Does there have to be a reason for everything? Perhaps in Lisbon I fell in love with the place where we stayed: Estoril. Sunny, beautiful sandy beach, lovely park, luxurious hotels. I just felt so good all the time we were there. Even the jeering Benfica fans before the game didn't upset me, holding up five fingers to the coach windows as a sardonic reminder of our 5-0 defeat by Sporting Lisbon two years earlier in the Cup-Winners' Cup quarter-final. We gave them their five goals all right: and we put a stop to their damn firecrackers and rockets. They'd been masters of Europe, but we showed them how to play the game.

To be fair to the Portuguese, they were gracious losers, showering us with praise and presents until it was time to leave Lisbon. One paper, *Seculo*, called our display 'A notable exhibition by Manchester'. *Bola*, Portugal's leading sports paper, headed their report: 'A Beatle called Best smashed Benfica.' And that did it. Portugal had their 'El Beatle', even if he was an import. Spain had El Cordobes, their long-haired Beatle bullfighter. Portugal adopted George Best and overnight entered the swinging sixties. The morning after the match every bikini on the beach wanted my autograph; some wanted a snip of hair. The men were just as bad. I was having my first taste of adulation, and I'd be a liar if I said I didn't enjoy it. For the moment.

I could appreciate, too, the sort of reception that was awaiting us back in England, and it was more than a sense of boyish fun that made me buy the biggest sombrero I could find in Estoril. Later in the month I was opening my first boutique. Something out of the ordinary would attract attention and make good publicity. Sure enough. As we were about to emerge from customs I stuck the sombrero on my head and moments later every waiting photographer shot his shutter. Within twenty-four hours the photo was all around the world. Football's Beatle home in triumph.

Not all the publicity surrounding Georgie Best was so intentional, though. Many times things just happened, because that's the time it was. It was the 1960s: young people were dictating the culture even if it was often manipulated by the media. Everything was changing, or so we thought. It was a lovely exciting time; a revolutionary time; and I was right in the middle of it. Young people suddenly had money in their pockets to buy records and magazines and they wanted young heroes. I bridged the gap between the pop world and football, wearing my hair long, dressing in smart Carnaby Street gear. My photograph and opinions could be found in more pop magazines than in football magazines. Then, too, the north of England had become fashionable. The groups were coming out of

Liverpool and Manchester; Liverpool and Manchester, with Leeds, were dominating the football scene. Everton were League champions in 1963, Liverpool in '64 and '66, United in '65 and '67, City in '68 (we were runners-up), Leeds in '69 and Everton again in 1970.

Furthermore, football itself was changing, moving away from its cloth cap image. More and more show business people were being seen at matches, even having their own boxes. Eventually, they became either shareholders or directors. All that began in the sixties. And at the same time there developed the singing and the chanting of adapted pop songs; what Arthur Hopcroft described beautifully as 'a plainsong of the terraces. It was created in Liverpool, where the city character, with its pervading harshness of waterfront life and bitterly combative Irish exile content, was given a sudden flowering of arrogant expression with the simultaneous rise of its pop musicians and of both its leading football teams. More than any other English city, Liverpool experiences its hope and its shame through its football.'[1]

Manchester would run it close: a football city completely divided. There was no in-between. You were either United or City, and for both players and fans the rivalry bordered on real hatred. The derby games were vicious; tackling you wouldn't take Attila the Hun to see. Today, I don't know; it doesn't seem to be there quite the same. Perhaps there aren't enough home-grown players – players who've come up through the youth sides – to carry on that life or death tradition of a derby game. In the sixties it really was black and white. If we lost to City, or vice versa, it was a week of misery for the losers and their fans.

So much of that sixties' excitement has gone now; all that promise has faded away and in the greyness of 1980, the survivors content themselves with nostalgia. In those days, however unimportant in an overall context, Britain dictated the music and the fashion; England won the World Cup; Celtic and United were the kings of Europe. Today, the music has become hard, more harsh and often ugly; the football is panzer-like. The fun has gone.

One other factor contributed to the growth of my pop image: I was single in a team in which virtually everyone else was married or engaged. Denis Law might have been king for the Stretford End fans and Bobby Charlton the star of the stands, but I was the one wearing

[1] *The Football Man.* Arthur Hopcroft. Collins, London. 1968.

the Chelsea boots, the square waistcoats, the turn-back cuffs and the tailored shirts. I had the long hair. Consequently it wasn't unnatural that ninety per cent of my fanmail came from young girls – all around the world.

To exploit this new-found adulation I had decided to open a boutique in Sale, but no-one was prepared for the scenes that occurred on the day we opened. After all, it wasn't as if the shop was in the city centre. We were five or six miles out, stuck in a suburban shopping area between a betting shop and a small printer. Yet two hours before the official opening there were three or four hundred fans – mostly schoolgirls – hammering on the plate-glass window to attract my attention. They scrawled 'We luv George' with lipstick all over my car; some idiots even tried to take the wheels off. Paddy Crerand had his shirt ripped trying to get to the champagne reception; girls fainted in the crush and ended up sipping champagne with Denis Law, Malcolm Allison and Mike Summerbee. Oh yes; I was friendly enough with City players off the field. Come to think of it, we even sold trousers in Manchester City blue, as well as scarlet, purple and mustard. We had all the 'in gear'; we were Sale's answer to Carnaby Street.

What happened at Sale, though, was nothing to what happened the following November when Bobby Charlton, Nobby Stiles and I went to the opening of the new Market Centre in the middle of Manchester. It was like a riot. Something like a thousand people there, quite a lot of them women with young children taking a break from their shopping. The police tried to control it, but all of a sudden there were scarf-waving fans rushing everywhere and girls shouting 'We want Georgie'. They ripped down Christmas decorations and tore the balloons from the Christmas tree. Shoppers were knocked off their feet. It was all too much for Nobby. He escaped to the safety of a nearby post office.

Incidents like these were lapped up by the press with the enthusiasm of an alley cat for a bowl of cream. New cars, new girls, new business ventures; they all appeared in the papers so often I wonder that people didn't tire of Georgie Best long before they did. I know I did, although I don't deny there were times in the early days when I got a kick out of seeing my name or my photo in the paper. When it got to the stage that everything I said, did or thought was news, then it became too much.

Some will say that this is the price of fame. Others that I

encouraged the publicity. And they'd be right to a degree. What I did not set out to do was create a monster or a myth; a legend. Georgie Best superstar might have been a child of the times, but he was very much a product of the media, especially of the newspapers. Georgie Best was news, which meant he helped fill and sell papers. If he's out somewhere, having a quiet dinner with a girl, photograph them. If he's standing in a pub with his friends, find out what they talk about. It's all 'news'.

No matter what it was, if my name was associated with it there'd be an item in the newspapers. Even the most crazy schemes would hit the headlines; and when I look back now, we came up with some great but quite impractical ideas for businesses. One of them was to moor together a pair of large barges on a river in Cheshire to make a floating discotheque. There were plans for restaurants; plans for a teenagers' supermarket. Several people were involved in that one, including Bob Lang from The Mindbenders group and Jennifer Moss (Lucille Hewitt) from *Coronation Street*. But apart from making news, little came of them. Often, more often than not, the idea would come from someone else and I'd just say yes. That was my trouble; I could never say no. I'd meet someone at a party, or in a club, and he'd have this great idea for making money. All he needed to get it going was capital – usually mine, because in those days I was making good money out of football alone and I had nothing to spend it on.

That was probably part of the problem. The other players, when we'd finished training or after a match, had their homes and families to care for. I was always at a loose end once we'd finished in the morning, and it relieved the boredom to play the tyro tycoon. What was it I was going to be? A millionaire by thirty? Not the way I went about it. Saying 'Yeah! Great!' to everybody who came up asking for four, five thousand to set up this and that with the promise that in such and such a time we'd take out so and so. Only I never bothered to follow the deals through to see what was happening to my money. I was twenty, twenty-one; what was money if it wasn't to play with? Like so many people of that time, I thought it was never going to end. This is what I'd be doing for the rest of my life. All right, I might have to stop playing football one day, maybe at thirty-five, but when you've just turned twenty, thirty-five is so far away it's not worth thinking about. Especially when you've come from a council estate in a city like Belfast. Saving's something they tell you to do in the television commercials; like buying whiter-than-white soap powder or test-driving the latest-model car. Nice to dream about but you never actually do it. As the money comes in it goes out. That's the way they live in Belfast; from one day until they're gone.

Manchester United did help, making sure the players joined insurance schemes so they'd have something when they were thirty-five. It all sounds rosy explained to you at seventeen by an insurance salesman, but by the time you get to thirty-five, with inflation it's peanuts. And that's supposed to set you up for the rest of your life if you haven't been able to make a go of something else. The clubs should do much more, I feel. Perhaps employ or have available someone who can advise the youngsters, not only on financial and business matters but on all aspects of life, warning them of the dangers. I know too well it wouldn't be easy, because when you're that age you want to do only one thing: play football. I was exactly the same.

You think you're street-wise, or you become street-wise over the years. Yet when it comes to financial matters most footballers are lazy. They don't want to think about facts and figures. And this makes them easy game for the hundreds of con-men waiting to take advantage. 'Give me your money', they say, 'and I'll invest it for you'. Invest; that's the magic word. All they need do then is bring along a piece of paper and say 'This is doing that and this is doing something else'. You nod your head, but you don't know what they're on about. Nor do you have to be a mug for it to happen to you. It's happened to most of the great players at some time: Bobby Moore, Denis Law, Pelé, Johan Cruyff. Players who should have been able to retire and never work another day of their lives if their affairs had been handled properly.

The more I become involved with other aspects of football, apart from simply playing, the stronger I feel that there is a responsibility to the youngsters, whether it comes from the clubs themselves or the players' union. Too often you're left to learn through experience, and by then it can be too late. You end up with nothing; or if you're lucky, running a little pub somewhere, drinking yourself to death on fading memories. Take someone like Ron Davies, the big Welsh international centre-forward who played for Southampton in the sixties and early seventies. A terrific header of the ball; scored more than 200 League goals; transfer valued at around £200,000 in 1970 and still good value when I played with him for Los Angeles in the mid-seventies. A player who gave a lot of service to the game, and yet the last I heard of

41

him he was working somewhere on a building site. They say the Georgie Best story is a tragedy, but there's the real tragedy of football. It creates its heroes then just as easily throws them aside.

At least when I began in the boutique business I had no great illusions of making money. It was only a little shop, and both Malcolm Mooney, my partner, and I knew it would never be our fortune. We'd met at a party, talked a bit, discovered we had a common interest in clothes, and in the way these things happen we became good friends. Opening a boutique was originally his idea; something he'd wanted to do for a while. He knew the rag trade, but he also knew that you have to be very lucky to do much more than pay your way. Same when we moved from Sale and opened the shops in central Manchester – Edwardia and George Best Rogue – except that we tried to set a higher standard. We both put in more than we ever took out, although Malcolm would take out his wages as manager. For me the boutique was always somewhere to hang out in the afternoons if I had nothing else to do. As soon as we closed for the day it was straight down to the pub.

One of the things about Edwardia was its situation: just off Deansgate, which is to Manchester what Fleet Street is to London. I remember meeting a girl at a party in London who said that the reason why the London School of Economics made the news so often was because it was just around the corner from Thames Television. The same applied to Georgie Best in Manchester. If the papers needed a quick quote or a bit of gossip, I was usually just around the corner; and if they couldn't find me they could always ask Malcolm Mooney or Waggy – Malcolm Wagner, a close friend who owned the hairdressers next door. As long as they could print a story with George Best's name in it. I think I must be the only person in Britain who has featured on the front, centre and back pages of a daily newspaper – all on the same day!

In addition to the clothes, the girls, the fan clubs and the boutiques, the cars I drove also helped cultivate the playboy image that would one day turn against me. I think I could resist girls more than I could cars: every time I saw a new one I fancied a change, even if I'd had mine a matter of months. I had only to walk past a showroom. Funnily enough I'm not car mad at all, so it must simply have been something to spend more money on. Certainly I began humbly enough, with a little Austin 1100. Then it was a Sunbeam Alpine sports, after which came a succession of Jaguars, nearly all white, a Jensen, a Lotus, a Rolls Royce, and the most fearsome of all, a 160 miles per hour silver-grey monster called an Iso Rivolta that set me back seven thousand pounds and frightened me to death every time I drove it. Most of the time I was parking these exotic cars outside Mrs Fullaway's little council house, parking alongside the guy who was spending his hard-earned wages coming to see me play football, doing something he would only ever dream of.

What amuses me now is the way these 'smart' and 'exotic' cars became 'fast' cars, just as the 'pretty girls' became 'models' and 'starlets', when the football started going sour and the image changed from swinging young man about town to reckless playboy. 'A few drinks with close friends' became 'sessions with hangers-on'. It didn't surprise me when people said they were fed up with reading about Georgie Best in the newspapers. I was fed up with reading about him as well. But I couldn't go around saying, 'Hey, look, I don't write this stuff. I don't want it to appear.' I learnt early on that there was nothing you could do to stop it, and it's useless trying to sue. You're lucky if you get an apology and a few hundred pounds for your trouble.

People might say that I get as much out of the publicity as the newspapers do, but there have been times when publicity was the last thing I needed. What I have done, though, is use the papers; for money. And that is something the press itself taught me. It was back in the mid-sixties when a crowd of us used to go over to Majorca every summer: some of the lads from Manchester; a couple of Swiss boys who came down in their Mercedes towing a speedboat behind; a few Londoners including a real comic pair called Laurie and Brian; and a Birmingham crowd that sounded like the Quality Street gang. Chalkie White, Lobster Lenny, Johnny Hart, Johnny Prescott the boxer, Alex Harley who played for Manchester City and Birmingham. Plus loads of girls from all over the place.

They were great times, full of laughs. Days you'd spend sitting on the beach, joking, playing cards or Scrabble, talking about what you'd been doing and who you were with the night before. Fellas and girls. You could guarantee that if there were twenty of you in a group, ten guys and ten girls, any one lad would have been out with three or four of the girls and vice versa. There were no jealousies or anything: it wasn't that kind of scene. Sex was no big deal. If you fancied someone and they fancied you, that was great; it was nice and thank you very much. But it didn't tie you down. Which is what that 1960s thing was supposed to be all about. Freedom. You'd maybe spend the next day on the beach if you wanted to and you could be good friends. There was never any embarrassment or guilt about it. In fact, whenever any two started getting serious about each other, they'd get hell from the rest of the crowd.

In most ways we were no different from a crowd of factory lads from Leeds, except that we had more money and we could stay on longer. We were all going to Spain for the same thing: cheap drinks, sun and sex. But people took it all so seriously. It used to make me laugh when, every so often, one of the more lurid Sunday papers would do an exposé about what went on at Spanish holiday resorts. Big deal! We were doing the same thing as people in Leeds were doing. The only difference was that we were lying out on the beach all day in the sunshine, drinking plenty of wine and watching half-naked women running around.

We were doing nothing new; not when you read what people were getting up to in the twenties and thirties, and especially during the war years. All we did was make no secret of the fact that we saw sex as something we did when we felt like it. At least we weren't suppressing our feelings; and I'm inclined to go along with Jerzy Kosinski, the Polish-born author who wrote the book *Being There*, from which came the film starring Peter Sellers and Shirley MacLaine. He said that to his generation (about ten years ahead of mine) sex was one of the few ways in which the individual could define himself regardless of external pressures. I like that.

It was while we were on one of these holidays in Spain that a fellow from a newspaper came up with a proposition: a feature on all the different girls I'd been out with while I was there. They had all the photos; they'd had a photographer building up a dossier on me over a couple of weeks. A new girl every day for Georgie Best. That was the sort of thing they wanted. I tried to spell it out for him that I wasn't interested: that we were just a bunch of friends having a laugh, a giggle, and we didn't want any aggravation. We'll pay you for it, he said. And then came the crunch.

'If you don't agree to it, we'll do it anyway because we've got the pix. So you might as well agree and get something out of it.'

That was it. I lost all respect for the press after that, and it soon got to the stage when I'd give them stories whenever I needed some quick cash. Tell them anything; same old story over and over again but with a change of names. They never bothered to check it out, and that's the way it went on year after year. It backfired, though, when Mike Parkinson wrote his book.[1] Made it look as if all I was interested in was jumping into bed with every girl I laid eyes on, and as soon as I was finished throwing her out again. It made most of the girls out to be no-good scrubbers as far as I was concerned, which just wasn't true.

What annoys me most, though, is the way other people get involved. Don't the people who write and print the trash stop to think for a moment what they might do to other people apart from me? My family, for example. Or someone else's family. When it was rumoured Angela and I were getting married, they were phoning Angela's mother twenty-four hours a day. They even gave Angela a fictitious brother to hang a quote on; which was embarrassing to say the least for Angela's mother. Recently some story cropped up and they wanted a quote from me; except they didn't know where to find me. So they phone Belfast; no joy. They call Angela's parents; no-one there. They even contacted an old friend whom I hadn't seen for twelve years. Eventually they found out where Angela's grand-mother lived and started to annoy her. It didn't matter to them that she'd been ill in hospital and was very nervous. They needed a back-up for their story; anything to make it a bit more interesting. How Mrs Fullaway ever coped I'll never know. There was a time when people were banging on the door all the time, and often she had to call the police to remove the reporters and photographers from the close.

The pressures of a public image do not all stem from constant publicity, however much that may have nurtured the image. There comes a time when you have to build your life around what other people are doing. I couldn't take the dog for a walk in the rush hour, for example, because motorists would be so busy honking at me that they'd run up each other's backsides. Which, if it wasn't so funny, would be serious. If I'm going to a movie, or a show, I always try to get to my seat when the lights have dimmed rather than be plagued by people wanting my autograph on half a cinema ticket. I arrived early for a Billy Connolly concert once and there was pandemonium. The star of the show had to wait to go on his own stage while his audience mobbed me.

People with me find it even more difficult to cope unless they're in

[1] *Best: an intimate biography.* Michael Parkinson. Hutchinson, London. 1975.

the public eye themselves. Which is why so many people in show business and football move about together. They feel comfortable in each other's presence; they can afford to be themselves, not the image people have of them. It's why I go to a club like Tramp in London; not to star gaze or eye the birds as one newspaper told its readers. I go because Johnny and Jan Gold are close friends who make me feel at ease as soon as I enter. Oscar and Jackie Collins are the same. We can sit at a table over dinner and maybe not say a dozen words but it doesn't matter. Johnny or Oscar might disappear halfway through the meal to do some business, but I don't mind. Why should I? They make me feel at home, and there are few public places where I can feel like that. I took my young brother to a Chinese restaurant in Edinburgh and the meal was ruined because he couldn't cope with some women who were staring at us. The more it annoyed him, so I began to get irritated with him because he was noticing it. In the end we went home and watched television. Probably should have stayed there in the first place.

Even going to the lavatory used to be hazardous. Denis Law and I devised a secret code, if we wanted to go off for a pee when we were at receptions and big dinners. Just look at each other, nod, and leave the room together. For protection, really. It's amazing the number of people who want to shake your hand at quite the wrong moment, and so you frighten them off because there are two of you. It's like the old Bill Shankly story. Same thing; he's in the loo. Fellow beside him looks at him, does a double-take, spins round saying 'Hey, you're Bill Shankly', and pisses all over his trousers.

The whole business of image and pressures becomes self-perpetuating, too. There comes a time when travelling by bus is no longer possible; and then it reaches the stage when walking past a bus stop means stopping to sign autographs for half the people there while the remainder mutter abuse about you. So you cross the road to avoid the bus stop and you become a big-head. Or, because you have to travel about the city, you isolate yourself in a car from door to door. To take the analogy a step further, you travel in a chauffeur-driven car, sitting in the back reading the newspaper, and another image is created. The quiet lad from the council estate has become a star, but in order to live with his stardom – and for his stardom to be real for his fans – he has to change to a new lifestyle. Paradoxically, those same people who put him on the pedestal of fame feel they retain the right to topple him; or conveniently forget him.

46

Chapter 4

West Ham United 1, Manchester United 6; 6 May 1967

United are the peerless champions

from Bob Ferrier

A monumental performance by Manchester United confirmed them their Championship, virtually obliterated West Ham, and left London with the marvellous concluding statement from Matt Busby's team that if the capital is to have the Cup final then Manchester is once again the centre of the universe. For the ragged, ragamuffin red-and-white battalions which invaded the field at the end, screaming for Busby, there has never been any doubt about that.

United had clearly spurned the thought of scrambling the solitary point that they needed. They devastated West Ham with intent, with the power, the pace, the professionalism of their play from the beginning.

A Charlton goal in the second minute, then three in ten minutes, left West Ham demoralised, concussed, and at the heart of a ravishing first-half performance stood Bobby Charlton. His goal was astonishing in its speed, its audacity, and the lightning reaction which Charlton displayed on seizing at a quarter-chance. Law cut Stiles through perfectly. Stiles was blocked, the ball broke loose but offered only the tightest of chances. Charlton went at it with a feverish venom that seemed almost out of character, thrashing the ball irrevocably past Mackleworth for a quite sensational goal.

Bobby Charlton, probably the best-loved player in our game, went on to play a first half that surpassed even his performance against Portugal in the World Cup semi-final. His touch on the ball, delicate and stunning, his control (once he turned past seven successive West Ham players with the same move, that quick flick with the outside of his left foot), his command of the entire midfield when he chose – here was a vintage performance from a most wonderfully gifted player at the very height of his maturity.

West Ham could find no answer to Charlton – precious few defences in the world could. They lost their second goal after seven minutes when Crerand headed home unerringly an Aston cross, high out of reach of

Match report reproduced by courtesy of *The Observer*.

47

Mackleworth's left hand. The third came after ten minutes when Foulkes challenged the goalkeeper to a left-wing corner. When Foulkes landed, back to goal, he found a largesse of space in which to turn and hammer the ball home comfortably.

Three goals, two from half-backs, made the point. It has been a turgid season for West Ham, and here they were with a goalkeeper playing his second league match, and a centre-half with less than a third of a season under his studs. Determined running by Hurst and Peters took West Ham occasionally to the frontiers of the affair but they never reached any control of the game.

Best's goal after twenty-five minutes brought a climax to Manchester's bewildering opening. Stiles cut one inside the fullback, Best came in, checked the ball with his right foot and with his left, breathtakingly quick, shot it under Mackleworth's dive.

With Sadler and Dunne indomitable in defence, Law was well able to indulge in his gamut of Italianate gestures. These in turn never prevented him from always being perfectly positioned, as when he headed powerfully at Charlton's free-kick and only a fully stretched and thrilling save by Mackleworth stopped him.

Thus both the match and the Championship were virtually settled at half-time. In the first minute of the second half John Charles came up-field in possession. With United drifting back, West Ham sprinted ahead, Charles was left with nothing but a shot on. Stepney went at it late and was perhaps unsighted.

The second half was distinguished only by Manchester's superiority – they were often able to walk the ball – some odd refereeing decisions, one marvellous save by Stepney from Peters' head and two further United goals. A mystifying penalty was given to United after sixty-three minutes as Stiles worked a short corner on the right. Law scored. Ten minutes from the end Law again, in one of his classic set-pieces, forced in at close range a low Best cross that Mackleworth could not hold.

This may not be United's greatest Championship win, their greatest team. But certainly in the history of the club they can never have had such devastating forwards as Charlton, Law and Best.

West Ham United: Mackleworth; Burkett, Charles; Peters, Heffer, Moore; Redknapp, Bennett, Boyce, Hurst, Sissons.
Manchester United: Stepney; Brennan, Dunne; Crerand, Foulkes, Stiles; Best, Law, Sadler, Charlton, Aston.

What better way to win a League Championship? We could have settled for a draw, as we'd done at every away match since the New Year, for the point would have been enough to make sure of the title in the end. But there was something about going down to London. You felt you had to show you were the best, even when the League table proved you were. There was always somebody ready to snipe; to remember we'd been beaten by a goal at Spurs back in September. Of course, that person would conveniently overlook the fact that we'd beaten them at home in January by a David Herd goal, one of the fifteen he scored that season before breaking his leg while netting his sixteenth in our 5-2 win over Leicester at Old Trafford.

We really turned it on for the fans that season, even if the goals tell only part of the story of how exciting and entertaining our football was. As well as the Leicester game we scored five against West Brom in the first match of the season and against Sunderland – David scored four in that. There were fours against Burnley, Blackpool – to avenge a 5-1 drubbing in the League Cup – and away to West Brom, a seven-goal feast that one, with David Herd getting another hat-trick.

We suffered some bad defeats, too: 3-0 at Stoke and 4-1 at the rapidly rising Nottingham Forest. But these were early in the season, and by Christmas the Boss reckoned we'd have the Championship if we could keep winning at home and take a point from our away games. He was right, and when the season ended we were four points clear of Forest and Spurs, each with 56 points. We'd scored 84 goals – West Ham, in sixteenth place, were next with 80 – and our defensive record, 45 against, was bettered only by Forest and Leeds. When we were champions two seasons earlier our record was 89 for and 39 against, proving, if nothing else, that we were not just a team laden with goalscorers. We had a superb, well-organised defence which saw us through many a close encounter. It was just that our philosophy wasn't defensive. Even if we were several goals down it never occurred to us to stop playing our natural attacking game.

Our sixth-round FA Cup tie at Wolves in 1965 provided a perfect illustration of that. Within fifteen minutes we were two goals down and were soon reduced to ten men when Denis Law went off for a short spell with concussion. Not that a knock on the head stopped him heading in John Connelly's corner to pull us back to 2-1 at half-time. Other managers, in such circumstances, might have told their team to play it tight and wait for the opposition to make the mistakes. Not the Boss. 'Attack, attack, attack' was all he told us. And attack we did, tearing them apart right from the kick-off. First David Herd equalised, and then I put us a goal up by curling a corner straight into the net. That was roughly on the hour. In the sixty-eighth minute Paddy Crerand crashed one in from the edge of the penalty area and seven minutes later Denis drove in a free-kick from twenty-five yards out. It was magic, Brian, as they tell the man on television when they're not feeling as sick as a parrot. Wolves pulled one back towards the end, but there was no way they could stop us taking United into the FA Cup semi-finals for the fourth successive year. We made that five in 1966, and for the third time running we failed to get to Wembley.

In 1964, as Cup-holders, we were beaten by West Ham while Preston knocked out Swansea in an all-Second Division tie. Had we gone through to Wembley against Preston, there would have been some checking through the birth registers to see who was born first on 22 May 1946: Howard Kendall or myself. As it was, Howard Kendall went to Wembley with Preston North End, I watched the match on television, and he became the youngest player to appear in an FA Cup final.

In 1965 we met Leeds in a hard, bad-tempered affair at Hillsborough. A goalless draw that was 'a disgrace, not only to football but to both sides. As a match, indeed, it resembled an ugly, unmade bed.'[1] The referee, a Mr Windle, was partly to blame for letting certain players audition their opponents for *Emergency Ward 10,* and it came as no surprise to learn that he was attacked after the replay at Nottingham Forest, even though this game was much less tempestuous. Probably because he blew his whistle for a free-kick every time opposing players came within kicking distance. We shouldn't have lost, because we controlled so much of the game. But Gary Sprake had one of those games he'll prefer to remember – I should think he still has the woodwork – and minutes before the end Giles flighted over a free-kick which Bremner glanced in. That was it. The next year, 1966, Everton also beat us by the only goal of the match.

Quite why our games over the years with Leeds should have been so acrimonious may be considered a reflection of the thinking of the two managers. Sir Matt Busby, I feel, wanted to create a team that would entertain by expressing its united skills, and would win matches because the sum of those skills would be superior to the opposition's. In 1959 he had expressed his concern at the way English football was developing when he wrote 'We are breeding a number of teams whose outlook seems to be that pace, punch and fitness are all that is required to win all the honours in the game.

[1] *There's Only One United.* Geoffrey Green. Hodder and Stoughton, London, 1978.

They forget that, without pure skills, these virtues count for precisely nothing.'[1] The teams that won United the League Championship in 1965 and 1967 were, I like to feel, rather like a fine clock, each part lovingly hand-made for its specific purpose.

Leeds, despite the abundance of talent in their formidable sides of the 1960s and 1970s, were inevitably predictable, technical and boring. Like Don Revie, their manager, they were hungry for success, irrespective of how it was obtained. Yet there were days when they could play the most marvellous football and the players actually smiled. Next match: destroying rather than creating; dour, hard-tackling, hard-running; 1-0 from a set-piece. Unfortunately their success, following that of England in the World Cup, produced numerous imitators who thought the oil well was found by manning the midfield according to magical mathematical formulae. I suppose we were the old, Leeds the new, and as in all schools of politics, philosophy or whatever, the protagonists fight bitterly for their beliefs while others wait to catch the wind. Unhappily for the game, Manchester United were to fade sooner.

I wonder, too, what effect the presence of John Giles in the Leeds line-up had on our matches. He had played on the right wing for Manchester United when they won the FA Cup in 1963 but was transferred to Leeds, then in the Second Division, following a disagreement with Matt Busby after the 4-0 defeat by Everton in the next season's Charity Shield. I think, for him, there was always that certain element of proving a point which easily rubs off on players as volatile as those playing for United and Leeds at the time. It doesn't take much for a little bit of niggle to become a whole lot of aggro.

With players like Denis, Paddy, Nobby Stiles and myself we were forever running the risk of explosive situations, the more so as some teams deliberately set out to upset our rhythm by making one or more of us retaliate. To the man on the terrace or the television pundit it looks all too much like a display of bad temper, whereas so often the reason is frustration. Especially when skills are nullified by deliberate breaking of the law, such as obstruction or shirt-pulling, which go unnoticed by the referee. For example, you first-time a pass straight to the feet of a team-mate and go for the return pass which will leave you with only the goalkeeper to beat. It's the classic breach of

[1] *The International Football Book, No 2*. Ed. Stratton Smith. Souvenir Press, London. 1960.

a packed defence and you've achieved it. Except that a defender grabs you by the shirt long enough to prevent you from reaching the return. The crowd moan because they think you're too slow; the referee hasn't seen it because he's watching the man with the ball; the linesman's waiting to flag you offside. You know you've done something special, something skilful, and you've been robbed of fulfilment. It's a bit like the boyfriend on the sofa with big sister (not his). He's made all the right moves and he's all set to score when little brother comes in for a drink of water: for the third time that evening! That's the frustration which makes you lose your cool on the football field.

Referees, I know, can't be expected to see everything. They're only butchers and bicycle salesmen after all. I went through eight minutes of a Cup tie once without a boot on my left foot, and the referee said afterwards that he'd noticed me bend down, assumed I was tying up the lace, and hadn't noticed I wasn't wearing a boot because the game was so tense. It was at that.

It was a fifth-round match against Burnley at Old Trafford: the round before that tie against Wolves. We were 1-0 down with under ten minutes to play when my boot came off in a tackle and, because we were laying siege to their goal, I simply had no time to put it back on. When I threw it to the sideline, people kept throwing the thing back at me, so I had to run around with a boot in my hand. Not that it made any difference to my game. I laid on both goals – one for Denis and one for Paddy – and one of those passes was made with the bootless foot. The next week the wags were addressing their letters to the Bootless Wonder; the newspapers, of course, were considering what action the government might take to stop such acts of youthful spirit. And it was only 1965.

*   *   *

Three times now I've written that being at Manchester United felt like belonging to a great big family, and twice I've crossed it out because it sounded like a cliché. The fact is, though, that it's the truth, cliché or not. The club did have a special feel to it, a quality you became aware of immediately. Part of it stemmed from tradition, much of it resulted from the type of people, the character of the men who ran the club. Not just Matt Busby, but Jimmy Murphy, Jack Crompton, and also the Board members. They were men of strong beliefs, yet they were fair. They could admit they were wrong.

When I first heard I was going to Old Trafford for a trial, one or two people in Belfast told me I was wasting my time because I wasn't a Catholic, and for a time this stuck in my mind. But the more I became involved in the club and came to know the people employed there, the more I saw that this was a fallacy. It basically wasn't true; indeed, it was the other way round. There were more non-Catholics, not just in the administration of the club but among the players. I guess it was just one of those rumours that were built around Sir Matt because no-one could think of anything more pernicious to say about him.

He did become larger than life, but not to himself or those closely associated with him. Legendary figures are often disappointing when you come to meet them, especially in football. Probably because what built the legend was so often distorted, as I well know. But I've never heard anyone who has met Sir Matt disagree with the general consensus that here is an outstanding man. There's the same feeling, too, about Bill Shankly, the former manager of Liverpool and, like Sir Matt, a Scot. It isn't always the big things they've done that make them great, so much as the little things which leave their imprint on another person's life. Two things I remember: one indirect but obviously reflecting Sir Matt's values, the other direct.

When I first went to Old Trafford, the young lads all knew their place and quickly learnt never to be out of order. We were part of the family, but as in the family there was a hierarchy to be respected. We would mix, and be encouraged to mix, with the first-team players – the élite – but there was never any cheeking them; not even a Reserve team player. Nor were there any cliques at Old Trafford under Sir Matt's leadership. You see them at so many clubs; the little groups who stick together. We never had that at Old Trafford until things started to go bad at the end of the sixties. Then it became very cliquey – twos and threes talking behind others' backs. That it had never happened before, in my time there, made it all the more upsetting.

My other memory of Sir Matt was his capacity to remember people and things about them. A small example. The first time my father went over to Old Trafford to see me play, he brought a couple of his pals with him. He's a bit like me in that respect; I don't like travelling on my own to new places. The next time my father went to a game he had one of these friends with him again, and Sir Matt not only remembered his name but also where he was from and what he drank. Little things, but things that make a person feel important in himself, and that can't be bad.

One thing he wasn't, though, was soft, despite what many people said about him being easy on his players, especially me. I saw players go in to see him, fully determined to demand this and that and tell him exactly what they felt they were worth. Time after time they came out with a sheepish smile on their face; but not feeling put down, for in that respect he was tremendous. You might be called into his office for a dressing down – it happened to me numerous times – and he'd get really stuck into you. Then, just as you were getting up to go, he'd wink at you. You knew you'd done wrong, but at the end of it all you knew you were still pals.

That's how he managed to keep everyone so happy: personality and understanding. And that is why so few players asked for a transfer from Old Trafford. Even if they weren't regular first-team members, players were so happy being part of the set-up. The position was similar, and remains so, at Liverpool, where the reserve strength is such that they could probably field two First Division sides and fight out the League Championship between themselves. Buying talent is not always difficult when you have the money, but keeping twenty to thirty accomplished players happy when they're not all getting regular first team football is. Managers like Shankly and Bob Paisley, his successor at Liverpool, have that knack. So, too, did Sir Matt Busby, and it is that, perhaps more than the League titles and the Cups he won, which made him for me such a great manager and a tremendous man. You have only to be at Old Trafford today and see the many old players who still call him 'Boss' to know you're in the presence of someone special.

I didn't give him an easy time, I know that, and people still say it would all have been different had he been tougher with me. But what else could he do? He fined me, but that was only money. He suspended me, and that must have hurt him as much as it hurt me because it removed an important component from his team. As he said himself, 'We couldn't shoot him. We might have felt like smacking his bottom, as a man might smack his own son's bottom. But this is not allowed in a player's contract.'[1] It must have been so frustrating for him, and yet I knew I could make it up to him by turning on some magic during a game and all would be forgotten until the next time. Rather as a child, having upset his parents, makes amends by doing something they appreciate. And then, because he acts rather than

[1] *Soccer at the Top*. Matt Busby. Weidenfeld and Nicolson, London. 1973.

thinks during that period of growing up, he goes out and thought-lessly hurts them again.

There is also in me an element, I am sure, of what Edgar Allan Poe called the Imp of the Perverse: doing something 'merely because we feel we should *not*'. Not consciously, but instinctively through impulse. 'We act', to quote Poe, 'for the reason that we should *not*. In theory no reason can be more unreasonable; but, in fact, there is none more strong. With certain minds, under certain conditions, it becomes absolutely irresistible . . . the wrong or error of any action is often the unconquerable *force* which impels us to its prosecution . . . It is a radical, a primitive impulse – elementary.'[1]

Might as well ask why I would stay out late at night and miss training the next morning as ask why I took on too many defenders and lost the ball instead of passing it. The Boss was forever on at me about that in the early days; that and not taking a tumble in the penalty area when I was tackled heavily. The reason for the latter was pride: I didn't want anyone to think he was able to bring me down. I'd sooner ride the tackle and perhaps lose possession than fall in the hope of winning a penalty.

Holding on to the ball developed when I was a kid; no doubt because I was finding myself better than my pals and so thought the ball belonged to me; which it often did. It was the same when I played in the Juniors and Reserves at Old Trafford, and it continued over into the first team. The frustrating thing was, as far as the pass-the-ball brigade were concerned, my penchant for falling on my feet. Three times I'd try to do too much and lose the ball. The fourth time I'd do something even more adventurous – or outrageous – and end up putting the ball in the back of the net. Why I did it, I don't know, except that I enjoyed so much having the ball at my feet and I loved the feeling of carrying the ball past someone. Even when the professional footballer in me saw the sense in allowing the ball to do the work with a telling pass, I would still try to do it all on my own.

There was one game, the play-off of a Fairs Cup semi-final against Ferencvaros in Budapest. We were 3-3 on aggregate after the home and away legs. In the play-off we were two goals down before John Connelly pulled one back for us ten minutes from the end. I picked up the ball in one of our many attacks, dribbled past five, maybe six of their players, and had only the goalkeeper to beat. Yet instead of

---

[1] *Tales of Mystery and Imagination*. Edgar Allan Poe. Collins, London and Glasgow.

booting the ball past him, I tried to waltz it round him: put the icing on the cake. Instead I got mud on my face – literally, by falling over the goalkeeper. One of their defenders was able to clear the ball, and but for that we'd have drawn level.

The lesson was not lost on me, though, and I managed to overcome the imp at least once. That was in the European Cup final when I broke clear for my goal in extra-time. There was a moment after I'd slipped past Cruz, and Henrique was coming off his line to narrow the angle, that I thought of taking him on and walking the ball into the net. It was that momentary flash of imp and for once, when it really did matter, I overcame the impulse.

Today, now I'm approaching the end of my playing days, I do move the ball around more. As Bobby Moore told me when we were together at Fulham, you let your head do the work your legs used to do. But there was one game, I do remember, in the mid-sixties when I passed virtually every time I received the ball. We'd lost the previous game, and on Monday morning, at the post-mortem, I'd been criticised for holding on to the ball by none other than Dave Sadler, my room-mate. I didn't say anything then, but when we got back to Mrs Fullaway's we had a right old dose of the verbals. The outcome was that the next game I passed every possible ball to Dave – and he was playing centre-half at the time.

If there were any ill-feelings, and I have my doubts, they were soon over and done with. Dave was too gentle a guy to hold grudges for long. After he was married he and Christine, his wife, used to visit Mrs Fullaway regularly to play cards with her, Dave and I getting expansive with the notes and Mrs Fullaway occasionally upping her stakes from threepence to sixpence if she thought she was holding a good hand. When we were lads – Dave had come up to Manchester as an amateur from Maidstone – we used to go around together, and he drove down to London with Danny Bursk, Mike Summerbee and me for the World Cup final in 1966. Four lads in a white Jag that was stopped by the motorway police for going too fast. Staying at Mrs Fullaway's sister's council house when we could just as easily have afforded a good hotel – if there was any accommodation available. London was packed solid. For all that I'd been down there to play football a number of times, I knew few of the places to go to, and it amused some people later to learn we'd spent much of Saturday night bird-watching at a place called Tiffany's. Not apparently the most in-place in swinging London. I certainly don't remember

William Hickey saying I had my own barstool there.

Of those three who went down with me for the World Cup final, Danny was one of the few close friends I made outside football; maybe a year or so older than me, but then so were many of the people I met early on. Few lads at eighteen, nineteen, had the money to go to the clubs I did, as regularly as I did, and it was inevitable that I'd become acquainted with people older than myself. It was the same with girlfriends in those days, too. Some of them would be older than me.

What I valued in my friendships with Danny and also with Malcolm Wagner was their acceptance of me as a person without making demands or expecting favours. At the same time they'd be honest enough to admit that knowing me had its advantages. For a start they were both United fans. Over the years we had ourselves a load of laughs and good times, but one incident, I feel, illustrates the strength of the friendship we three enjoyed. Moreover it doesn't involve me, except as a bystander. Danny was with me in Spain when his father died, and his family phoned Waggy (Malcolm) for the best way to contact us. To Waggy, the thought of a close friend learning of his father's death by telephone or cable was out of the question, so he immediately cabled us that he was coming out to Malaga, caught the next plane from Manchester, and told Danny the sad news personally. That is what I call friendship, and it rankles when I think of how often they were labelled among the hangers-on and the bad influences when the press decided it was pedestal-shaking time.

Danny also warrants fame of some kind as the recipient of one of my few letters. He was in Israel at the time, working on a kibbutz following the six-day war. One Sunday he was at Selwyn Demmy's flat in Manchester, a usual Sunday afternoon haunt, when a call came telling him to report to London: the next day he was in Israel, just like that. The following year, though, he was back home and off to Majorca with us for the summer spree. He'd been with me when I first went there in 1965, when it was just the two of us in the same hotel for two weeks and most of the time was spent with the same two girls.

Times changed, and by 1968 a group of us were taking our own villa: first home got the choice of bedrooms, last home usually ended up sleeping in the car or down on the beach. That was the year the papers made a big thing about me flying back to Manchester for a haircut. 'George Best pays £56 for a 12/6 haircut'; that sort of thing.

They really love you in the bus queues when they read that, but I suppose it was my own fault. I should have known the press would take me seriously. What happened was that Danny and Waggy were holidaying in Majorca with me at different times during the summer and, rather than hang about there on my own, I flew back with Danny to do a few things in Manchester until Malcolm was ready to fly out. Like a good many loners I don't enjoy being alone for too long. Anyway, I was sitting in the Village Barber, Waggy's shop, one day when we see the pub over the road crawling with people. Naturally, being curious, we wandered over for a look and discovered there was a flood. We also found the press there in force, the pub being just around the corner from Deansgate, and they soon lost interest in the flood when they saw I was back in town. Which is how the haircut story came about.

Mike Summerbee I'd known from the time I was seventeen, and the fact that he was a City player made no difference to our becoming good friends. We even went into business for a while, trying to make the Manchester bloods trendy by selling them Ravel shoes. They were too up-market for Manchester, though, and Mike and I were probably the only ones there wearing them. Funnily enough, the café where we met, a little old place called the Can-Can and now no longer, was close to where Mike later opened his own shop and where one of my former businesses, Oscars, is.

Like my relationship with Danny and Waggy, my friendship with Mike was based loosely around the freedom of either person to do as he pleased. You might arrange something, but if the other didn't turn up you didn't get up-tight about it. You just assumed he had something better to do that night, and you'd have forgotten all about it when you next met. Mike and I would often be found on Sunday afternoons at Selwyn Demmy's, where there'd always be some of the lads and a few girls chatting, having a drink or watching television. Living in digs, as we were at the time, it was good to have somewhere to go and relax.

Sometimes we'd meet up on Saturday night, depending on how you felt; usually whoever was playing at home would go over and meet the other's coach when it came back. We even shared a flat in Crumpsall for a while; somewhere private to take a girl or sit around playing cards with the lads. I think it was coming home from there one Friday night – early one Saturday morning – in December 1967 that I skidded on some ice and ploughed into the back of a parked car. Both cars were something of a mess, though mine was easily replaced the next week with a new S-type, white of course. Smoothing things over with the Boss wasn't so easy: to say he was livid would be understating it. Not that I could blame him. Waking to learn your star player has a bruised head, a cut knee and has not long been in his own bed is no way to start the day when your team is travelling to Newcastle. All I can say is that I'm glad we came away with at least a point.

The law didn't let me off lightly either. Seven months later I was fined £25 and banned for six months for careless driving: most inconvenient because I'd promised Mike Summerbee that I'd drive him to his wedding, what with being his best man and all. Instead we travelled in chauffeur-driven style out to the church at Mottram in Longdendale, which was probably just as well because we spent the night before the wedding at the Piccadilly and it was very, very late before we got to bed. The cup of coffee with the vicar in the vestry was much, much needed.

It was idyllic up there in the black stone parish church of St Michael and All the Angels, looking out over the dales and appreciating the perfect peace away from the weekday bustle and noise of the city. The only sign of people, somewhere, at work was the puffs of grey-blue and white smoke merging into the green of the hill fields. I was so struck by the beauty and tranquillity of it all that I said to Mike: 'You know, we only have to open the door, jump that wall, run down through the fields and we're free.' It was a feeling which came over me in that moment: a little bit of it humour to ease the tension before the wedding, but a lot of it expressing my own desire to burst away from all the adulation and the glory, the clothes-touching in the street, the total lack of privacy.

It wouldn't have worked anyway. Every reporter and cameraman in Manchester, it seemed, was sitting outside the church waiting, blocking the entrance for their one last shot or their precious footage of film. I'd heard of wedding photos, but this was ridiculous. That was life, though. No time to pause a moment to appreciate the old stone cottages with their century-old slates sagging, to watch the schoolkids playing in the yard, or to study the sundial in the little square. Just jostling people and a rush to get into the cars and out of the public eye.

The public eye was probably the main reason for my eventual decision to move away from Manchester and live in America. From the moment I made my name as a first-team player, every man, woman and child in Manchester, it seemed, wanted to have some part of my life. The number of people over the years who grassed on me was amazing: little wonder that I came to think of the city as a village. Even in the mid-sixties, when the playing side was going well and the publicity was all favourable, I'd sometimes go off somewhere quiet for a night out; not get home till late and maybe once or twice skip training or arrive late. Every time the Boss would know where I'd been. First thing in the morning there'd be a phone call telling him that Georgie Best was in such and such a club. I'd turn up for training some mornings and you could see the look of amazement on his face that I'd managed to make the effort. According to his informant I'd been boozing and wenching through till dawn, whereas I'd been at home watching television with Mrs Fullaway and had had an early night. I reckon I must have had half a dozen doubles running around Manchester at one time, some of the places I was meant to be and things I was supposed to be getting up to.

Looking back on it, I did get away with more than I should have in those days, but Sir Matt was human and he knew he had, in me, a natural, special player with talents to light up the dullest game. Why try to discipline me into conforming? He knew I was fit, provided I had enough sleep, and on days when I missed training I was always happy to go in later on and play about with a ball on my own. Most of the training under Sir Matt was with a ball, very little running for the sake of it. Just a few laps to loosen up and then work with the ball; five-a-side, games using small goals, that sort of thing. Pre-season was the hard work, with cross-country running to build up stamina. But once that's over and the season starts, a good player shouldn't need to spend all his practice time building up stamina. For one thing he gets enough running during a game, and most top players get through forty to fifty games in a season.

Certainly at Old Trafford we were fortunate in having excellent facilities, but it was the quality of the players, not the way we trained, that made us such an exciting and successful side. I remember players like Denis Law, Bobby Charlton, Maurice Setters – players worth a lot of money – sharpening their ball skills by going in and out of the dividing posts in the car park. And this was a concrete car park with bits of broken glass and sharp stones lying about. Bill Foulkes used to take himself off to the gymnasium, hang a punchball from a rafter at a height he could barely reach, and practise heading until he was thumping the ball with the middle of his forehead. Then he'd increase the height and start all over again. We were that sort of team. We knew where our talents lay and we developed them, sharpened them, put them to use when we were playing together as a team.

Not that we simply went into training, did our thing, and went off again. We were a team in many senses of the word. Most mornings after training a group of us – Bobby Charlton, Nobby Stiles, Paddy, Denis, Shay Brennan, a few others – would go up to the little kitchen above the offices, have a cup of tea, sit around, chat about football and things in general, have a laugh with Mrs Burgess, the lady who took care of the kitchen. It's important, I feel, that players get to know about each other because it helps, when you're on the field, to understand what goes through someone's mind at different times. You develop a rapport. It was the same after a game; on a Saturday night. Paddy, Denis, Noel Cantwell and their wives would often go to a little Italian restaurant called Arturo's; sit there to all hours of the night talking. Maybe someone would play the piano and they'd sing a few songs. And if I was in town with the boys, once in a while I'd drop in and have a drink with them, maybe a plate of spaghetti. The fact that I was younger and they were established players made no difference.

Indeed, that was the great thing at Old Trafford under Sir Matt; everyone had a feeling of belonging. From the groundsman, the two women who did the laundry – Mrs Ramsden and Mrs Taylor – all the way through the office and backroom staff to the top. Everyone was made to feel important in his or her own right, and they all seemed to be great characters. Johnny Aston and Joe Armstrong; Jimmy Murphy, Sir Matt's right-hand man, a lovely man, everybody's pal. Whereas Sir Matt might remain a little bit aloof – but not so aloof that he wouldn't put on a pair of boots and join in a five-a-side – Jimmy would take you off for a beer and a chat and become one of the boys. It was a marvellous set-up; and yet it was only a matter of years before they were talking of drawing lots to decide who'd room with whom on away trips in an attempt to break up the little cliques.

Chapter 5

Edinburgh on a sunny April morning made cold by a biting wind whipping in from the Firth of Forth. Running becomes a double necessity: to keep warm as well as the prime objective of losing weight. Dallas lopes along ahead of me, his tongue lolling, his head turning from time to time to enquire, from curiosity or with impatience, how I'm making out. Further down the beach, closer to the water, two racehorses are exercising, their stride as easy and rhythmic as Dallas's; consuming the ground without effort while I force my feet over the sand, the dried sweat pricking my neck, my lungs struggling against the wind and my knee stiffened by the cold. Training at Easter Road seemed to go too quickly, so I've set myself to run four miles by lunch and there are two to go. The horses come nearer, the lads keeping a watchful eye on Dallas, who watches them pass by. A wave of the hand from the lads and I'm back on my own again.

Yet I'm making progress. I could feel it in myself on Saturday against Celtic. The Parkhead fans saw it, too, switching to applause after giving me a hard time when we came out for the warm-up. The Sunday papers were generous as well, and several named me as their player of the match. This against a team containing such players as Danny McGrain and Bobby Lennox and in spite of the fact we lost 4-0. The little touches were still there, the passes still pin-point to where the man was; or should have been had he read the game properly. But most pleasing was the way I could run with the ball, take on players and go past them. The stamina was improving and the legs were showing willing to do the work.

It hadn't always been so since my return to Edinburgh a month earlier. The first game I played, against Rangers at Ibrox, I had to come off because I was feeling so ill; partly because of the treatment I was having for a stomach upset, but also because I was in such terrible condition after all the alcohol. The next game, a Cup quarter-final at Berwick, the manager pulled me off because I wasn't doing him, the team or myself any favours. That's when I decided to put in some extra training down on the beach, something I used to do during my first few seasons in America. In fact, the first year I was in Los Angeles the team trained on the beach some days, down among the high school girls with their maximum exposure. A bit different from Portobello, windswept and deserted except for the returning horses and an elderly couple in an Escort looking out to sea.

A shower would be nice; hot and penetrating. In LA we'd go straight into the sea, fool around in the surf with the girls, lie in the sun for an hour or so, then stroll up to Fat-Face Fenners for a few beers and a sandwich. Now, there's still a mile and a half to go, the dog's getting bored with waiting for me to catch up, and there's a twenty to thirty minutes drive home in a sticky tracksuit before I can shower. Nor will there be any beers with the boys but, funnily enough, apart from missing the company I don't mind that.

I've gone a month now without a drink and already I'm feeling better for it. Okay, it's only a month, and the situation is made somewhat artificial by the Antibuse. I *know* I can't drink, because if I do I'll be ill. Yet this knowledge that there's no escaping into alcohol – plus the thinking I've been doing for the book – has given me a greater awareness of myself as a person. And it has made me more aware of those around me; of my responsibility to them, as people and for the trouble they are going to on my behalf. To Angela for her patience and her concern; to the people at Hibernian – Tom Hart, the chairman, and Eddie Turnbull, the manager – for their confidence in me. They must have taken some stick when they signed me on; more so after the February affair. I'd like to prove to them that their efforts aren't being wasted.

I begin to see myself in a different light, too. My attitude to life seems to have become more positive. Being in Scotland helps. I feel close to the people, which is not so surprising as one of my grandfathers was born in Glasgow. My father comes over here, it's just like going around the corner for him; he knows that many people. Not so much in Edinburgh, perhaps, but when he goes through to Glasgow. For Angela it has meant giving up most of the things she'd have been doing were we still in London, or in the States, but she realises how much I need her if I'm to straighten myself out.

Even acknowledging that is a victory of sorts; recognising that I can't get through life on my own and that there's nothing wrong with relying on somebody else. Too often in the past I've thought, no, they won't be interested in my worries. I guess I've usually underestimated myself, or been wary because I've assumed people were interested only in Georgie Best, rather than George Best. It was a point Angela's mother made recently.

'You know what's wrong with you?' she said, having a little go at me but in a way meant to help; not as unwarranted criticism. 'You don't know how important you are to other people. How big you are; how good you are in yourself. When you walk into a room you don't realise your worth. You should walk into a room feeling bigger than you are. You don't do that. You should walk in feeling you're the most important person in that room, even if you're not – and I'm not saying you are', she added. 'You shouldn't feel inferior and hold yourself back.'

The more I've thought about it, the more I've come to agree with her. I've never been confident like that in company. Yet I've seen people in the show business world, people with comparatively little talent, act as if they're at the top of their profession; and in a funny sort of way you have to admire them for it. My way of overcoming shyness was to stand in a corner, out of people's way, with a drink. Gradually, after a few drinks, I might loosen up sufficiently to chat to one or two people. Nor was this lack of confidence in myself confined to being in the presence of others. Only of late have I been able to call a restaurant, somewhere I'm not known, and use my name to book a table. Not to be pushy, but maybe take advantage of the manager recognising me and seeing that I get a good table. That's why in the past, when I knew a place and felt secure there, I would return time and time again.

Such familiarity could have its embarrassing moments, though. I once took my girlfriend of the time, Jackie Glass, to a restaurant in Manchester where the waiter – Italian and football mad – pulled back my chair to allow me to sit down while Jackie was left standing. Fortunately she was a girl with a sense of humour, as she so beautifully illustrated at another restaurant: San Lorenzo, I think, in Knightsbridge.

That night I was in one of my more talkative moods, helped on no doubt by a couple of bottles of wine, and we were having a good old giggle about things. She was working at the time for a French scriptwriter and I was getting the inside story of some French actor's love life. Sitting next to us were three youngish Frenchmen of indeterminate sexuality, complete with a poodle tied to the table leg. Throughout the meal they entertained themselves by talking about Jackie, in fairly loud French, saying what they'd like to be doing to her and generally being obnoxious about the two of us. What they didn't know, of course, was that she was telling me everything they were saying, which made us fall about even more. At first I was fuming, but Jackie said 'Don't start anything, leave it to me. I'll sort it out.' For a moment I thought she was going to stand up and wrap a plate of food around their heads. But no; she acted super-cool and just kept translating what they were saying. Eventually we finished our meal, paid the bill and stood up to leave. To get out, however, Jackie had to step over the poodle, and in doing so she gave it a little nudge, forcing it to move. 'Oh!' she said, turning to the three French-men and speaking in fluent French. 'I hope I didn't step on your dog's cock.' To see their faces was worth putting up with all the stuff they'd been saying throughout the meal. It was magnificent; the perfect exit line.

It was Jackie to whom I left the much-quoted note: 'Nobody knows me.' Everyone made it out to be full of significance, and in some ways it was true. But at the time it was a joke. Rather similar to the comment Jackie made when asked by a columnist what was special about our relationship. 'We have some beautiful silences', she replied. Being an intelligent girl she was forever telling me things about myself, trying to sort me out. She was the one who got me reading books. Anyway, this particular day – I was returning to Manchester – I wrote the note for her as one would a quick farewell note; sort of like, I put the cat in the fridge and the milk outside. In its way it was a bit like John Lennon saying the Beatles were more popular than Jesus Christ and the whole of Alabama fell on his head. When you're famous, people take you seriously. You're allowed to be funny only if you're labelled a comedian.

There are times I wonder what would have happened had I married someone like Jackie; not necessarily her but one of the girls like her with whom I had a long-term relationship which then became friendship. The Boss was always on at me about getting married, but his idea of a nice little wife and mine were way out of line. When the papers broke the news of my 'engagement' to Eva Haraldsted, a Danish girl, in 1969 he couldn't get me in his office fast enough to demand what I was up to 'marrying a foreign girl you have only known a few weeks'. Why, he went on, couldn't I be like everyone else and marry someone a bit nearer home? I somehow think his idea of marriage, for me, was spending my evenings at home in front of the television while my little wife from Whalley Range fed me regularly with meat and veg and made sure I was out of bed in the mornings in time for training. I'd have broken out inside a month; not to go chasing other women, or even to get drunk with the lads, but to escape from the regularity of it all, the boredom of being in one place all the time.

Today it's different. I'm more than ten years older, and I've seen there's more to life than football and Manchester United. Which is not to say I wouldn't love to go back. I'd play for nothing for just one good season in the English First Division, though I know there's little likelihood of it happening. So for the moment I'll stay on at Hibs, see the season through, and await developments from the States. Already I should have reported back to Fort Lauderdale for training. But Florida is out. New York, too, despite one good offer. My hopes are that a West Coast club will show interest: somewhere in the sun with a nice little stadium and good support. In the meantime, the four miles run and the sun behind the clouds for the day, it's back to the flat for a shower, a cup of tea, and a bacon sandwich.

Chapter 6

Northern Ireland 1, Scotland 0; 21 October 1967

Best inspired the Windsor victory

Scotland's hopes of winning through to the European Nations Cup next May, which looked so bright when they defeated England last season at Wembley, now hang on the slender thread of completing the double against England at Hampden next February.

They got a severe jolt at Windsor Park [on Saturday] with many Scottish reputations trampled on and finally buried by a Northern Ireland side which, inspired by the footballing genius of George Best, rose above the handicap of a below-average attack to batter and humiliate the Scots to an extent not even remotely suggested by the 1-0 margin in their favour.

It would be so easy to go overboard in this moment of Irish victory. How much safer it would be to ponder over the strength – or rather the weakness – of the opposition. And let it be said right away, this Scottish team served up one of the saddest, sorriest displays ever. It is now crystal clear that the team which earned such a shining reputation just a few short months ago at Wembley is a thing of rags and tatters.

Drab, lack-lustre, uninspired. Trot out all the adjectives and it describes the Scots.

From a very early stage they lacked almost everything we have come to expect from them – forward ability, shooting power, strength and, most surprising of all, spirit and determination.

Manager Bobby Brown is left with numerous problems. Whether Billy Bremner, Jim Baxter, Jimmy Johnstone and Bobby Lennox can solve some of them on their return to the team remains to be seen. But one thing is certain: this Scottish side, sputtering and smouldering like a damp squib, needs an injection of the traditional Scottish fire and fury. When they needed fire and fight they had tip-tap powder-puff football.

When the fight of the Irish boys started to creep into the game anything resembling teamwork crept out of the Scots. The whole game kept running away from them and the longer it progressed the bigger became the gaps in a nerve-ridden Scottish defence. But only George Best had dynamite in his

Match report reproduced by courtesy of *The Irish News*, Belfast.

boots and hunger in his heart.

Do not for one minute detract from the merit of Northern Ireland's win, for it was a victory thoroughly deserved, but at the same time there were some Irish reputations buried along with the Scots. Inside-right John Crossan never really got a grip of the game, continually labouring in midfield.

To crown it all he missed a second half penalty just after the goal in 71 minutes. He tried to roll the ball in at an upright but Ron Simpson seemed to anticipate Crossan's direction and dived to the exact spot before the ball reached it.

Centre-forward Derek Dougan had another poor international. He did a tremendous amount of running around, but he was indecisive and frequently caught flat-footed by Ron McKinnon. However, we saw the birth of a new star. He is Glentoran right-half Arthur Stewart who took this game in his stride. Stewart is a real diamond. He has a glittering international career ahead of him and not for a moment did the occasion threaten to prove too much for him. His passes were made quickly, decisively and accurately. McKeag, too, showed much to promise for the future. Though taking time to settle, once he cottoned on to the fact that Willie Morgan, wearing the No. 11 jersey but generally operating on the right wing, seemed to have only one way of beating him – on the outside – he quickly gained control of the situation.

But the player who really brought about the downfall of the Scots was left-winger George Best. He repeatedly tied the Scottish defence in knots in his own simple, straightforward, graceful way. Doing the obvious but doing it so quickly, slickly and with such calm certainty that the opposition had no time to stop him or cut off his passes. He was terrific and rose in stature as the game went on.

It was Best who carved the opening for the goal in 69 minutes. He took a swift ball from John Parke, swept smoothly down the right and accelerated as he veered towards the penalty area. Left-back Eddie McCreadie was caught in the halfway hell of uncertainty – whether to cover Simpson or tackle Best. He wasn't given time to make up his mind. Best swept the ball into the middle and Dave Clements raced on to it, slickly brought it under control, and a strong raking drive glanced off McKinnon's boot well out of Simpson's reach.

From then on we had the unusual spectacle of an Irish team impudently taking control.

Northern Ireland: Jennings; Parke, McKeag; Stewart, Neill, Clements; Campbell, Crossan, Dougan, Nicholson, Best.
Scotland: Simpson; Gemmell, McCreadie; Greig, McKinnon, Ure; Wallace, Murdoch, McCalliog, Law, Morgan.

That was my game for Belfast, showing them perhaps for the only time what the boy from Burren Way could do when the mood took him. People there still talk about it as the greatest individual performance in an international, and it pleases me that I could give them something memorable; something to pass into the Belfast folklore. Two years later the army had moved into Northern Ireland and I was making headlines of the wrong sort for withdrawing, injured, from the side to play the Soviet Union in a World Cup qualifier.

My injury was genuine; no-one disputed that. But it raised once more the bitter club or country controversy which happens every time a Football League club fails to release a player for his country or, as happened this time with me, plays him immediately before the international and he is injured. That the Irish, Welsh and Scottish teams suffered more than the English in this respect served only to increase national ire, and the outburst from Irish Football Association president Harry Cavan – that the export of young Irish players to the English League clubs should be banned – came as no surprise. It had been said before. But Manchester United did pay my wages and my first duty lay with them. That they should have to play a League Cup replay against Burnley two days before the Moscow game was unfortunate, but it was a fact of life. As regards the risk of injury, I had been playing throughout the season with an incredible bruising – haematoma – of the shin but, because I was scoring at almost a goal a game (thirteen in fourteen), both the club and I were reluctant to give the leg a rest. The whack against Burnley settled the issue.

Whether or not Northern Ireland would have qualified for Mexico had I played in Moscow is one of those questions best answered in the taprooms. Yet defeat there was undoubtedly a saddening moment for an Irish people suffering the breakdown of their society in what could loosely be called a civil war. During that uneasy summer before the troubles, the prospect of Northern Ireland reaching the 1970 World Cup finals was a major topic of conversation. We had a strong squad, with experienced players like Pat Jennings, Terry Neill, Dave Clements, my old pal Eric McMordie, and Derek Dougan – all First Division players in England. Moreover, we had begun our campaign well with a 4-1 win over Turkey in October 1968 in Belfast, a game in which I scored one of my favourite goals. Taking the ball on my chest, with my back to the goal, I let it drop to my knee, juggled it until a defender had come in close behind me, flicked it to one side and then hammered my shot home from the edge of the penalty box. At the time we were having trouble overcoming a resolute defence and that goal, especially the way it came, was just the boost we needed.

The Russians, when they visited Belfast the following September, played it much tighter and held us to a draw. It was not a game to remember, but no-one at Windsor Park that evening should ever forget the unreal atmosphere. Some 40,000 ventured out, but for many their minds were not concentrated on lifting their team into the World Cup. All around them festered fear and hate as the city set foot into a decade of murder, violence and self-destruction. They stood cheerless. Unable to raise their own spirits, they found their players similarly depressed by the events of the past months. The troubled city handed the phlegmatic Russians an unintended psychological advantage.

Today my visits to Belfast are few: once or twice a year perhaps. Yet it remains home: those 'ugly red-brick streets', as one writer saw them, mean more to me than Manchester or Los Angeles ever could. There, amid the tight-eyed soldiers, the suspicion and the rows of desolation, live my memories: of the boy drinking lemonade on a city centre treat with his mother; of the child, bright and eager in the summer sun, chasing beside his grandfather to a dustbowl known as 'The Hen Run' for his first football match; of the truant, rebelling not from lessons but from a philosophy of education which favoured middle-class rugby union to working-class football. They're never talked of in the way men reminisce in pubs or clubs or beds. The friends of my youth are no longer found kicking a ball about the empty fields at Bells Bridge behind the sewage works. The years have made them fewer and the troubles have sent so many elsewhere. Those remaining, fame has set apart.

So, whenever I return, I travel down Ravenhill Road and glance quickly along Donard Street. I hurry through the barricades and look in Woolworths, the magical Woollies with its myriad delights to occupy the truant on a cold afternoon. On my way to some out-of-town function I drive past houses with bricked-up doors and planks nailed across the windows. And occasionally, amid the squalor and the despair, three or four old people stand at doorways staring at the car; there so long they'll never want to move until they're gone. Then, in the evening, I go with my father to his little sports club and sit laughing and drinking among the Catholics and the Protestants as the comedian cracks his jokes about the Pope and Ian Paisley. I listen to their talk and I see their love for me in their smiles. But we have so little in common now. They are living through a hell they have come to accept as part of life and living. I am the folk hero home for a day. They laugh, they drink, they show no fear. And to me that is more disturbing than the flak-jacketed soldier at the end of the street with his back to the wall and his rifle raised ready. This is not Belfast as I remember it, and yet it is still home. My family live here.

Belfast for me is the Donard Street of my grandparents or the wastelands of the spreading Cregagh where we roamed in gangs determined not by denominations but by streets and friendships. The religious aspect was there; it always has been. But the most we ever threw at each other were names. We saved the lumps of dirt for the rivals from another street. Most of the time, though, every free moment was spent on football, on the fields or on the street. School breaks were the same. From Nettlefield Primary School I'd dash to my Granny Withers in Donard Street for my lunch, then it was back to the school playground for football. The quicker you got back the more often you had the ball, because the game soon degenerated into a free-for-all; forty-five or fifty a side, and if you managed a dozen touches of the ball you were a good player. Keeping me in shoes must have been the despair of my parents, for one pair would last little longer than a couple of months. Shoe manufacturers were always advertising the 'indestructible' shoe, but playing football on concrete all day we had no trouble wearing them out.

The Americans, anxious for knowledge in their desire to foster soccer, forever ask how many hours a day I put into practice as a child. They can't understand that it wasn't like that. Our schools didn't always have playing fields and gyms; we didn't set aside so many hours a day to practise football. We kicked around a ball at every possible opportunity from dawn to dark because more often than not it was the only – as well as the cheapest – form of entertainment. It stimulated us, it tired us out. I would keep a tennis ball in my pocket so that every journey to the fish and chip shop on the Castlereagh Road became a cup final full of amazing dribbles and delicately executed wall passes. A tennis ball! exclaim the Americans in wonderment, as if this might be the answer to the problem. But if you can control a tennis ball on an uneven pavement, think what you could do with a football on an even pitch.

Not that it was all football. The Cregagh was a developing estate with new houses and new streets providing homes for young families moving out of the old confined areas of the inner city. There were kids everywhere, and there was space for them to play and fight and dream. I don't have total recall. But I do remember the rat, and I doubt if I will ever forget trying to jump the river. That could have changed at least one course of my life.

The rat was one of hundreds you would see around Bells Bridge; every time drains were laid for a new street or foundations dug, the rats would dart from their hiding-places pursued by terriers and children with sticks. One day we chased one into a tree trunk, and we all dared one another to put a hand in and get this rat out. I suppose we were out to kill it, but no-one was willing to risk a hand. For a start the thing looked massive; for another, being cornered, it was vicious, or so we kept telling ourselves as an excuse for being chicken. Eventually one of the lads put his foot inside the trunk, only to let out a fearsome howl as the rat bit right through his Wellington boot and into his flesh. That was enough for us; we fled, leaving him there screaming until workmen came down to investigate. The story went that they took him to hospital with this rat still hanging on to his boot, but whoever heard the story after that version would no doubt have been given an even more grisly account.

Jumping the river was something we all did; but only one way. It wasn't really a river; more of a stream only a few feet wide. On each side was a concrete slab with a sewer pipe running through the water, but as one side was lower than the other it was easy to jump from the high side to the low. No-one – in our gang anyway – had managed to jump the other way. The day eventually came when George Best could no longer resist the challenge; especially when I announced my decision and all my pals told me I'd chicken out or that I wouldn't make it. I measured out my run-up with all the care of a fast bowler in a Test match or a long-jumper in the Olympics, took one last look at the distance I had to clear, burst into a sprint and launched myself into space. Threequarters of the way across I knew there was no way I was going to make it; not properly. Nor was I going to fall short and land in the muddy water. I was going to crash on to the concrete slab. I put my arms up to protect my face, but the pain as I landed on my elbows was nothing to what followed immediately. Projecting from the front of the slab was an iron pipe some four or five inches long, and as the rest of my body bent and smacked into the front of the concrete, the pipe hit me. Not in the stomach or the legs, but right in the balls.

The pain was incredible, but with my pals there jeering at me there was no way I would show it. I just hung on until I could crawl up on to the slab, by which time the others had all gone off to play somewhere else. How I managed to get home I'll never know; I was doubled up and could hardly walk. I tell you, standing in a wall for a free-kick never worried me at all after that experience. Once I reached home – there was nobody there – I locked myself in the bathroom, threw cold water over myself to ease the pain, and cried my eyes out. I wouldn't cry in front of the others; such is the power of pride. But even worse than the pain was having failed in front of all my mates, and for weeks afterwards they were at me to try again. There was never any chance of my even thinking about it.

Family life, in my child's mind, seemed to centre around my grandparents' home in Donard Street, where we lived until moving up to the Cregagh. For some reason I always went to the primary school near there and so was in and out of my grandparents' house almost every day; more so than my sisters. But Sundays were special, my grandfather being a good, religious man. Not deeply so, but God-fearing and a respecter of the Lord's day. Every Sunday, then, the family would come together at Donard Street, attend church in the morning, we kids would go to Sunday school in the afternoon, and then there'd be church again in the evening. There was no getting out of it; my grandfather was strict about that, and yet not in a way that made you hate it all; in a lovely way, a way that made you feel part of a tightly knit family.

Even the ban on Sunday television was never a hardship, because we could always watch when my grandfather took his afternoon nap. While the rest of the family were busy chatting, we'd crowd around the set, the sound as low as possible so that he wouldn't hear. It made the programmes twice as exciting, especially as one of us would always have to sit on the stairs listening for him getting up. He or she would have only the picture. And as soon as there was a noise upstairs, the set was switched off and all the chairs moved back as if nothing had happened. Then it would be time for tea: those Sunday teas with my granny's home-baked cakes full of jam.

I suppose I so enjoyed being there because I was always my grandfather's favourite. I had been named after him, as was my uncle George, and rather in the way that Matt Busby ruled over

Manchester United, so my grandfather was the patriarch of the Withers family. He was a lovely man; tall, greying hair, striking in appearance and much respected. To me he always looked too young to be a grandfather. And then he died.

I was taking my eleven-plus at the time; not at Nettlefield but up the top of our street at the local school: Cregagh Primary School. School work never gave me too much trouble in those days, I was good at arithmetic and English, and the examination was going well. I felt confident I would pass and so gain the grammar school place my parents were hoping for.

Come the final day of the examination I walked up to one of the local shops to buy myself a couple of new pencils and a rubber, already thinking of the task ahead. Consequently my mind was only half attentive when the woman behind the counter asked me what I thought was a very daft question.

'When's your grandfather getting married?'

Thinking she must be cracking a joke, and not wanting to appear as if I wasn't listening, I started to laugh and rushed out of the shop and on to the school. Once there I never gave her words another thought until I'd finished my paper, enjoying that feeling of relief that the ordeal was at last over. And then it struck me. What she had said was 'When is your grandfather getting buried?' I couldn't wait to get out of the classroom to race home. The house was empty, so I rushed next door to Melda, my mum's best pal down the years and a second mother to us kids. Whenever something went wrong and our own mother wasn't there it was next door to her. The story just burst out of me, full of questions and demanding explanations. And that is how I learnt my grandfather Withers had died.

No-one had told me at the time because of the examinations. They didn't want it to affect me, though everyone was so shocked at the time that I'm surprised I noticed nothing unusual. Perhaps children don't. Even when I was told, I didn't want to believe it, yet at the same time I knew it must be true. It was the first time anything emotionally disturbing had really happened to me and I didn't know how to react. So I went out by myself and began walking until it was dark. They found me cried out sitting underneath a lamp-post.

The funeral left from Donard Street; all the family there just as on Sunday; everyone going up to the coffin to pay his or her last respects. Except me. I remember so little of that day, nothing of the bustle that surrounds any family gathering, but I do know I couldn't bring myself to look into the coffin. And then we moved out of the house, through what had once been a tiny shop at the front, and on to his church. From there the men went to the cemetery and the women returned to the house, as is their way in Ireland. There would be tea, and cakes, and drinks, but for me the house could never be the same. It was the passing of my childhood.

*   *   *

'It intrigues me and satisfies me nowadays to observe that the English schoolboy still rebels against any attempt by authority to obstruct him from football as my own generation did. It pleases me out of all proportion to the local significance of the circumstances to watch organized rugby . . . change instantly to improvised football the moment the teacher's back is turned.

'I remember clearly the bitter sense of imposition I used to feel at being made to pick up, and run with, that ridiculous ball with its pointed ends, when I could kick a round one naturally. I have always felt that compulsory school rugby in any area where football is the paramount sport – and that means just about every town outside South Wales which has any pretension to being an industrial employer – is an infliction of crass snobbery. It is even bad for rugby . . .'[1]

Only on one point do I differ from Arthur Hopcroft. Being mad about most sports I actually enjoyed playing rugby. I was fast, quick on my feet, and I made a nifty fly-half for a brief time. But football remained the number one sport for me, and it frustrated me to play with the oval ball when I could do something so much better with a round one. By now I was becoming special at football; people were stopping alongside the fields where we played simply to enjoy watching me. They were making complimentary remarks to my parents. And yet this institution was preventing me from expressing my one major talent – at that time.

This institution was Grosvenor High School, and I was my parents' pride as I set off to go there on my first day of term. Their son, going to a grammar school. Most of my pals from the estate were going to the local secondary modern, Lisnasharragh Intermediate. Whereas I had passed the dreaded eleven-plus, few of my friends had even bothered to take it.

[1] *The Football Man*. Arthur Hopcroft. Collins, London. 1968.

But as well as pride there must also have been sacrifice for my parents. We were an average, right-down-the-middle family; not paupers, because my father was in employment most of the time and my mother usually had a part-time job in the fish and chip shop or the ice-cream factory. But we had no money put away, and Grosvenor High School meant a special uniform and bus fares. So, like my parents, I could feel proud at going from a council estate to the grammar school for I knew what it involved.

I sometimes wonder how different it might have been had they only played football. For the more frustrated I became at being denied the game I loved, the less interested I became in my school-work. The worse my schoolwork became, the more often I'd be kept behind for detention, writing out lines for punishment. Detention meant going home on my own, walking to the bus stop through a predominantly Catholic district. And in Belfast that means one thing. Trouble. The uniform was an immediate giveaway, and a small skinny Protestant kid on his own was too great a temptation. If I improved my ball control on broken pavements with a tennis ball, I developed my acceleration, my body weaving and my sidestepping trying to prevent my books and cap from being taken off me.

From disenchantment to disappearance was an easy step. Playing truant came naturally. Either at first break or at lunch I'd hide in the toilets or up in the roof until everyone was inside. Then it was around to my Aunty Margaret's to hide my schoolbag behind her dustbin and off to town; past Van Morrison's Cyprus Avenue on to the Upper Newtownards Road and into the centre; wandering through the shops, nicking fruit from the greengrocers to make up for the school lunch I all too often missed. Days too cold or wet I'd use my bus fare to buy bright red wine gums, suck them until my throat looked inflamed and retire home pleading tonsillitis. That ruse eventually backfired when my mother sent me off to hospital to have my tonsils out.

Aunty Margaret's dustbin didn't serve its purpose for more than a month or so, either. She returned home from work early one after-noon, found my schoolbag there, saw me collect it at three-thirty, and informed my mother. I was playing football at the bottom of the street when my mother walked past to the bus stop, but I thought nothing of it. When she walked past an hour and a half later, all the laughter gone from her face, I knew I'd been rumbled. Not only had she seen my aunt; she'd been to the school and discovered how frequently I'd been missing classes. There was no mistaking the tone

76

of her voice when she said she'd see me 'at home in ten minutes'. I ran away then, but Belfast in late autumn is no place for spending the night under a hedge.

So ended my days as a grammar school boy. I was given the chance of returning and reforming, but it meant dropping into a lower-grade class to catch up on my studies. Or I could go to the secondary modern with its football and its neighbourhood friends. It was no contest, and from my first day at Lisnasharragh my world was filled once more with football. Football at breaks, football for the school, football for Cregagh Youth Club. Even football in the classroom. Art classes seemed set aside for choosing the football teams: all the boys clustered in a corner while the girls played at painting and giggled about the boys.

Not about me, though, unless it was my physique. I was so unbelievably thin; apart from my legs, which were strong, my body was a disaster area. I took part in a school gymnastics display once, and for days beforehand I couldn't sleep at the thought of people looking at this apology for a body stripped down to vest and shorts. I was sure everyone would laugh at me, just as the girls did. They made my life hell, though I suppose I made it worse for myself because I always fancied the prettiest ones. Usually, too, they were the ones with boyfriends twice my size, if not bigger. Several times I came close to getting my head kicked in by the school Romeo and his little mafia for looking too long at his girl. Husbands had similar ideas in later years, but by then I had my own mafia. And anyway, I rarely had to bother looking.

Yet all the hang-ups about my size; all the embarrassment at being the only kid in short pants when the others wore long trousers; everything lost significance when I was on the football field. There I had a world of my own, winning the ball, directing play, cutting defences with long balls, setting up goals, scoring them. I was di Stefano, Tom Finney and Puskas all rolled into one. The games are faded far from memory now, but I do remember one year playing in the final of the Youth Club Cup at The Oval, which is Glentoran's ground. For us, it was the same as it would be for an English kid to play at Old Trafford or Anfield. And for me it was especially memorable because Glentoran was the club my grandfather had supported.

The youth clubs, or boys' clubs, play an important part in growing up in Ireland, especially for lads dreaming of a football career. So many of the youngsters who go across to England are spotted playing for their youth club team; and at the same time there are many who get missed. I'd like to know how many scouts took one look at me and said straight away, 'too small'. But then I was fortunate in having someone like 'Bud' McFarlane running our club. Bud was the second team coach at Glentoran, he had a good football brain, and he knew people like Bob Bishop.

Bob Bishop helped run the famous Boyland Youth Club and was also chief scout in Ireland for Manchester United. It's part of the Georgie Best legend that he sent Matt Busby a telegram saying simply 'I believe I've found you a genius'. But he was much more than just the man who set me on the path to Old Trafford. I remember him as a great character who really gave his time and energy to helping kids in Belfast. He had a little place outside the city, at Helens Bay, where every weekend he would take half-a-dozen youngsters from Boyland, and one weekend I was invited down there. For lads like us, from council estates or the inner city slums, it was just like camping out. Everyone had to chip in, helping prepare the meals, wash the dishes. First thing in the morning we'd go for a run; much of the day we'd spend kicking a ball around. It may not sound much, but to any kid growing up in Belfast it was a weekend to treasure.

Even then, after going down to Helens Bay, there was no knowing what would come from it. Bud and I had been disappointed before, knowing the scouts were about and yet hearing nothing. Not even the Irish schoolboys' selectors were interested, and that was after our Cregagh Under 15 team had beaten their representative side 2-1. 'Too light, too small', they said, forgetting the old maxim that if they're good enough, they're big enough. Then, because Cregagh and Boyland played in different leagues, Bud arranged a match between our Under 17 side and them. I was not quite fifteen at the time – too small, too light – but I scored twice and we beat them 4-2. That was enough for Bob Bishop. Off went the telegram, and back came the reply from Old Trafford: 'Send the lad over and let us have a look at him.'

The day they told me was one of those moments in life when time stands still. I was so thrilled. As usual I was kicking a ball about in the street, and I can remember being really annoyed because I had to leave the game and go into the house to see the gentleman who had come to see me. I went in, and there, sitting at the table with a cup of

78

tea, was Bob Bishop. I knew something was up because of the flush on my mother's face. It was similar to when we heard I'd passed my eleven-plus. He asked how I was, asked how my football was going, and then he came to the point of his visit.

'How would you like to play for Manchester United?'

I couldn't believe him; couldn't see how he could mean it. Manchester United! Even an Irish club would have been too much to expect. But the most famous club in England. I couldn't do anything but laugh. And then he explained. There'd be a trial for two weeks during the school holidays; it would all be arranged. There'd be another lad, Eric McMordie, going across with me. But already I'd stopped listening to the details. All I wanted to do was rush back outside to my friends.

'I'm going to play for Manchester United', I screamed at them. 'I'm going off next week to Old Trafford.' I never dreamt that I would ever play for them. But just to go there. It was like a dream.

For the journey my mother bought me my first pair of long trousers and I felt grown up: all five feet of me. They were also my only pair, and when I returned to Manchester to stay, Mrs Fullaway had to alter some of her sons' clothes for me to supplement what was in my suitcase. But that's the way it was, and for years after it was the same for others. I'd see the new lads arriving with their one suitcase: wee Irish and Scots lads shy and unsure in the presence of Georgie Best. And I'd look out some extra clothes for them; something to help them feel more at home. It was my way of remembering; and I suppose my way of saying thanks.

Chapter 7

The café was small, but large enough to have a waitress. The tables were square, wooden and covered with plastic. A few pictures decorated the walls. We sat down, Mrs Fullaway and me, and, in the way you do, looked about us. Part curiosity; part trying to attract the waitress. At another table sat my uncle and aunt, but it didn't surprise me to see them there. Mrs Fullaway, seeing me look across, asked if they were people I knew. I explained they were an uncle and aunt.

'Oh, I'd like to meet your mother's sister', she said, which struck me as odd because this aunt was actually my father's sister. Still, I gave my uncle a little nod to suggest we might join them, but he shook his head and I let it pass. This uncle and aunt, I explained to Mrs Fullaway, were the parents of my cousin, Gary Reid, who was shot in Belfast in 1974; caught in crossfire between the army and rioters while on his way home. He didn't die immediately, but we all knew he would never recover. He existed for eight days.

No sooner had I finished telling Mrs Fullaway this than my aunt stood up and came across to our table. Her face was quite devoid of expression or emotion; there was no knowing that any relationship existed between us. And when she spoke she called me Mr Best. It was weird.

'Mr Best', she said, 'I wonder if I could have your autograph? It's for my son, Gary. He's such a fan of yours, you see.'

Which is when I woke up, shaking. I tried to get back to sleep but my mind was too alert. From the street came the sound of tyres over a wet road, and when I looked out the window I saw that it had started to snow. In another room Dallas stirred. Another car crunched through the fresh snow and beside me Angela slept on. Sleep, I knew, was not going to return quickly or easily, so I left the warm bed and went through to the kitchen to put on the kettle for tea. It was almost two o'clock, and looking through the kitchen window I saw, with some relief, that I was not the only one awake. In the gardens the snow was beginning to settle, but it was still not so thick that it was sliding off the high-pitched Edinburgh roofs.

The tea made, I went through to the living-room and sat down at the table with a pen and the pad I'd been using to jot down ideas as they occurred to me.

Gary had dreams of leaving our city,
To escape in style like Walter Mitty;
What seemed more suited to his talented feet
Were Anfield or Old Trafford, not Thistle Street.

His family were close; he loved this place
And getting away was becoming a race;
A race young Gary was destined to lose,
This Belfast Boy with no political views.

He yelled he'd be back in a minute or two,
Some chicken chow mein and some ribs would do;
But hurrying home with their supper that night
He became one more victim of the senseless fight.

Just thoughts, but having written them I felt easier in my mind. Except that I was too awake to sleep and my thoughts were again returning to Belfast. Not to my own days there, but to life as it must have been for my parents in the years after I'd left. And especially I thought of my mother, for it was her, more than anyone in the family, whom my fame and public image affected most.

At first my being away from home made little difference to their lives, unless it was having one mouth less to feed and some extra money coming in. I went home frequently then; perhaps only for a day or a weekend but often enough for them to see how well I was. If it gave them the chance to be that much more proud of me they rarely showed it to me; and certainly never in public. Not that I'd have wanted it any other way. The longer I was in football, the more I came into contact with parents of whom I'd have been embarrassed were they mine. The mother of one player – after a game at Burnley – grabbed hold of my arm as I was leaving the ground and literally dragged me into the little tearoom they had at Turf Moor. There, in front of other people, she proceeded to tell me in no uncertain manner how her son was a better player than me, how he'd grown his hair long before I did, and that he was worth more money than I was. Just because he played for Burnley he wasn't considered fashionable.

'Good luck to him', I said. 'I'm not going to argue with you.'

There were a number like that. Getting more out of the game than their sons were. If my mother had done anything like that, I think I'd have disowned her.

My parents, if anything, went the other way, preferring to lead their own lives rather than become involved in mine. Indeed, my mother would become embarrassed when people approached her in the street to congratulate her when I'd done well. My father could enjoy it a little more when he was with his pals, but for most of the time he was content to let life revolve around him. Even when he watched me play he'd rarely comment on my game. He understood that I knew enough of myself not to need praise or criticism. Although I do recall him once telling me to learn to 'take it against any team without getting steamed up'. That was after one of my more petulant displays, against England in 1966, when I thumped the ball over the stand at Windsor Park.

By 1966, however, the newspapers were covering more than just Georgie Best's football career. The car accidents, however minor, were made to sound sensational. If I hit someone, few newspaper reports if any would mention it happened in that half-light, half-dark period around lighting-up time, or that a person, holding an umbrella low to keep off the driving rain, stepped from the pavement in front of the car which was moving slowly at the time. 'George Best knocks down pedestrian' had my mother on the phone in minutes, and she would then have to be reassured that everything was all right. I wasn't going to be prosecuted and thrown in prison. There was a rumour in 1968 that I'd been killed in a car crash. It circulated like wildfire before I arrived back in Manchester to show it was a malicious hoax. But for several hours my family had to live in uncertainty: so, too, did the family of the girl I was driving home from London.

Then the footballer became the playboy and every aspect of my private life was under scrutiny. The football began to go sour around 1970 and the stories became sourer. They struck my mother hardest, for I had always been her favourite, her first-born, and there was no way she could defend me now or attempt to protect me. Telling her not to believe half of what she read was to no avail. As mothers do, she turned my shortcomings into self-criticism, asking where she had gone wrong and questioning her beliefs: just as after the death of my grandfather, she grew very introspective, searching through her

82

religion for a reason why he had been so suddenly taken.

Nor did I help by staying away from home for long intervals. At first I'd be back in Belfast every month, it seemed. Then it was every three months; then every six. And as the visits became less regular, so it became more difficult to return. Or perhaps it was simply becoming easier not to return. I could have written, but I didn't. Even early on it was Mrs Fullaway who wrote to my mother with news of my welfare. I remember telephone numbers but never birthdays. Yet a birthday remembered takes on such importance; as does one that is forgotten. My mother shouldn't have needed to phone Mrs Fullaway every week to see how I was; I should have been phoning her. But, like my father, she didn't want to trouble me. It was the same with money. The press knew before I did that my father had been on unofficial strike for seven weeks in 1970 with no money coming in except the social security and what my two eldest sisters could contribute. At that time there were three young children to support. So many times I told them they had only to pick up the phone, but I've come to realise that that is not the same as being there to help out.

In public, too, life was becoming more of a strain for my mother. Where once the problem had been to cope with being a minor celebrity, she now had to bite her tongue as she listened to people around her running me down. Occasionally it became too much, as happened one night when she and my father were leaving their social club. While my father waited to call a taxi, my mother went into the ladies' cloakroom where another woman, recognising her, asked if she was Mrs Best.

'Yes', said my mother, trying to back out of the room as quickly as possible.

'George Best's mother?' continued the woman, going up to her.

'Yes', replied my mother, hoping she might want an autograph or a photograph the way many people did. 'I'm Mrs Best.'

'Well', began the other, 'I think your son's a disgrace to Ireland. He's . . .'; and she laid into my mother with a full rundown of all my failings. It was nothing new for my mother, but this time she snapped. Up came her hand and she smacked the woman right in the mouth. Immediately realising what she had done, she dashed from the cloakroom in search of my father.

'Dicky! Dicky!' she yelled at him. 'Jump into the taxi. We've got to get away from here!'

They didn't go back to the club for weeks afterwards, but today my father laughs at the story and I wish I'd been there to see it.

However, I was so busy with – and creating – my own problems that I had little time for anyone else's. The irony of it was that, in seeking an escape from my own life through drinking, I was creating an image which was, in turn, causing my mother to find solace the same way. It was not immediately obvious, but as the 1970s progressed it became more so until, somewhere between 1972 and 1975, one of my aunts called on me to return home.

'We're getting worried about your mother', she told me. 'She seems so depressed all the time; there's no get up and go about her any more. Come home and talk to her.'

But I knew already, from what my sisters were telling me, that something was wrong. During the time I lived at home I had no recollection of my parents arguing. Now, it seemed, they were. My father would return home from work, my mother would have been drinking during the afternoon, something would be said, angry words spoken, and my father would go off for a few quiet drinks with his pals. When he went home he'd find my mother in a worse condition. She couldn't see what she was doing to herself, but then neither could I see what I was doing to myself. And I was dragging both of us down.

They put on a party when I went back; a get-together for most of the family. Rather like the New Year's Eve parties of better days when the whole clan would gather in true Scottish tradition and there'd be home-made treats for the kids and a jolly singsong with much laughter and cheer. This time the laughter and cheer were muted, and not just because of circumstances within our family. Belfast was adjusting to the reality of everyday existence in the shadow of violence. The armed troops, introduced we thought as a temporary measure, were now a regular feature of street life in the city.

My mother's reaction on my return – tears, hugging and kissing – I took to be one of affection and relief at having me home. But as the evening developed and members of the family arrived, she became teary, crying instead of joining in as she once would have. I talked to her, trying to reassure her that I would always land on my feet. Hadn't I always? But I was getting nowhere. Every now and then she'd go off on her own and I knew she was having another drink. Not that it cheered her up; it only served to make her more depressed.

Long before the evening was through she had ceased taking any interest in what I was saying. She could only sit beside me, touching my arm or my hand and weeping.

The next day, arriving back in Manchester, I felt so lost that I did what was now almost habitual: opened a bottle of wine and drank it on my own before going in search of company. Drink. It's the Irish problem that transcends politics and religion. And for so many in Northern Ireland today it's the only escape. I'm sure my mother wasn't the only woman in Belfast drinking cheap wine in the afternoons and hiding the bottles from her family. Many wives and mothers must see their husbands and children off in the morning and wonder what the evening will bring. For my mother there was, in addition to that worry, the concern of what was happening to me. I would have liked to take them away from Belfast, but by this time I had no proper home of my own. I was living the life of a gypsy, trailing from one place to the next in search of something I couldn't define. Eventually I left Manchester and went to America, putting myself even farther away from Belfast. But the newspaper stories kept my family misinformed of my activities, and for every good story there were ten to break my mother's heart.

My mother died in October 1978. She collapsed one morning after my father had left for work and was dead when my sister found her. I was in Los Angeles at the time, though I'd been in Europe several weeks earlier, playing football. I hadn't gone home to Belfast, and I didn't know there were newspaper reports saying I had disappeared during the tour. Now it was too late; too late also for the pangs of conscience that would trouble me for years after. 'If only you'd been at home more, George, it wouldn't have happened.' My aunt's words filled my mind all the way back to Los Angeles after the funeral. And there, within weeks of my mother's death, I learnt I had been banned by FIFA, the world football authority, from playing anywhere in the world. By playing several invitation matches for an American team in Europe I had, unknown to me, broken the terms of my registration. I'd become an outlaw.

Chapter 8

Real Madrid 3, Manchester United 3; 15 May 1968

Manchester United in final at last

from Geoffrey Green

After 11 long years and four attempts at the semi-final round, Manchester United have reached the pinnacle of the European Cup. In this giant palace of the Bernabeu Stadium [in Madrid], they reached the final and became the first English club to do so.

On May 29 at Wembley they will fight out the climax with Benfica, the champions of Portugal.

Manchester United now stand as the heroes of England, having suffered and survived the scar of losing the league title at the last stride only a few days ago, and they must take the field at Wembley as the favourites.

Seldom could there have been a more hazardous or remarkable journey than Manchester United made tonight as they recovered from the depths of despair at half-time to beat Real Madrid, the champions of Spain and the symbols of Spanish football power, on aggregate by 4-3.

To the end, their goal by Best at Old Trafford was worth its weight in gold after all. This, indeed, was a fairy story. As I sit here, with 125,000 people pouring dumbfounded and stunned out of the stadium, I can hardly believe it.

It was a match of great character. In the first half, Real had the freedom of the game and built themselves into a 3-1 lead by goals from Pirri, Gento, and Amancio, to a lone and almost lame duckling by comparison from Dunne, for United, a long forward lob of some 40 yards which trickled home past Betancourt as he was muddled by Zoco, with Kidd challenging close in.

That goal hushed the stadium, but Real at that moment seemed in no danger. All that looked in prospect was this lead probably to be built on in the second half. After all, the great Amancio, like a matador, had teased the Manchester United defence with masterly footwork and passes of his cape, as it were. At his side were Grosso and Velazquez and Perez, building up an almost non-stop barrage.

For half an hour Manchester held out, with Stiles snapping angrily all the

Match report reproduced from *The Times* by permission.

time at Amancio's heels, and often failing. Brooding disaster hung in the air, and suddenly the storm broke. In the last quarter of an hour of that opening half, four goals suddenly tumbled out of the night – a header by Pirri, from Amancio's bending free-kick; from Gento, as he burst through after Brennan had missed a long through-pass from Pirri; then that long straggler from Dunne; next a dazzling shot on the turn from Amancio out of a crowded ruck.

So it looked all over, with the Spaniards 3-2 ahead on aggregate, and with more to come, we thought. The vast crowd was in a symphony of sound. They resembled a man who has two bottles of wine inside him, pleasantly intoxicated and feeling that there is nothing much wrong with life.

Manchester, in that first half, had played a tactical formation of 5-3-2, with Sadler, wearing the number ten, drawn deep in defence at the side of Foulkes, and only Best and Kidd to forage up front. This gave Real Madrid the initiative, and it seemed all over. Already the night was peppered with goals and chances.

This was fiesta time for the hot-blooded crowd, whose wrath flamed out as Stiles stabbed at the fleeting Amancio. Flags and banners waved; the air was full of fireworks, rockets, and there was a hot juicy feeling of expectant victory in the air.

The stadium at half-time must have seemed to Manchester United like a sheer, granite cliff of sound that was falling about their ears. But the twist was in store. Now the fairy tale began to weave itself, and from nothing a magical recovery was born.

It was born from a change of tactics which saw Sadler at last moving up into attack and Manchester stirring to 4-3-3 and even 4-2-4 as they almost threw caution to the winds. There was the crunch. It brought justice because in the end it was English temperament, fibre, and morale that won through.

All day the sun had beaten down like a hammer, and the night, exquisitely still, was humid. It should have favoured the Spaniards, but it was they who withered, leaving Manchester United to pass into history in a blaze of splendour on a night of enchantment.

Turning to attack, United came back into the match with just over a quarter of an hour left when Foulkes headed on a free-kick by Crerand which the alert Sadler slipped in on the run. That made it 3-2 on the night, and 3-3 on aggregate.

Then, with 12 minutes left, the remarkable story was completed. Crerand took a long throw down the right touchline, and Best showed his peerless genius as he beat Sanchis and Zoco in a corkscrew run, sped up to the right by-line, pulled the ball back diagonally, and there, of all people, was Foulkes, that veteran warrior of 16 years, the defensive centre-half, now following up in a moment of inspiration to turn the pass in at the far corner. It was a brilliant stroke, and it won Manchester United the battle.

The hour and a half sped like five minutes, though the closing seconds seemed an eternity, with 21 players in the Manchester United half, and Real Madrid battering their heads against a red wall to save themselves.

But not even Amancio, supple, alert, industrious, and brilliant in footwork, could rescue the monarchs, and in the end the sleek, self-assured football of Real, which they had unfurled in the first half, died in the dark.

One has to search in the recesses of memory to recall such a night, and I cannot do so.

Real Madrid: Betancourt; Gonzalez, Sunzunegui; Zoco, Sanchis, Pirri; Grosso, Perez, Amancio, Velazquez, Gento.
Manchester United: Stepney; Brennan, Dunne; Crerand, Foulkes, Stiles; Best, Kidd, Charlton, Sadler, Aston.

David Sadler and I walked straight off the field, through our dressing-room and under the shower. Four years earlier we had shared that first sweet taste of success by bringing the FA Youth Cup back to Old Trafford. Now Dave, with his goal, and I, with my corkscrew run up the right flank, had taken Manchester United to the last stage in achieving the club's long-standing dream. We sat on the floor in our playing strip, letting the water pour over us. Outside, in the Madrid night, a hundred thousand silent Spaniards found their way to bars, cafés and eventually to bed. Their noisy celebrations had been brought to a premature end at half-time, even if they were not aware of it at the time.

It was then Matt Busby showed that his genius as a manager did not rest alone on his ability to find or buy players. So often he had told us before a match, 'Go out and enjoy yourselves', that people came to ignore him as a tactician. True, we rarely played the numbers game, but as we trailed into the dressing-room at the change-over he set about not only rebuilding our morale but also making significant tactical changes. First he reminded us that we were only a goal down on aggregate so we might just as well attack: we would have in any other game. And then he pushed Dave forward out of the defensive position he'd adopted throughout the first half. 'That might surprise them', he said, and he was right. Our new-found aggression produced two goals and we were bound for that momentous night at Wembley.

Manchester United were not the first British club to win the European Cup; that accolade rests with Celtic in Scotland. We were, however, the first club from the English Football League to do so, and our 4-1 win over Benfica at Wembley climaxed a memorable career for Matt Busby, brought him a knighthood, and set the seal on a great chapter in the club's history. My regret is that we failed to reach the final again in 1969 when, in the semi-finals of the European Cup for the fifth time, Manchester United were drawn to meet AC Milan at San Siro in the first leg. United had gone down 4-0 at this venue in 1958, in the semi-finals that followed the Munich disaster, and for many in the club it was an emotional return. However, thoughts of getting away with a win or a draw were dashed by goals from Sormani and Hamrin either side of half-time. And in the second leg at Old Trafford Milan played their defensive game so well that we were in the seventieth minute before I finally slipped Anquilletti to put Bobby Charlton through for the club's 100th goal in the European Cup.

That goal was just what we needed to lift our game. We knew now that their massed – and masterly – defence could be penetrated, and narrowing the deficit gave us heart to endure for another twenty minutes the provocation and dubious tackling so characteristic of many Italian teams. Our attacks were no longer tentative forays; they were mounted with a confidence that threw the Milan defence into uncertainty. And when a goalmouth scramble ended with Denis Law stabbing yet another rebound over the line we felt sure we were there. But no! A Milan boot hooked the ball out of the goal and the French referee, badly positioned in my opinion, ruled against any goal. Denis was positive he scored; so, too, was Willie Morgan who was following up and could well have booted the ball into the back of the net had he been unsure that it was fully over the line. Even the television film and photographs published later seemed to establish that we had been robbed of an equaliser.

Harsh words have been spoken since on the subject of Italian clubs ensuring victory by having their bank manager on the bench, and bribes scandals in the Italian game have done nothing to refute the allegations. Yet we could still have turned that match had our fans not reacted in such an appalling manner to the referee's decision. No sooner had he rejected our appeal for a goal than the Stretford End mob launched an amazing selection of missiles, one of which laid low the Milan goalkeeper, Cudicini – or so he claimed. That stopped play for some minutes, and in doing so it put an end to the rhythm we had built up prior to the disallowed goal. Had we simply got on with the game we might well have forced a draw or even gained a victory. It had taken us time, but as so often before, when all looked lost, we had finally clicked and there would have been no stopping us.

Defeat by an aggregate of 2-1 put us out of the European Cup; and more than a decade later United have yet to re-enter the competition. In the meantime, Liverpool have won the Cup three times and Nottingham Forest twice, and in some minds the memory of Manchester United's glorious years has faded. Certainly, in the eyes of some who saw us knocked out by AC Milan that May night in 1969, the glory days had come to an end. In my heart of hearts I think I was already one of them, though my reticence – and my youth – held me back from saying so in public.

For me, that 1968-69 season had been one of mixed emotions and growing personal uncertainties. Conditioned from the beginning to live with success – to expect it even – I was finding it difficult to adjust to the doldrums of a middle-of-the-table existence. Only once in my professional career had I gone a season without a trophy, and that was 1965-66 when we went so close in three competitions: semi-finalists in the European Cup and the FA Cup and finally fourth behind run-away Liverpool in the League. In just four seasons I had won two League Championship medals, a European Cup winners' medal and been voted Footballer of the Year in England. At the end of 1968 I was named as European Footballer of the Year ahead of Bobby Charlton – the first time two players from the same club had occupied the top two places. Now, on the eve of my twenty-third birthday, I sat down to look back over a season which, apart from our run in Europe, was ordinary: eleventh in the League, with only four more goals to our credit than the 53 scored against us, and beaten in the quarter-finals of the FA Cup.

Of those fifty-seven goals, nineteen were mine and Denis scored fourteen. No-one else scored more than ten, whereas the previous season, when I was joint leading goal-scorer in the First Division with twenty-eight goals, three others scored ten or more. Whether or not our slump was reaction from winning the European Cup, or taking time to recover from the two vicious World Club Championship encounters with Estudiantes I don't know. Injuries took their toll, with John Aston breaking his leg in the third match of the season and Bobby Charlton and Tony Dunne sidelined for long spells.

We'd suffered from injuries before. Then, however, there had always been young players waiting to stake their claim or Matt Busby's shrewd assays of the transfer market to keep the clock ticking smoothly. Now, when he bought the necessary replacement, his decision, in my opinion, was the wrong one. Willie Morgan might have been Burnley's answer to George Best, but he was no John Connelly, the England winger purchased from Burnley in 1964 to replace John Giles and transferred on in 1966 when the Boss felt John Aston was ready for First Division football. Moreover, it took Morgan a season to settle in and by that time, for me personally, the damage was already done. I had begun my period of disillusionment, though many would say I had taken my first steps on the path to self-destruction.

Some time after he returned from the moon, the American astronaut Buzz Aldrin took a long look at life and wondered what more it had to offer. The only answer he could find at the time was nothing; and so, rather than live each day with the thought of that, he turned to drink. Eventually, I understand, he became an alcoholic. When the story broke, people were generally sympathetic, as I've found they can be. Even the press were understanding. He had, after all, been to the moon.

The way I look at it, maybe he should have been prepared for the pressures that would arise from going to the moon. Here was an intelligent man, chosen for a specialist rôle in a highly technological operation. Yet all the years of planning amounted to nothing when the bottom dropped out of his high.

Where, then, does that leave a Belfast boy with one God-given gift who found himself a legend before he was twenty-one; living a larger-than-life existence; having hundreds of letters a week with two or three specially employed girls to answer them? Fame, honours, cars, businesses, more money than I'd ever believed possible. Neither background nor education – what there was of it – had prepared me for these. And although I enjoyed them, they remained a secondary part of the high I was experiencing by playing for Manchester United. Performing with players whose own skills I respected and appreciated and playing for a manager who understood my own special talents. 'Let him develop his own way.' I entertained. I gave pleasure to thousands of people every week. Little tricks that took their breath away; goals that were a flash of magic. There was one at Chelsea in 1966 when I flicked the ball from my right foot to my left as I was falling off balance and still smashed it in off the crossbar. But I could afford to be adventurous and even outrageous. I was there to exhibit my genius.

Then, in one season, the mood changed at Old Trafford. Without fully understanding them, I felt the undercurrents pass through me like that classroom realisation when I knew my grandfather was dead. Knowledge came before the confirmation, which only several more seasons would bring. It was almost as if the established people at the club – players as well as backroom staff – thought that winning the European Cup was the ultimate achievement. They were happy now to relax and rest on their laurels. But to me, with a whole career ahead of me, it looked as if the future contained nothing but grafting about in the middle of the table, losing as many games as we won. There were players who needed replacing, if not immediately then certainly in another season. I could see that. Surely the Board and the management could. But where were the replacements coming from? Where was the forward planning that, in the past, had produced new players at just the right moment? This was the richest club in the British game; the best supported. It had one of the greatest traditions in the world. There was a time when every youngster dreamt of going there. Where were they now? Why were the Arsenals, Birmingham Cities and Sunderlands contesting the Youth Cup finals? United hadn't reached that stage since we won it in 1964. And in the years to come Crystal Palace and Millwall would stamp their name on the trophy; the latter as a Third Division club!

In retrospect I can think of two, maybe three, answers. The first is that the extensive scouting network, which once kept a stream of talented youngsters flowing to Old Trafford, had aged with the years and not been replaced with younger, more aggressive scouts. Where were the successors to lovely Joe Armstrong, who, for Matt Busby, limped around the schoolboy grounds of England in search of lads with that extra something he felt and knew would stand United proud in future years; lads like Duncan Edwards, Bobby Charlton, David Pegg, Denis Viollett and Brian Kidd? Dave Sadler, too, was recommended by Joe. Lads kept arriving at Old Trafford, of course, but within the quantity there was not the quality of old.

Secondly, the club's success might have frightened off youngsters who thought as I did. How can I break into this team of world-famous players; every one of them an international? The answer to that, of course, is that they weren't worth having if they didn't feel they were good enough to win a place.

A third possibility is that parents were being offered a reward – or incentive – and the best lads were going to the highest bidder. It has always been said that clubs were prepared to leave a little parcel on the table for the parents, though that certainly didn't happen to mine. If I cost United anything, it was the £150 donation they sent to Cregagh Youth Club. Plus whatever Bob Bishop's bonus would have been for 'discovering' me. But what does it matter if clubs are offering incentives to parents in order to sign youngsters? Most of the parents are lower-middle- or working-class folk who could always use some extra money, and were there a limit to the amount that could be offered, everyone would know where he stood. It might cost five hundred pounds or more per player, plus the cost of maintaining a successful youth scheme, but what is that today when clubs pay more than a million pounds for someone who is not an established international?

Which returns the theme to Willie Morgan; or more specifically to the purchase of a player, for almost £100,000 in 1969, who had appeared in just one international for Scotland – that unforgettable Northern Ireland-Scotland match in 1967 – and was not to reappear for his country until 1972. This was not the type of player Matt Busby had bought in earlier days to see the club through an emergency; as a replacement for an injured or out-of-form player. With a few successful exceptions, such as Tony Dunne and Alex Stepney, he had gone for experience. John Connelly has been mentioned already. His contribution was immediate: fifteen League goals in his first season. Albert Quixall, transferred from Sheffield Wednesday in 1958 for a record £45,000, scored around ten goals a season from then until 1963. Then, like Connelly, he was transferred elsewhere when his job was done.

But for me, the man who epitomises Sir Matt Busby's shrewdness in buying the right player was David Herd. His father and Sir Matt had been friendly since Sir Matt's Manchester City days before the war, and the Boss knew David was Manchester United mad; would play his heart out for the club. David had turned professional with Stockport County, where he had the distinction of playing alongside his father, and in 1954 he'd gone to Arsenal. When United signed him in 1961 he was in his late twenties, had recently won his fifth cap for Scotland, and possessed one of the fiercest shots in the game, though I gather it had taken time to develop. Sir Matt bought him when he was at his peak, as his record of League goals from 1961-62 until he broke his leg testifies: 14, 19, 20, 20, 24 and 16. Among his Cup goals were two in the 1963 FA Cup final win over Leicester City. He would, I am sure, have kept scoring for United for another season or two, and yet it is significant that Dave Sadler was already established in the first team to fill the gap caused by David Herd's injury.

Denis Law and Paddy Crerand, both signed in 1962-63, were bigger signings in terms of money and reputation, but they, too, illustrate Sir Matt's all-round expertise in the transfer market. He knew who was available – and when – by being *in* the market the same way as a good stockbroker knows what is being bought and sold at any given time. He kept an ear to the ground. He knew when Denis Law had grown disillusioned with playing in Italy and was waiting in Switzerland to mastermind the coup that was worth 236 goals for Manchester United. He had a gentleman's agreement with Jock Stein of Celtic that United would have first option should Paddy Crerand ever want to move. It was football's equivalent of the stockbroker's old school tie connection.

Why, then, did it end? Were there suddenly no more experienced players wanting to move to Old Trafford? I find it hard to believe. Alan Ball, I feel sure, would have loved to play for United and was just the player to instil the enthusiasm and fire which seemed lacking after 1968. Were the people associated with the club really doing their utmost to maintain the standards that had been set in the 1950s and 1960s, or had complacency set in? If the lesson to be learnt from United's decline and fall was don't sit back and enjoy the brief moment of success, Liverpool heeded it well, buying in or producing players to replace first-team regulars as soon as the management felt the moment was right. Sentiment has little place in the preparations for success; only in the celebration of it. I look at the players Liverpool release and replace so easily. And then I look at our European Cup side and what followed. In 1968, Paddy Crerand was a year off thirty, Bobby Charlton was thirty, and Bill Foulkes was thirty-five or thirty-six. Yet where were their replacements? Who was standing by waiting for the moment when one of them was injured or called it a day? Bill retired after the European Cup success and had to come back again because the defence lacked a strong central defender. Surely someone must have seen the need for his replacement several years earlier, no matter how well he was playing.

Although it took me a long time to speak about it to anyone but a few close friends, inside me I felt what was going to happen to the club and it hurt. Perhaps I should have spoken out, but I was only twenty-two. Who was I to tell the greatest club in the world that I thought something was intrinsically wrong with the set-up? Not just with the team, but at other levels as well. Who was I to walk into

94

the boardroom and protest that the lovingly built machine was falling into disrepair? We'd won the European Cup. Had I been three or four years older I might have been able to accept the responsibility of carrying the team with my skills and my experience. But as we began the 1968-69 season all I wanted was to keep on enjoying the game; to play alongside the type of players with whom I'd become accustomed to playing.

Unhappily it would never be like that again. Where once I entertained, I now found myself one of two up front in a four-two-two or, if I was lucky, one of three in a four-three-three. Plus a goalkeeper, of course. Saturday afternoons and Wednesday nights meant taking stick from overmanned defences as I twisted and turned to set up chances or score the goals. Now it mattered if I lost the ball in mazy dribbles because we no longer won it back so quickly or so confidently. My goals became all-important because others weren't scoring them so frequently. Instead of revolving around me, the team now depended on me and I lacked the maturity to handle it. I began to drink more heavily, and on the field my list of bookings grew longer as my temper became shorter.

By January 1970, when I was suspended for four weeks and fined £100 for 'bringing the game into disrepute', I'd had only five bookings in seven seasons of League football; in 1970 alone I was booked four times. Interestingly, I think they were all in the second half of the game, by which time I'd taken more than I could stand and would suddenly explode. The moment it happened, of course, I regretted it intensely; but by then the little man was going through his point duty routine and my name was in his book. The press put it down to my Irish temper; petulance was a favourite word. But do they look at themselves when they're caught in a traffic jam or if the bar hasn't opened on time? For ninety minutes I was expected to have my ankles systematically kicked so that today each one is bloated and unrecognisable from what it once was.

'Bringing the game into disrepute', incidentally, was knocking the ball out of the hands of referee Jack Taylor, a butcher, at the end of a bitterly fought League Cup semi-final against Manchester City. Again it was a moment of frustration: a way of showing my disappointment at the sort of game we'd played. Unfortunately for me i made the mistake of committing my crime before the television cameras – and it was seen by millions, folks! But the kids watching my tantrums on television would take notice that such heinous acts were not countenanced by those in higher authority and would be punished with due gravity. They would also have noticed that the dangerous tackling – four players received warnings in the first half alone – did not bring the game into disrepute. No-one, at the time, did ever get around to saying what the 'game' was. I don't think it was football.

As my interest in playing football diminished, so too did my interest in those outside activities which rode on the Georgie Best image. I became an agent's nightmare. I'd agree to something and then fail to turn up, either because I felt sick in my heart at what was happening to the game I loved so much or perhaps at times simply out of perversity. There was a television commercial, around 1969 or 1970, for which I was to receive something like £20,000. A men's toiletry called Fore, with Georgie Best running through Hyde Park pursued by Afghan hounds and beautiful models who couldn't resist the fresh-flavoured golf course smell of his after-shave or his armpits or whatever. That sort of thing. Though what connection there should be between Georgie Best and golf I just don't know. Hole in one, maybe!

Anyway, everything was set to film this commercial on a Sunday; they even provided a helicopter to fly Waggy and me down to London from Bangor, where I was playing for United in a friendly. Waggy, in theory, was there to do my hair for the commercial, but in practice he was there to ensure I was around when the cameras began rolling. They were leaving nothing to chance, this lot. They booked us in for the night at a hotel right on the Park, and they even had Vivien Neves as one of the models – enough to make any red-blooded male get out of bed at seven o'clock on a Sunday morning.

Saturday night I trooped off to Tramp so William Hickey would have something to write about on Monday. Waggy trailed along in hot pursuit, but as the evening wore on and Saturday night became Sunday morning his watchdog days were obviously numbered. 'Don't worry, Waggy', I told him. 'It'll be fine. Go back and have some sleep. I'll see you in the morning.' Poor lad, he was almost asleep on his feet. The next thing he knows is that it's seven o'clock and Ken Stanley, my agent, is on the phone. Where's George? Waggy's heart sinks. Ken Stanley's has already gone down with all hands. Over in the Park are cameramen, a director, models, an advertising executive with £180,000 of television advertising wrapped around this commercial, and a pair of beautifully groomed Afghan hounds.

96

1964. A youthful eighteen but already displaying the genius that drew comparisons with Matthews and Finney and was to make Georgie Best football's first 'pop' idol. *Colorsport*

Left: 1965. Nineteen, and enjoying every moment of my footballing life. *Daily Mirror*
Above: 1967. West Ham and England captain Bobby Moore is left watching as I round the last defender to set up one of our six goals that clinched the 1966-67 League Championship for Manchester United. John Aston is the United player in support. *Central Press*
Right: 1969. With Sir Matt Busby. The fulfilment of his greatest ambition – winning the European Cup at Wembley the previous year – was the turning-point of my career, though neither of us realised it at the time. *S & G Press Agency*

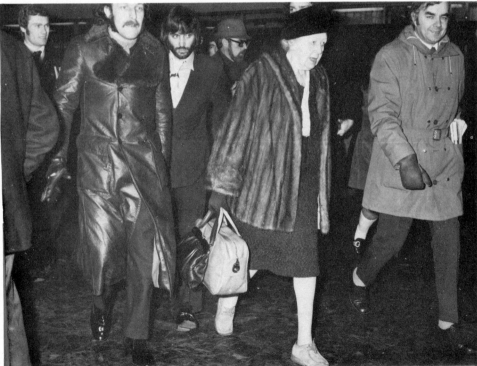

Top: 1967. Lap of honour with the League Championship Cup: (l-r) Nobby Stiles, Shay Brennan, Bobby Charlton, John Aston, Denis Law, Alex Stepney, Sir Matt Busby, Pat Crerand, myself and Tony Dunne.
Bottom: Arriving at Euston, late for an FA Disciplinary Hearing, accompanied by Malcolm Mooney (foreground left), one old lady, and various gentlemen of the press. *Central Press*

1970. The third (top) and fourth of my six goals against Northampton Town in my first game after serving four weeks' suspension for bringing the game into disrepute. *S & G Press Agency*

Above: 1971. Escorted from the field by Tony Dunne and Bobby Charlton at Stamford Bridge after being sent off by referee Norman Burtenshaw – for arguing with one of my own team-mates! *S & G Press Agency*
Left: My father, Dick Best. Some of his best advice – 'take it without getting steamed up' – I'd have done well to heed. *The Guardian*
Left opposite: 1972. Happy days are here again – for the time being. With Denis Law on my first day back at Old Trafford after 'retiring' in May. But by the end of the year I had quit United and football once more. *Central Press*

1968. Celebrating one of Manchester United's most famous victories: winning the European Cup semi-final against Real Madrid after being down 3-2 on aggregate in Madrid at half-time and coming back to win the tie 4-3. *Ray Green*

Now Waggy really starts to work. He knows one of the girls I was chatting up in Tramp and phones her. I'm not there, but she remembers me talking to someone else later on. She knows her name but not her address. Oh yes, she's a model, and can she go back to sleep now, please. Waggy consults Ken Stanley; they confer with the advertising executive and the director. Vivien Neves feels unloved, the cameramen drink coffee, and the Afghan hounds look longingly at all the trees. Waggy could quite happily go back to bed, but the advertising executive has £180,000 on his mind. The director is fuming. They begin to phone agents in an attempt to locate the girl. It takes time. It is, after all, Sunday morning; or it has been when at last they get an agent who knows the girl's address in St John's Wood. Waggy phones. The girl thinks twice about answering but eventually does.

'It's Malcolm Wagner. Is George there?'

'It's for you', she says. 'Malcolm.'

I lean across her and take the receiver.

'Waggy', I tell him, 'bring my boots. We're going back to Manchester.'

There's heavy breathing and whispering at the other end, and I can picture Ken Stanley and the advertising executive leaning on Waggy as he starts to talk. He knows I won't want to do it now because, yes, I'm worried that I'm five hours late and I'm scared what they'll all think of me. I'd rather catch the train and run back home. Unfortunately I've got Waggy on a bad day. No sooner does he arrive at the flat than he grabs me by the shoulders and shakes me like an Afghan hound with an Afghan rabbit. In the end, what can I do but laugh. He's so angry and so grimly determined. Then he lets go of me and begins to laugh too.

'You enjoyed doing that, didn't you?' I said as we climbed into the advertising executive's car. But he didn't say anything; just put his head back and closed his eyes to dream of Vivien Neves. She was nice. So was the advertising executive. The cameramen thought it was all great fun – they were on Sunday rates – and the director forgot he'd been cursing me all morning. The Afghan hounds had a pee and we got on with the filming.

I wonder at times if I put myself in those difficult situations so that someone would make the decision I felt was inevitable yet did not want to make myself. I would have to break with Manchester United, even football, regardless of how much I loved the club and how much it would hurt to do so. To which people might reply that if I felt so strongly I should have stuck it out through the bad days because, in the end, the situation improved. But to me it didn't really; only the results improved. They have never returned to the standard at which I wanted to play. Maybe I set my sights too high; maybe I was being a perfectionist. Or a romantic. But for me, my relationship with Manchester United was a love affair; it wasn't a marriage. And when the flame that lights the love affair has gone, there can be but one ending, no matter how painful its determination. Which doesn't stop you, in later years, closing your eyes and remembering how good it was.

For it was good. On the days when we put it all together we were magnificent. Those who were fortunate enough to see both the 'Busby Babes' of the 1950s and the more mature team of the 1960s are entitled to argue forever over which was greater, and I would dare only to venture that we might have been the more entertaining because we played outside the disciplined framework of our predecessors. The reason for this, I feel, is that each player was chosen for his part rather than developed for it as many of the 'Babes' were by Jimmy Murphy and Bert Whalley, the team coach who died along with eight of the players, the secretary and the trainer in the Munich disaster. In 1958 there were still good youngsters to bring through, such as Shay Brennan and John Giles, but recourse to the transfer market was an essential part of building one last great side for the 1960s.

That we were a great team should not be questioned, and it saddens me when people remember us only as the side which won the European Cup. Before that we were at the top for five seasons. Our strength was consistency over a period of years, for once he found the right blend the Boss held it until the last. Then it was too late for changes. The proportion of home-grown players to purchased players was roughly the same, although of the European Cup side only four – Stepney, Dunne, Crerand and Law – were obtained on the transfer market. And Tony Dunne cost a mere £3,500 in 1960; certainly one of Sir Matt's wisest buys.

Alex Stepney cost considerably more, but he repaid every penny with that marvellous save in the European Cup final, and there are many who argue that we wouldn't have won the League Championship in 1967 without him in goal. He was never flash, but he was very good and some of his saves were quite unbelievable. An indication of his ability was his selection for the England squad, for the overall standard of goalkeeping in England must be the highest in the world.

The two fullbacks were lovely players. Shay Brennan, a Manchester lad born and bred, was a touch player, as you might expect from a former wing-half. I don't think I ever saw him tackle anybody, but he probably never had to. His positional sense, like Paddy's, was marvellous. Tony Dunne was one of the fastest footballers in the League at the time. You'd think you were past him and he'd be back in front of you before you knew it. It was no coincidence that some of our best moves and many of our goals began at the back with these two.

The halfback line was put together beautifully. Paddy was the constructive halfback, as Matt Busby was in his playing days, while Bill and Nobby were more physical. I wouldn't say they roughed people up, but they did make them move. Even though we had a reputation for being a footballing side, no team had an easy game against us. These two, in the heart of the defence, could take care of themselves, which is what every team needs. But there's a difference between being hard and being dirty. The reputation Nobby Stiles had in Europe and in South America – assassin was their nicest word – was quite undeserved and was based almost entirely on his superb marking of Eusebio in the 1966 World Cup and the 1968 European Cup final. Big Bill Foulkes I admired for the way he always got on with the game; nothing was ever going to disturb his concentration. He did once get upset with Nobby for relaxing when we scored our sixth goal against West Ham in 1967. The little man had the temerity to congratulate Bill on winning his fourth Championship medal and the big fellow apparently was not amused.

The heart of the side was the midfield linking of Paddy with Bobby Charlton. It is said that United gained its style for the 1960s the day Bobby moved from the left wing to play as a deep-lying forward, but the deployment would not have been so instantly effective had Paddy not been there beside him. For me, Paddy made the team tick, making up for his lack of speed with an almost uncanny positional sense. His passing was tremendous – forty or fifty yards right into your path – and above all else he was a great competitor. Even towards the closing of his career he always seemed to give us that slight edge when it mattered most, and if I ever had to choose a team to play in a Cup tie, Paddy would be my first name. Off the field he was wonderful company, with a deep, romantic feeling for the game.

It was obvious to anyone listening to him talking about football why Matt Busby wanted him at Old Trafford.

Bobby Charlton, to me, was perhaps as enigmatic as I was to him. When I first started playing with him he struck me as being as shy as I was, but the closer you got to him you saw he had a lovely sense of humour. To outsiders, though, he always looked a bit strait-laced, and it didn't help when he was put up on his pedestal as the epitome of all that should be good in football. It still makes me smile when I recall the howls of anguish which greeted his comment on television that a certain player should have been 'professionally fouled' outside the penalty area to stop a goal in the Leeds-Chelsea Cup final. You'd have thought Mary Whitehouse was proposing . . . well, I hate to think what.

Much was made of my decision not to play in Bobby's testimonial match, for by then it was generally well known that we didn't get on. But to have done so, I felt, would have been little less than hypocritical. It wasn't that I didn't admire him as a player: he was one of the best I've seen and it was a pleasure to be in the same side. But as his career was coming to an end and the team was struggling, it seemed to me he was putting so much of the blame on himself; as if it was all his fault. Which, of course, it wasn't. On a more personal level, I began to feel that he saw himself as better than most of us; not as a player but as a person. I know he found it hard to accept that I could be excused from training when all the others were expected to turn up; and I'm sure he disapproved of my lifestyle. I know I frustrated him on the field when I first played in the team because I would try things that didn't always come off. But ironically, by the end of his career, the wheel had turned and I was the one frustrated because he was trying things that were no longer coming off. I wish he had retired several seasons earlier, and I suppose at the time I said so aloud too often. I wasn't the only one who thought that way, but the others kept their feelings to themselves in public. Today it seems so far in the past, and if I was asked now to play in a testimonial for him I wouldn't hesitate to agree.

Up front there was speed, artistry and usually someone solid. The sudden departure of John Connelly upset the balance of the attack for a time, because he was one of those wingers who can go wide to give the attack breadth or cut in to score goals. But then I began hitting them in and it didn't seem to matter. Moreover, we were never a forward line that relied on just one or two people to score goals, even if we did have Denis Law, so fast and lethal anywhere near goal and also a wonderful creator of openings. David Herd, of course, was there to thump them in regularly, and when he and Denis were injured the youth policy had ready replacements in Dave Sadler and Brian Kidd.

Then the production line dried up. Youngsters brought forward to cover injuries were found wanting and so were the expensive buys from other clubs. Funnily enough, looking at United's League position from 1970 to 1972, I find they were eighth each season; not exactly disastrous, but none the less a tumble from the heights of the 1960s. Those respectable eighth positions, however, could not disguise the signs. Manchester United were in decline, and in 1974, six seasons after standing supreme as champions of Europe, they finished bottom but one in the First Division and were relegated to the Second. I wasn't there to see it happen. On New Year's Day, at Loftus Road against Queen's Park Rangers, I had made my last appearance for the club.

Chapter 9

Manchester United 0, Leeds United 0; 23 March 1970

The night of 22 United heroes

by Eric Todd

At five past ten last night Manchester United and Leeds United helped each other off the field and brother grasped the hand of brother as the crowd gave them a tremendous ovation which every man deserved as never before.

After another 120 minutes' hard struggle in pitiless conditions their FA Cup semi-final at Villa Park still remained in a state of deadlock and these two grand sides will have another try at Burnden Park, Bolton, tomorrow night.

Whoever reaches Wembley, there to do battle with Chelsea, will have arrived the hard way and if fortune decrees that Manchester or Leeds win the trophy, nobody surely will complain that they haven't worked for it. This was Hillsborough in duplicate except, of course, that the paying customers were given extra value for money and certainly for entertainment. The weather gods, who rarely look benignly on meetings between these two Uniteds, sent heavy rain before and during the match and the state of the ground was enough to break the heart of any conscientious groundsman. But both Manchester and Leeds provided the skill and the determination expected of them, and for whole-hearted endeavour and physical fitness we may not see its like again for some considerable time.

This game had everything and I would not presume to name one outstanding incident for they were far too numerous to mention. There were a dozen or more near misses, a disallowed goal by Clarke, breathtaking saves by Stepney from Jones and Gray, the sight of Best ploughing through the mud all on his own and then leaving the ball behind within speaking distance of Sprake and of Bobby Charlton fouling his brother and not apologising. I could go on all night and the way things went it looked as though I might have to.

Manchester, as they had done at Sheffield, were in command in the first half, during which they missed some easy chances and were desperately unlucky with others. Kidd in particular strove and suffered, flinging himself

Match report reproduced by courtesy of *The Guardian*.

bravely at everything that came across from either wing and failing by a whisker to connect with at least three centres or corners; Sartori, too, chased everything and everybody, Bremner included. Behind them Sadler more than compensated for the absence of Ure and Stepney was no more than a spectator, at least in the first half when Leeds were committed almost entirely to defence and an uneasy defence at that.

Only those people who know Leeds by heart could have expected such a show of retaliation. It had been thought that Hunter would be missed, as indeed he was before the interval, but Madeley in the end proved himself a capable deputy. Bremner was the captain supreme, the inspiration incomparable. He drove his men as never before and distributed the ball with an uncanny precision.

Leeds finished so strongly that it seemed they must score and assuredly they would have done so if it had not been for Stepney, Sadler and Stiles, who made light of a violent attack of cramp. On a night such as this, however, cramp was a modest price to pay and on such a night tempers were kept remarkably well under control; Edwards's enthusiasm, more than anything else, led to him having his name taken for a foul on Gray. Cooper has a gashed shin but should be all right for tomorrow.

Manchester United: Stepney; Edwards, Dunne; Crerand, Sadler, Stiles; Morgan, Sartori, R. Charlton, Kidd, Best.
Leeds United: Sprake; Reaney, Cooper; Bremner, J. Charlton, Madeley; Lorimer, Clarke, Jones, Giles, Gray.

To say I left the ball behind within speaking distance of the goal-keeper was putting it very kindly. As far as most people were concerned I fell over the ball and landed flat on my face in the mud. The Leeds fans thought it was wonderful; our supporters weren't so impressed. I lay there wishing the ground would open up and bury me, but then my sense of humour got the better of me and I remembered the woman in the hotel. I picked myself up with a rueful smile and got on with the game – whenever Paul Reaney, the Leeds defender, gave me a chance to.

The hotel was of the olde-worlde variety, somewhere outside Birmingham; we'd returned there on Saturday night after losing 2-1 to Chelsea at Stamford Bridge. The woman was of the modern variety; chic, self-possessed, and more interested in John le Carré than attempts by footballers to chat her up. Which is why I didn't try. It wasn't that I hadn't taken any interest: you always keep looking in the hope that there might be some little sign. But I wasn't going to be told to get lost by some classy bird with exquisite legs who kept her nose in a book all Sunday long. So I let it pass and spent a long, boring day playing cards or watching the television. Monday night's replay would come around soon enough.

At the time I was growing a beard, drinking too much over longer periods, and getting depressed easily. The depressions were usually brought on by football, for even though we were enjoying a reasonably good season the old thrill had gone. Wilf McGuinness, who'd taken over as 'chief coach' following Sir Matt's retirement, was a numbers man. We now had team talks and diagrams on blackboards before matches; everyone had a specific rôle on the field, unlike Sir Matt's day when it was all off the cuff and we were told to go out and enjoy ourselves. Not that I held it against Wilf. He was young, he had modern ideas, and he must have been influenced to some extent by the thinking of Sir Alf Ramsey, for whom he'd been a training assistant during the 1966 World Cup. Probably, in retrospect, he was too young for the job, purely and simply on the grounds of his age. He'd grown up with people still in the team, had even played alongside them, and in some quarters there was resentment that he now held the reins. It wasn't that he lacked the qualifications. The year before he took over at Old Trafford, he was appointed England's youth squad manager, and he had already devoted his life to Manchester United; as a player until he broke a leg in 1959 and then as a trainer.

Denis Law, in his autobiography, refutes the suggestion that some of the senior players would not play for Wilf. It is his view that he eventually failed at Manchester United because he introduced an approach to the game that was totally alien to United's previous style. Younger players, however, saw things differently. Dave Sadler, for example, felt that not everyone would play for Wilf and, as a result, he wasn't getting one hundred per cent effort from the team. 'You just had to look at what happened when Sir Matt returned', he said. 'The situation changed at once.' It certainly did. When Sir Matt took over control of the team from Wilf in December 1970, United were fifth from bottom in the League. By the end of the season we had climbed to eighth with only five losses from nineteen games.

My biggest worry with Wilf, though, was his determination to keep an eye on me; probably because I was single and my reputation with the girlies wasn't designed to give a football manager an easy night's sleep. Thoughts of me dissipating all that hard-earned energy must have kept him awake for hours on end, and whenever we were away from home he seemed to spend every moment of the day trying to anticipate my next move. I don't know why he bothered, and in later years, when we could both laugh about it, he wasn't so sure either.

'If I'd known then what I know now', he told me once, 'I'd just have left you to get on with it. Just let you do whatever you wanted to do, because I'd have been better off not knowing about it rather than trying to keep an eye on you.'

But in those days, struggling desperately to establish himself as the boss, he linked my off-the-field activities with what I did on the field. And sometimes, as at Villa Park that night against Leeds, I gave him evidence which, if not necessarily correct, was certainly circumstantial enough to hang me.

On the morning of the match, shortly before lunch, I'd had enough of sitting around the hotel. I was bored, my nerves were twitching with irritation and my face was driving me mad. So I decided to shave. That made me feel considerably better; indeed, so good that I automatically said hello as I passed the bookish lady on the stairs. When she said hello in reply I couldn't help but stop dead and turn to look at her. I also turned my inward smile to an outward one.

I had no idea what to say to her, but she made it easy by asking me to autograph a photo she had in her room. I said of course, and went into the well-tried routine, asking her how long she'd been at the hotel, what she was doing there; the usual line of chat that almost every man uses with a woman and yet invariably succeeds with. She was married, but she said it in a way that made me realise things could have been better. And all the time we talked I had one thing going through my mind; two things, actually. I kept thinking I had a game that evening and so there wouldn't be much time for the other thing. There was also the problem of lunch. If I didn't appear soon, Wilf would be doing his gumshoe act.

'Look, I'm expected at lunch', I told her. 'Perhaps I could come up after?'

'To autograph the photo?' she asked. There was a hint of a smile and a little bit of cheek in her flat Midlands accent.

'Of course', I replied.

My change of mood must have been obvious over lunch. Whereas I hadn't been at all talkative in the morning, now I was at least making some attempts at conversation. I tried not to hurry through lunch, but it took me all my time to stay at the table when I saw my afternoon's appointment leave the restaurant. As I was soon to discover, I still didn't remain there long enough. Hardly was I in the lady's room, it seemed, than Wilf's banging on the door, and he's got the hotel porter with a master key to let him into the room.

I'd never seen him so angry. Me, I was just embarrassed, not so much for myself but for the woman. The porter was standing there, trying to look unconcerned, and there were players walking past in the corridor, going to get ready before we set off. 'Get to your room', Wilf was shouting, the sweat on his forehead shining. 'The coach is leaving in forty-five minutes. I want you downstairs ready in half an hour.' That meant half-past three, and I was in the habit of spending a few hours in bed before an evening match.

It was no good arguing with him. I had no alternative but to put on my sorrowful look and walk out of the room with as much dignity as possible. The door closed quietly behind us. I half expected a lecture, but instead Wilf marched straight down the stairs and into the bar where, by leaning over the banisters, I heard him order a large whisky. That was enough for me. I about turned and went straight back into the room opposite. I missed my few hours, but I did get on the coach in time. However, as I lay in the mud of Villa Park, I almost wished I hadn't. And I knew Wilf would be thinking it was all that woman's fault. He wouldn't realise that meeting her was the best part of my day, nor that I'd got more from my half-hour interlude than the obvious. It takes more than sex alone to make you drive down the M6 from Manchester to Birmingham as I was doing for some time afterwards.

Shades of 1965: we lost the second replay 1-0 by a Billy Bremner goal in the eighth minute. Perhaps if I hadn't fallen over in the mud; perhaps if . . . No, words like perhaps are meaningless. I'd have loved to go to Wembley as a Cup finalist, but it simply wasn't to be. Whether it would have lengthened Wilf's time in charge it's difficult to know. I somehow doubt it, for he was in a no-win situation. The club would still have found itself in the same dire straits the following Christmas because the seeds of discontent were already germinating. By autumn 1970 they were fully in flower.

For me, personally, life was a mêlée of emotions. There were good days and there were bad days, many of them broken only by long crazy nights of drinking. They were what I now think of as the Brown Bull days, a period of alcohol-inspired madness that led to the lost years of George Best. I had reached a stage where my life appeared to have lost its balance: the highs and the lows had become inextricable. One moment I was lying in the mud at Villa Park with jeers ringing

106

in my ears; another, I was sipping wine in the state rooms of Number 10 Downing Street as a guest of Prime Minister Harold Wilson at a reception for the West German Chancellor, Willy Brandt. As far as I can remember, I spent much of the time talking football to the Chancellor's personal bodyguard, which later earned him a reprimand from his boss. Not that I was the only footballer invited; Bobby Charlton was there too. The cynics naturally made a connection between our presence at Number 10 and the fact that Gerald Kaufman, then Mr Wilson's aide, was the prospective Labour candidate for the Manchester district of Ardwick; but they neglected to mention – if they were aware of the fact – that Mr Wilson had personally written to congratulate me after one of my performances which he'd been able to see.

That was March; in April I was in court as a defence witness for Paddy Crerand, and I was in trouble for reputedly spitting, swearing and throwing mud at referee Eric Jennings in the international against Scotland at Windsor Park. The spitting, however insanitary, was disgust at the referee's inefficiency, and it wasn't as if I was spitting *at* him. I'd done something personally satisfying with the ball, something that required a lot of skill, and I'd been prevented from completing the movement because someone pulled my shirt. I don't know if the referee didn't see it or didn't want to see it, but as a player I felt I had a right to protection; not because I wanted to be a special case but because the Laws of the Game state specifically that holding an opponent is a foul. Throwing the mud was, I don't deny, stupid, but it was only an underarm lob in his direction. It didn't hit him.

Paddy Crerand, however, had hit someone, which is why he ended up in court. The magistrate called the whole thing 'trivial and almost comic', which was a pretty apt summary. The 'childish exchange of discourtesies', which led to assault charges being made against Paddy, took place at Blinkers, a smart Manchester club which I frequented for booze, birds and the privacy of a quiet corner to have a meal without being mobbed. It just so happened that, on this particular night, one of the birds present was my much-publicised non-fiancée, Eva Haraldsted, to whom I was not particularly well-disposed, having paid her £500 out of court as settlement for her breach of promise writ on me. A few drinks and a wicked sense of humour made me take over the disco and play The Beatles' *Get Back* for her; only I kept playing it over and over again until the lad she was with took exception. As he had his brother with him, that would have made the odds unfair if I hadn't had Paddy with me. His presence put the odds in my favour, but they didn't see it that way until one of them ended up with a broken nose. Hence the charges, of which Paddy was eventually cleared.

For Paddy, these were not the easiest of times either. An old-fashioned attacking wing-half, he had no place in the modern, more defensively minded formations to which Wilf adhered. Players like him know intuitively what to do in situations as they arise during the game; they can't be programmed beforehand with diagrams on the blackboard. For that matter, nor could I, but Wilf could throw me up front and leave me to get on with what he saw me as: a goalscorer. Paddy wasn't fast enough for the all-action midfield man of the 1970s, and in 1969-70 he played in only half the fixtures, give or take one or two. In 1970-71 he played in the first three matches and then was out of the side until Sir Matt took over after Christmas. For the rest of the season he played in every game and the team ticked again. Whereas we'd scored twenty-eight goals up to New Year, we scored thirty-eight between then and the end of the season. At the same time we conceded fewer goals in the second half of the season: twenty-seven as opposed to thirty-eight. The return of Alex Stepney, who'd been dropped along with Paddy back in August, was a major factor, but even more important was the return of the old philosophy. If you attack, they're too busy defending to think about attacking you. We began the season with two, maybe three, forwards up front; we ended it with five. Of my eighteen League goals that season – including my hundredth League goal for United – twelve came in the second half of the season.

Yet the return of Sir Matt had hardly been an auspicious one for me. Earlier in December I'd received my fourth booking of the year following an incident at Old Trafford in which Manchester City's Glyn Pardoe broke his leg as he and I went for a fifty-fifty ball. Ninety-eight times out of a hundred nothing happens, but this time, because of the angle or the way we made contact, Glyn's right leg received a double fracture. It was an accident, as Glyn himself later said, but the referee, having consulted his linesman, put my name in his book. That night the plate-glass window at Edwardia was smashed and the following week's post brought dozens of poison-pen letters. Manchester takes its football very seriously.

My FA hearing set for January didn't take that booking into

account, though. It was concerned with three earlier ones, for which Sir Matt was going to plead a case on my behalf. Only I failed to make an appearance on time and eventually arrived at Lancaster Gate an hour and a half late. Considering the trouble I'd had getting there at all, being only ninety minutes late could almost be considered an achievement. I'd tried to get a flight from Manchester but the airport was fogbound, and when I raced back to the city centre to catch a train I just missed one and had to wait for the next. By this time, of course, Sir Matt had arrived at the FA without me, and within minutes the early afternoon papers were printing banner headlines of the 'George Best missing' variety. Most of Fleet Street, plus the television folk, must have been at Euston when my train arrived and there were girls everywhere wanting autographs. In the end I needed police help to get me away from the station, and two officers kindly drove me to Lancaster Gate. If only I'd been able to get out of bed in time to catch the 8.30 train from Manchester!

By the time I arrived the FA were ready to throw the book at me. Probably Sir Matt was prepared to hand it to them! The fine, £250, was the highest ever given to a player in England, and in addition I received a six months' suspended sentence. The money itself didn't worry me, but if they were making an example of me I felt it was unjustified. Especially when a member of the disciplinary committee told me that 'if you continually beat one man and then another, and then come back to repeat the dose, you will have to expect rough tackles. No-one likes to be made to look a fool. It's human nature.' If that wasn't a charter for every fullback in the land to take a hack at my ankles as I passed by, I'd like to know what was. No wonder I was becoming disillusioned with football. The artisans had taken over from the artists.

That was Monday. On Tuesday we went to Middlesbrough to replay our third round FA Cup tie, having drawn 0-0 at Old Trafford the previous Saturday. Middlesbrough were in the Second Division at the time, but they were a hard, more-than-useful side with a good little Belfast inside-forward named Eric McMordie prompting their attacks. It was a miserably cold night, the pitch was covered in snow, and they beat us 2-1. My goal was little consolation to the team or me as we drove back across the Pennines to Manchester. We were poorly placed in the League, we'd been beaten in the semi-finals of the League Cup by Third Division Aston Villa, and now we were already out of the FA Cup.

It was a bleak week. It would have been nice to get on a plane and fly off to Spain; anything but play football. Not even the shop was an escape. The way the rag trade was going generally, our prospects were gloomy unless we could find an influx of capital, and that meant merging with a London-based clothing firm called Lincroft. So, instead of being able to sit with Malcolm Mooney, quietly talking my way through the football problems, I was forced to concentrate on stock values, share capital and other unwelcome financial details. We were out of our depth and we knew it. Six o'clock came as something of a relief: time to go round to the pub and forget it all with the help of a drink.

The trouble with that kind of forgetfulness is that it takes time . . . and quite a few drinks. Not that I always drank to get drunk; far from it. Most of the time was because I enjoyed a drink, and especially because I enjoyed the company of the people I drank with. I'd loosen up, start to talk more than I might usually, and being with close friends helped protect me from the Georgie Best groupies, male and female, who wanted a touch of the star. Once the pub closed, some of the lads would go home; one or two of us would go off to a club – maybe Annabelle's or Blinkers – for a meal, a few more drinks, and a bird if you were lucky or you were Georgie Best. If you simply wanted to keep on drinking, there were always places that remained open for the grafters, the croupiers, the Bunny girls and the loners with a need for company. Manchester is that sort of town.

But for the grafters, the croupiers and the Bunny girls, six or seven in the morning is the end of their day. From a few quiet drinks it would be home to bed for a good day's sleep. Georgie Best was supposed to be training in a few hours, except of course he wouldn't be. He'd be lying in bed in his architect's dream house listening to Olga, his housekeeper, on the phone to Mrs Fullaway, her mother-in-law, because Georgie wasn't getting up for training and what should she do? Mrs Fullaway would tell her not to worry. The important thing was to let George catch up on his sleep. It had happened before. Sir Matt would understand.

Only this time Sir Matt didn't want to understand. When on Friday – as on Monday – I failed to catch the train for the journey south to London, he made up his mind to leave me out of the team to play Chelsea. He even phoned the shop and told Malcolm I needn't bother turning up later because I wouldn't be in the team. Mind you, I was in good company. Earlier in the week West Ham had announced their intention to drop Jimmy Greaves and Bobby Moore 'as a result of a breach of disciplinary rules'. Sir Matt must have been influenced by the star-dropping atmosphere of London, or maybe he'd grown tired of waiting around for me on railway stations.

I went to London all the same. I didn't understand why, but somewhere in my head was the thought that I could still talk my way out of the trouble I was in. The possibility that Sir Matt might be genuinely angry never occurred to me. I wanted simply to talk to him because I was so mixed up in myself that half the time I had no idea what I wanted to do. I needed to clear my mind of the muddled emotions and the pressures that were turning me into a nervous wreck. I knew myself that I hadn't always been playing well, but I didn't need the newspapers telling the world that my 'intermittent brilliance' was a luxury Manchester United could no longer afford. I was feeling that the club had let me down, not the other way round.

But then Manchester itself was in a fair old state of turmoil in those days. Top of the football world at the end of the 1960s, the city now found both its teams in trouble of some sort. We were staring relegation in the face; Manchester City were locked in a boardroom takeover battle. Attendances were on the decline, too, and crowd behaviour was getting worse. Perhaps I didn't need to talk to Sir Matt after all. Perhaps I needed someone who was not interested in football at all; someone who was neutral but understanding; who would see me for the mixed-up person I was.

They won without me at Stamford Bridge: 2-1 through a Willie Morgan penalty and a goal by Alan Gowling to end a run of ten games without a win. I watched the results coming through on the television and listened as the experts proclaimed how much better United had played without me. That did wonders for my morale. It was a good thing I was locked away in an Islington flat with a lovely, patient Irish actress named Sinead Cusack who let me talk as and when I wanted to. She made me cups of tea, and in true Irish tradition she helped me escape from reality for a while.

I'd first met her at the end of November when we were both on a chat show in Dublin, and we'd met again when I was in London a week or so later for a game at Spurs. I missed the train that time, too; arrived at Piccadilly just as it was pulling out of the station and they wouldn't let me on to the platform. This time I'd gone to her because, basically, I didn't know what else to do. One look at the photographers and reporters massed around the team's Russell Square hotel had convinced me there was no way of getting inside the place unseen, so I told the driver to keep going. It was then that I thought of Sinead. I realised I was taking a chance going there, but she was at home and she was understanding. For a few hours my mind began to slow down. Then the press caught up with us and all hell broke loose.

The mistake we made was going out to dinner. Until that time they had no actual proof that I was in Sinead's flat, for all that they'd staked the place out in case I might be. Now everyone arrived: photographers with telephoto lens to peer through the windows; television cameras; reporters offering money for an exclusive. My nice quiet weekend away from it all became a nightmare: I felt embarrassed for Sinead and she felt sorry for me. There didn't seem any point in talking about my problems any more; they were all too obvious. So we watched the television and saw pictures of the crowd outside the building while we sat imprisoned inside. Here hides Georgie Best, runaway footballer! The local kids thought it was great. After school on Monday about a hundred of them turned up, banging on the door and chanting 'We want Georgie Best' or other less pleasant things. In the end the police had to clear the stairways and the street, and that, plus the fiasco at Euston the previous Monday, led to questions being asked in the House of Commons about the waste of police time on my behalf.

Manchester United, meanwhile, suspended me for two weeks with a loss of pay, *The Times* devoted a leader article to me, and *The Guardian* took the mickey out of everyone as only it could. About the only good to emerge from the chaos was that it helped Sir Matt understand the sort of life I was being forced to live. It wasn't as if I deliberately went seeking that kind of publicity. Nor, for that matter, did Sinead, unlike some of my other girlfriends. She had talent and was developing into a fine actress. I still saw her from time to time afterwards, but that weekend put paid to any hopes I might have held for a more serious relationship. Mind you, the state I was in on one of the last occasions we met would have given her reason to rejoice that I was out of her life. I'd been out gambling and drinking in London, and when it came to bedtime I discovered I had nowhere to go. Out came the little black book and I dialled a few numbers. That it was four in the morning may have accounted for a distinct lack of response from the first numbers tried. But Sinead answered; maybe she was one of the few with a phone by her bed. No, she said, of course I couldn't come round. For one thing, her boyfriend was staying there. For another . . . But I was persistent and I'd always been good at the little boy lost line, so she eventually gave in and let me sleep on the couch — my usual place when I stayed with her.

I haven't always been so lucky, though. They haven't all been understanding actresses prepared to wake me up with a cup of tea and an ear for my tales of woe. There was one morning in London; a real morning after the night before. A poky, matchbox of a room with a narrow bed and someone beside me who must have looked ten times better at three o'clock in the morning after a few drinks. I had no idea where I was, I couldn't think what had woken me. The girl lay on her back with her mouth open, and then the doorbell rang again. And again. The girl stirred and eventually left the bed; I turned towards the wall in the hope of another hour's sleep. Some hope. Back came the girl with three of her cronies and a chocolate cake. At eight-thirty in the morning! It was her birthday surprise. The fact that she had a man in the bed didn't seem to perturb any of them as they plonked themselves down, stuffed their fat little faces with chocolate cake, and then proceeded to pass round a joint. It was all too much for me. I'd woken up with pretty models who liked to start the day with a smoke, but not chocolate cake. I grabbed my clothes, beat a line to the bathroom, and got out of there as fast as my throbbing head would allow. A taxi driver took me to Euston and I was back in Manchester for lunch.

The journey home with Malcolm Mooney after the weekend at Sinead's was not so quick. Neither of us was in a hurry, and we used the time on the road to talk. The merger of the two boutiques with the Lincroft group was going through in a few days' time, and already Malcolm was looking towards a future outside the rag trade. A restaurant, he thought, with a small farm to grow his own vegetables and some chickens. Dominique, the French girl he was going to marry, would work there with him. He'd been thinking about it for a long time, he said, and the way he told it the whole thing sounded perfect. Then the car broke down and we were six hours late getting back to Manchester. Which was all I needed: to be late for my atonement at Old Trafford, with the usual hordes of photographers in attendance to record my reconciliation with Sir Matt Busby. By the following month, when Sir Matt and Lady Busby came to my house-warming party, we were able to laugh about the affairs of January for the team was steadily climbing the League table to a safe position.

Everyone knew, however, that Sir Matt would not remain in charge longer than the end of the season, and in June he finally took his seat on the United board of directors. In his place arrived the former Leicester City manager, Frank O'Farrell, who, in the laconic words of Denis Law, came as a stranger and left as a stranger. He took up his appointment on 1 July 1971; on 19 December 1972 the Board announced his dismissal. For George Best, too, the Manchester United connection was all but severed.

Yet, under O'Farrell, the team began so well, losing only twice – 1-0 to Everton and Leeds – between the start of the season and the first week of December. It didn't even matter that we had to play our 'home' games on neutral grounds as a result of some lunatic throwing a penknife on the pitch at Old Trafford the previous February. We beat Arsenal 3-1 at Anfield and West Bromwich by the same score at Stoke. I scored my first two goals of the season in the West Brom match to begin a run of scintillating form that brought me another twelve goals from the next fifteen games, including hat-tricks against West Ham and Southampton. In addition there were three in the League Cup, in which we progressed as far as the fourth round where Stoke, after two draws, beat us 2-1 in the second replay. They were our bogey team in the Cups that season, later knocking us out of the FA Cup in the sixth round, again after a replay in which – as in the League Cup replay – I scored our only goal. But the FA Cup defeat was in March, and by then we were in trouble again. From being eight points clear at the top of the League in early December, we went eleven League games without a win, including a sequence of seven defeats. In an attempt, partially successful, to stop the rot, Frank O'Farrell dived for the club's chequebook, paying Aberdeen £125,000 to strengthen the defence with the very promising Martin Buchan, and a club-record £200,000 for the Nottingham Forest forward Ian Moore. Buchan was an excellent buy, but Ian Moore was already injury prone and even if he could score goals there was a big question mark over his ability to do so for long. For all that he was unlucky to be injured out of the game within a year of his arrival at Old Trafford, I doubt that he was ever worth the money spent on him.

To some observers it looked as if the team lost its momentum at the same time as I went off the boil. If that was so it reveals a basic weakness in the team itself, for no side challenging for honours – as United should always be doing – can afford to be reliant on just one or two players, no matter how good they are. More to the point, perhaps, is that we began the season with the same 'going forward' approach with which we'd finished the previous season, and the gradual return to a defensive attitude was pinpointing the team's essential weakness – its defence. Nobby Stiles had been allowed to go to Middlesbrough and, more important I feel, Paddy had retired to look after the Youth squad. No-one at the back, Alex Stepney apart, could stamp his authority on a match until the arrival of Martin Buchan.

No-one should have been surprised when the team came out of its fool's spring and went into sudden decline. Several of us knew the good times couldn't last but, as always it seemed, telling people the truth was not a popular pastime. For by now I was prepared to speak my mind; not to sit back and hope. I even managed to control my drinking so that I could turn up in the morning for training without the other players smelling booze on my breath. Then, in October, came the death threats. My house was placed under observation by the police – as well as by the constant star-gazers – and in one match, at Newcastle, I kept running and running to make myself as difficult a target as possible. The threats were probably the work of some crank, but when rumours are circulating around Belfast that you've donated several thousand pounds to the Reverend Ian Paisley, you take threats on your life seriously. Which is why, when the *Manchester Evening News* was informed that I might never return to England if I played for Northern Ireland in Belfast, I withdrew from November's European Championship game against Spain. Nor did it ease my troubled mind when one of my sisters was shot in the leg while leaving a dance hall. So I went back on the drink again; took the easy way out.

Ironically, it was in November that I was chosen as the subject of the television programme, *This Is Your Life*. This was your life, George Best, might have been more appropriate considering the months that followed. But in November, as far as the public was aware, I was riding high. The goals hadn't yet dried up, and people were already voting me as Sportsman of the Year in *The Daily Telegraph*'s poll ahead of Princess Anne, Jackie Stewart and Muhammad Ali. I'd won this title once before, in 1969, but after the ups and downs of 1971, winning it a second time brought me more satisfaction. Her Royal Highness got the better of me, though, when it came to the BBC television Sports Personality of the Year. But, as some wit joked before the programme, they weren't going to let some little Irish footballer come out on top of a princess on television, were they? So I had to be content with second place.

Because *This Is Your Life* is supposed to come as a surprise to the personality involved, I was lured down to London on the pretext of hosting a fashion show. And just in case I felt like disappearing, Waggy was there to make sure I was in the right place at the right time, even if a late-night visit to Tramp did bring back memories of another time he tried to keep tabs on me. This time, though, all went according to plan, and I'm glad it did. It allowed me to experience the warmth people felt for me. A feeling that sent a chill down my spine; one that was both frightening and gratifying. I experienced it again many years later when I went back to Ireland to open a building society office in a little village; the sort of occasion when you expect maybe a hundred people to turn up. But this day it was like the coming of the Messiah. They were there in their thousands; all ages. Many of the kids had probably never seen me play, and I'm sure some of the lovely old dears had never watched a football match in their lives, except on television. Yet there they all were to greet me. Not because I was a footballer; they don't look at me like that any more in Ireland. I'm some kind of cult figure to them and, in a nice way, they feel they own me. I'm part of them and I always will be; that's what they feel and that's the way I feel. Something of that was there when I appeared on *This Is Your Life*.

By New Year, though, the stories were all bad again. I was drinking heavily, missing training and, after a week in which my depression became blacker with each day, I was dropped from the team for the home match against Wolves. My friends tried to help me but I didn't want help; I wanted understanding. Perhaps being dropped was what I wanted; an act so definite that it brought my sense of self-destruction into focus; forcing someone else to make the decision for me. But then, having gone part of the way to destroying what I'd been building up, the depression relented and I wanted to join the world again. I spent some time in London with Carolyn – Carolyn Moore, Miss Great Britain, whom I'd been seeing since December. And I was happy to agree when Frank O'Farrell ordered me back to Mrs Fullaway's.

Living in my own house at Bramhall was getting to me anyway, never having a moment's privacy from people peering through the windows, ringing the doorbell and picnicking on my lawn. Sundays were the worst; coach parties and car loads of grockles coming to gawp at the house where Georgie Best lives. Lives? Most of the time I was restricted to skulking about indoors with all the curtains drawn; which made it even easier for the kids to snatch the goldfish from my ponds. If I wanted to go anywhere I had to ask the local police to set up diversions to ensure I wouldn't be followed by the pressmen who had the place under constant surveillance. Why should I be sorry about returning to Mrs Fullaway's? It would be a relief. I parked a friend of mine, Eddie Hindle, in the house as a sort of caretaker and I'm sure he had a much more enjoyable time there than I ever did. A proper character, Eddie; he could handle living in a goldfish bowl.

For that's what the house had become. A goldfish bowl. Yet, like many other ventures in my life, it had begun with great expectations. Like the businesses. It ended up the same way, too; somewhat out of my control with me not putting enough of myself into it. I knew what I wanted to have inside: sunken bath, comfortable study, big luxurious bedroom, lots of push-button gadgets. And I had them all. The television set disappeared up the chimney breast at the touch of a switch; the garage doors opened by remote control as you approached the house – or they sometimes did. But the exterior I left to the architect, and although he did explain to me what he was trying to do, I just wanted him to get on with it. I think now that I'd have been better buying an older house and renovating it inside. A house finished on the outside with white tiles to represent my 'clean simplicity' did look somewhat out of place in stockbroker Bramhall and was inviting criticism. None the less I didn't take kindly to people saying that it looked like a public loo.

Still, we had a good housewarming; even had to send the police to the local when we ran out of booze. Or so the story goes. Tommy Trinder, Clement Freud, Lionel Blair – danced with one of his girls once – Bob Monkhouse, Imogen Hassell – danced with her, too – and Derek Dougan were among the guests specially ferried by chauffeur-driven cars from the local pub because there wasn't room to park in the lane beside the house. I don't remember Vivien Neves coming though; probably had enough of me in Hyde Park.

As well as getting me back into digs, O'Farrell stipulated that I should train mornings and afternoons five days a week. Most of the time I managed it, but there were times when getting out of a nice warm bed just didn't seem worth the effort. On one such occasion

Waggy had scarcely begun his snipping for the morning when Frank O'Farrell was on the phone. George hadn't shown up at training; he wasn't at home. People were asking questions. Did Waggy know where I was? He didn't, but he assured Frank he'd do his best to find me and get me to The Cliff some time that day. He did find me eventually, after quite a bit of phoning round. Someone remembered seeing me in a club with a couple of girls, one of whom Malcolm knew. He drove round to her house and, sure enough, there I was, still in bed with both of them. No wonder I didn't want to go training.

It took Malcolm a lot of patient persuading but eventually I agreed to go training in the afternoon if he and Frank Evans, another pal, promised to go along and train with me. Waggy had worked out with me before when I did afternoon training; someone to talk to and stop making football seem too much like a nine-to-five job. There was so little enjoyment in it now anyway. But this day neither he nor Frank managed to get into a tracksuit, let alone do any training. One of the coaching staff, I don't remember who, made sure of that.

'What's this then?' he asked, walking straight up to us as we started stripping.

'Waggy and Frank are going to train with me this afternoon', I explained. 'Keep me company.'

'This gym's not for riff-raff', he replied. 'It's for professional athletes. You two', he said, pointing a finger at Waggy and Frank, 'out!'

That was the trouble with Old Trafford in those days. Everyone took life all too seriously. There was no fun; there was no satisfaction.

Somehow I saw the rest of the season through, but it was a struggle. The more I played, the more I wanted to get as far away from football as possible, and as soon as the season ended I took off for Marbella in the south of Spain. I should have been playing for Northern Ireland in the Home International Championship; I was supposed to meet up with United in Tel Aviv to play on their tour of Greece and Israel. All I wanted was escape, and escape meant somewhere sunny with plenty to drink. The *Sunday Mirror* paid me £4,000 for a 'George Best quits' exclusive, and at the time I thought an end to football was the answer. Then the time came when, eventually, I'd had enough to drink and, after moving on to Majorca to join Frank and Waggy, I made my way back to Manchester. There were the usual suspensions and fines but everyone wanted me to play again, even Northern Ireland. I reported early for pre-season training, moved in with the

Crerands as part of my 'new leaf', and took the field once more in United's colours.

I soon wished I hadn't. The season began disastrously: nine games without a win and in the bottom two or three of the table until 25 November, when we beat Southampton to move into nineteenth. That game, although I didn't know it at the time, would be my last for United for some time.

The days that followed the win over Southampton are little more than a jumble of memories now. They were scarcely clearer then. Buying a new Rolls Royce, missing training, drinking heavily, hitting a girl in a club and being charged with causing bodily harm, being dropped and then suspended, going to London, getting transfer listed. I woke one morning to find some vandal had deliberately scratched one side of my new car; another day I was told that my name had been removed from the window of Edwardia. Ironically the boutique was renamed Tramps! I thought of going to Spain but some time in this mad month Waggy had taken my passport to prevent any such occurrence. Finally, on 19 December, after several days' hard thinking and some despair, I delivered the following letter to the board meeting at Old Trafford.

'I had thought seriously of coming personally and asking for a chance to speak at the board meeting, but once again I am afraid when it comes to saying things face to face I might not have been completely honest.

'I am afraid through my somewhat unorthodox ways of trying to sort my own problems out I have caused Manchester United even bigger problems.

'I wanted you to read this letter before the board meeting commenced so as to let you know my feelings before any decision or statements are issued following the meeting.

'When I said last summer I was going to quit football, contrary to what many people said or thought, I seriously meant it, because I had lost interest in the game for various reasons.

'While in Spain I received a lot of letters from both friends and well-wishers, quite a few asking me to reconsider. I did so and after weeks of thinking it over I decided to give it another try. It was an even harder decision to make than the original one. I came back hoping my appetite for the game would return, and even though I like to think I gave a hundred per cent in every game there was something missing. Even now I am not quite sure what.

'Therefore I have decided not to play football again and this time no-one will change my mind.

'In conclusion I would like to wish the club the best of luck for the remainder of the season and for the future. Because even though I personally have tarnished the club's name in recent times, to me and thousands of others Manchester United still means something special.'

At this same board meeting Frank O'Farrell was dismissed as manager, and three days later Tommy Docherty took his place for a reputed fee of £15,000 a year. I thought I'd finished with Manchester United, but under Docherty there was one last, unhappy chapter to be written.

*   *   *

It was a warm evening for May. Too warm for lying in bed with little to do but watch television and feel sorry for myself. Waggy had brought some good books but I was too fidgety to read. Instead I just lay there, wondering if what they said was true. That I was lucky to be alive. Perhaps I was. Who knows what would have happened had I stayed on in Marbella with the Spanish doctor's magic potions?

I'd gone down there because there was nothing better to do in Manchester. No court cases; the magistrate said the girl brought two-thirds of the trouble on to her own shoulders and then put me on a conditional discharge for twelve months. No boutiques to sit in; Lincroft had bought me out in March. I'd sold the house, which meant I had nowhere to call home again. In fact there was nothing to do but drink and feel sorry for myself. I could just as easily do that in Marbella where a pal, Paul Cozzi, had a bar called the International. There was a hotel-cum-apartments nearby – the Skol – and they always managed to find me a room. Meeting the pretty lady from Manchester there was just a bonus, although she was to become more important to me than that in a few days time.

It was about a week after I'd arrived. We were down at Paul's as usual, sitting about, playing records, having some laughs, a quiet drink and something to eat. The plan was to go on to a club once Paul was ready to close, which he'd sometimes do early if business was quiet. Just sitting there I began to notice a numbness around the inside of my right leg; like it had gone to sleep. Walking about didn't help; if anything it seemed to make it worse. Every so often I'd feel some pain, and whenever I touched my leg I could feel the swelling getting worse. By the time Paul was ready to close for the night, my leg was throbbing like hell and I was in too much pain for anything except going back to the Skol. The manager there called out a local doctor, but his only remedy was to give me some pills and a spray. Whatever it was, he said, would clear up in forty-eight hours.

That was very reassuring! At three o'clock in the morning the pain was so intense that I thought I must be going mad. I might have flipped altogether without the lady from Manchester there to help me make it through the night. All the time my leg was getting bigger and bigger, and by five I'd had enough. I got her to phone Malaga and get me on the first flight to Manchester. It took some wheeling and dealing but she managed it. Then I phoned Waggy to meet me at the airport.

'I don't know what it is', I told him, 'but the doc who's looked at it didn't seem to know what the hell he was talking about.'

Waggy said he'd have his own doctor at the airport, and there was nothing to do now but sweat it out until morning.

The flight to Manchester was three and a half hours of agony. My leg felt as if it would explode at any minute; I couldn't put my shoe on because of the swelling and the perspiration was pouring off me. The other passengers probably thought I'd been on the drink again, sitting there clutching my shoe in my hand. And all the time I was urging the plane on to Manchester. Once there I could hardly walk off the plane and Geoff, Waggy's doctor, needed only one look at my face to know something serious was wrong. He took me straight out to his car, got me to pull my trousers down, saw the condition of my leg, and drove me straight to Ancoats Hospital. An hour later I was on a drip and they were telling me I was lucky to be alive. I'd had a thrombosis; a blood clot in a vein in my right calf. I'd been fortunate because it had travelled down the leg and not up.

No-one knew for sure what brought it on. I might have bumped into something; or it might have been caused by the change of routine; the period of inaction after being fit for so long. Whatever happened it frightened me to death. I'd never been ill in my life before; never been in hospital except to have a cartilage removed back in 1967. So I took it to heart when they told me to cut down on the kind of life I'd been living. For a while.

One of the first people to visit me was Sir Matt. One evening after dinner. Brought some fruit and sat for a while talking over the old times. I knew what he was thinking and I think he knew I knew it. But he waited until he was almost out of the room before saying anything. Just stuck his head back round the door as if it was an afterthought.

''Bout time you were back playing, isn't it?'

I listened to him walking down the corridor. He wasn't stupid. He knew I'd had a fright and wanted to get back into training. It was simply a matter of time and timing.

Paddy Crerand made the connection; Paddy McGrath, an old friend of Sir Matt and known around Manchester as The Godfather, provided the meeting-place. Nothing much was said, but it gave Tommy Docherty and me a chance to meet on neutral ground. Not that we were strangers, but this was more than a few drinks in a Spanish bar, which was where we first met. I'd heard the usual stories about him, of course, but from what I knew of him personally I quite liked the man. He certainly had energy.

The next meeting was a little closer to home – over lunch at Old Trafford cricket ground – and there we started to get down to business. Docherty said he'd like to have me play for him; I said that if there was anywhere I was going to play it would have to be for United. So we more or less agreed I'd go back. I told him I'd need time, extra training, and I specifically asked him not to rush me. Let me play in the Reserves for a few weeks, just to get a feel for it again. He agreed, said he understood my problems and was generally sympathetic. I actually felt then that this was it. I had a chance and I could make it. Whatever I did from now on it mustn't interfere with the football.

I knew the training would be hard, what with the leg and everything, but I didn't realise quite how tough. I was carrying too much weight as well and was having trouble shedding that. Still, with regular morning training sessions and afternoons in the gym with weights or running in the local park with Paddy and Bill Foulkes, I began to feel myself getting back into shape. I was only twenty-seven after all. In September I played forty-five minutes of Eusebio's testimonial match in Lisbon and in October, when Docherty suggested I play in a friendly against Shamrock Rovers, I readily agreed. I'd been training for more than a month now and I'd regained my appetite. The right leg no longer felt twice as heavy as the left and I was keen to try out my skills under proper match conditions. Except that we never did finish the game. Towards the end several hundred kids came swarming on to the ground to congratulate me on the way I was playing. It was stupid, but it gave me a nice feeling.

They say one swallow doesn't make a summer, and some good touches in a friendly didn't mean I was ready yet for First Division football. The manager thought otherwise. Four days later my name was on the team-sheet to play at Birmingham. I wasn't happy but there seemed no point in arguing, and a marvellous reception from the 50,000 crowd certainly lifted my spirits. Moreover we won – by a penalty taken by Alex Stepney. It was his second of the season and, after twelve games, made him the team's leading goalscorer with Brian Kidd and Sammy McIlroy. If I hadn't been so concerned with my own form I might have wondered what I'd let myself in for!

After that my game improved with every outing, and when I scored at Spurs in November I felt sure that it was all coming back. For there was a time when I was scared that I'd lost some of my old skills. I still wanted to be the best by my own standards; good wasn't enough. I wanted to give the crowd something to smile about on the way home. By Christmas I'd scored once more, and even though the team was badly placed in the League I wasn't feeling as depressed about it as I had been the year before. Perhaps because the challenge was more personal. I felt I had something to prove, and the chance to prove it came when we were drawn against Third Division Plymouth Argyle in the third round of the FA Cup. We were at Old Trafford, there'd be a full house, and I'd be able to turn it on for them again; to show that George Best was back in business.

Then, on the Tuesday before the Cup tie, we went down 3-0 at Queen's Park Rangers and I went down, too. Nothing heavy, but enough to make me think a party that night was better than sitting in front of the television. The result, as I should have known, was the inevitable: I missed training. Come Friday I went in as normal, and when no-one said anything about Wednesday or Thursday I gathered that Docherty was holding to his word. He did understand that there might be days when I would miss training. Saturday we reported as usual, had lunch, and returned to the ground an hour to an hour and a quarter before the kick-off. Usually I was the last to get ready, always hanging about the players' lounge talking, but this day I was keen with anticipation. I'd even removed my jacket to start getting changed when I remembered the team-sheet hadn't been pinned up. Not that that meant anything; there might have been injuries.

Nevertheless it was enough to make me put my jacket back on while I waited.

I was still waiting when I received word that Tommy Docherty and Paddy Crerand wanted to see me in the referee's room. Neutral ground. I knew then he was going to tell me I wouldn't be playing. And when he actually said it, the whole thing I'd been building up died in that split second. So much hope, so many expectations; so much hard work. Dashed in a single sentence.

'Why?' I mumbled, fighting back my tears.

'You didn't come in for training Thursday morning, so as an example I'm leaving you out.'

'Don't worry', Paddy said after he'd gone. 'He's just showing who's boss. You'll be back in next week.'

'Next week!' I cried. 'What about all that crap he gave me about if I miss the odd session it'll be all right? Just work harder; it'll be amongst ourselves.'

I didn't have to think what the press would do to me. The same old story all over again, or worse. I wondered if he'd have done it if we weren't playing someone like Plymouth and doubted it. It all seemed so unreasonable. Couldn't he have quietly pulled me aside on Friday morning and told me that I was out of order? If he had to drop me, why did he have to wait till right before the game?

'This is it', I told Paddy, my voice cracking with emotion. 'If I don't play today, I don't play again.'

He didn't know what to say and eventually he left me there, sitting in the referee's room, listening to the others getting ready, feeling the bottom drop out of everything. I didn't want to cry but I couldn't stop myself, and I felt better for it. Then I pulled myself together, washed my face, and walked into the players' lounge. No-one was surprised to see me there; there were still fifteen or twenty minutes to kick-off. People came up to wish me luck, the usual remarks, but then it gradually became obvious that I wasn't playing and I was left alone. I hadn't said anything. Couldn't. I didn't have the guts to say I wasn't in the team so I just sat there throughout the game. Afterwards I stayed around for a while and then I went home. I didn't go back for a long time.

Eventually, in November 1975, Manchester United released me from my contract, and for the first time in my life I was a free agent. Between times, though, I'd not stopped playing completely: there were occasional testimonials, some games in South Africa and two for

124

non-League Dunstable Town, who were managed by an old friend, Barry Fry, for whom I'd played in the Juniors in the early days. However, every appearance I made required permission from Old Trafford, and that really killed me because it was usually Docherty who gave the okay. Which meant, in effect, that he was still saying whether I may or may not play football. Indeed, one manager I played for made some very cryptic comments about the trouble he had to go to, getting me cleared to play. So, when the news of my release of contract came through, I had no compunction about getting Tommy Docherty to Old Trafford on a Sunday morning to sign the papers.

That should have ended the story, but there was one final footnote in 1978. I was living in Los Angeles at the time, and a friend in Manchester sent me a clipping from the paper about an investigation by the Manchester fraud squad into the arrangement by which I played my two games for Dunstable. 'A sum of £1,000 is thought to be involved' the story said. The investigation didn't concern me personally, and what came of it I never did hear. But I don't know that I really cared by then.

Chapter 10

'You must be mad, laddie', he said, an old man selling newspapers in the raw Edinburgh wind. 'You threw it all away.'

Who was I, warm in my Turbo Saab listening to Fleetwood Mac and waiting for the lights to change; who was I to disagree? He'd read the stories, good and bad; he'd categorised the failures. He didn't want to know I'd had some fun along the way. I may not have won as many medals as other players or appeared in FA Cup finals. I've never played in the World Cup finals. On the other hand I've done things most people only dream of: seen places, met all kinds of people, enjoyed the luxury of the best hotels in the world. It wasn't all sour. Life is not all regrets.

Like the Brown Bull, for instance. The nights spent there probably did more harm to me as an athlete than any other single factor. But I look back on them with more affection than I remember playing football in the mud and snow of a cold January night. The Brown Bull recalls wonderful friendships and one hell of a lot of laughs. Not that you'd think it if you passed by there today. It's not the most fashionable pub in Manchester; anything but. Nor was it in the late sixties, early seventies, and yet for a time it became an institution almost.

We found the Brown Bull quite by chance, looking for a place to drink where I wouldn't be annoyed by people driving me crazy. It didn't have to be that pub; it could just as easily have been the Salford Arms, which was just over the road, the Albert Vaults, just along the road, or even the Pen and Wig, which was a hundred yards or so closer to Edwardia and the Village Barber. But there was something about this dirty two-storey hotel curling round the corner by the traffic lights at the bottom of Bridge Street; something that made me slow down and suggest to Danny that we give it a look.

Inside it was empty except for an old fellow contemplating his evening pint and the lad behind the bar. You could tell business was quiet because he was asking us what we'd have before we were through the door. We ordered, and gradually we fell into conversation with him; learnt he was American, name of Billy Barr, and grew to enjoy his company. During the night there were probably no more than ten people in there at one time, and none of them appeared very interested in George Best. It couldn't have been better. We had one last drink with Billy while he washed the glasses and we knew we'd found our local.

The trouble was, of course, that the place soon earned itself a name; not just in Manchester, either, but in Birmingham and London. From being a nice quiet place where our crowd of fifteen or sixteen could let off steam, it became an 'in' place, packed to the doors. Footballers, pop stars, acting folk in Manchester for the night all wanted to see the famous Brown Bull. After hours were busier than regular hours. Sometimes there'd be people staying there and the parties would go on all night. Granada studios weren't far away, and quite a few visiting actors and actresses found it easier to climb the stairs to bed than find a taxi or make their way back to another hotel. It's probably a good thing I don't remember the names of the young actresses who used to doss down there. Some of them must have become famous since then.

For me, living in digs, the place was like a second home. Many a night Billy would give up on us and leave me to close the place. Many a morning I'd wake up on an old mattress in the junk room, looking bleary-eyed at the people on the top of the buses; good folk going to work when I should have been thinking of going training. They were mad times but a lot of laughs. The 'Black Cow' Sir Matt called it once when he was telling me to keep away from the place. A hard-drinking pub in a hard-drinking town. Not that it's anything to be proud of; simply a truth. I've been in other places around the world where people are supposed to drink, but there's nothing to touch Manchester. I've seen lads there go for days on end and still look as though they've had only one or two.

Some of the sessions we had were unbelievable. Crazy. I drank a pint of vodka one night as a bet; straight down in one go just for the hell of it. We thought it was a great laugh. Same with the drinking games like Jacks. You have a pack of cards and the first one dealt a jack has to order a drink. Anything he likes; any concoction he can imagine. Sometimes they were putting vodka, brandy and whisky together and topping it up with soda water. The next jack tastes it, and the third jack has to drink it down in one go. The fourth jack pays for it. And then we'd start all over again. If you didn't finish the drink in one go, you had to buy a drink for the fourth jack. People would

127

come into the pub, think we were out of our heads – we sometimes were – and end up joining in. Other times there'd be arm wrestling on the bar, picking up chairs by one leg, seeing who could do the most push-ups. Gunfights with soda syphons; some nights the floor was awash.

Saturday nights were often card nights. The same little school as a rule: Billy, Les Davis who worked at Granada studios, a lad called Brian Hafferty and myself. We'd start up about midnight and quite often go through until five or six, the girls sitting around talking or making coffee and sandwiches. It was usually poker but the stakes were never high; not by gambling standards. If you won thirty or forty pounds in a night you thought yourself lucky.

When Billy left the Brown Bull to take over the Grapes, our crowd moved too. It wasn't far to go; for the television people it was even closer than the Brown Bull. Today, whenever I'm in Britain, I look at faces on the television and I think: I've seen you before. Knocking them back at the Grapes, perhaps. They tell me Billy Barr has moved to Canada these days, and I should think Manchester is poorer without him. He took care of the people he had to take care of and I for one missed him when he moved from the Grapes. The night he told me he was giving up the pub business altogether, he slipped me an envelope containing three or four hundred pounds. 'Appreciation', he said, 'for you and the boys. I know . . . it wouldn't have been half as successful without you.'

But for all of us there came a time when the mad drinking had to stop; especially for me because I was supposed to be playing football. Whereas at twenty-two or twenty-three I could drink heavily with little visible effect, the harder the drinking became the more it started to show. You don't think it does but people close to you notice. Disillusionment with football didn't help either, though when the chance came to play in an indoor six-a-side league in Toronto, I thought why not. I'd written my letter of resignation to Manchester United, the man in Canada was talking in lots of noughts, and I figured a change of towns might stop me taking out my quick temper on the general public. First, though, there was a court case to attend and that had little to do with being drunk or losing my temper. If anything I'd kept it remarkably well considering the strain I was under.

Most of the day had been spent driving about town or sitting in the car, thinking. I didn't want to talk to people, least of all to Frank

O'Farrell or anyone from the club, so I kept shy of my usual daytime haunts. Perhaps if I had been able to sit with Frank O'Farrell and talk my problems through it would have saved us both a lot of heartache, but that never seems to have been my way. Run first and face the music afterwards; that was me. Smile, say sorry, and wait for forgiveness. Only this time I didn't want forgiveness. I thought I wanted out; out of Manchester United and out of football.

Which is why midnight found me sitting in a quiet corner of Reuben's club chatting to a lad called Dougie Welsby, who owned the Queen's club. It wasn't a busy night, not even the fact that Georgie Best was on the premises could bring them in that night, but a few people were about, including what sounded like a hen party. We couldn't see the girls, but you could tell from the joking and laughing that they were having a good time. Had been having a good time for most of the evening by the sound of it. Occasionally one of them would go to the bar for more drinks, and her return to the table would produce another howl of merriment. 'Guess who's at the bar, girls? Georgie Best!'

Eventually one of them, a long-haired blonde they called Stevie, came over and asked me to dance; more to the point, she attempted to drag me off my stool and out on to the dance floor.

'Sorry', I said as politely as possible, 'you know I don't dance in clubs'.

If I had the right girl, we'd been through this scene a few months before. When she went off I thought she'd taken no for an answer, but five minutes later she was back, not wanting to dance this time but to give me a real mouthful. 'Pretty crude verbal abuse' is how the magistrate put it later: 'big-headed bastard' was one of her more flattering comments. Dougie tried to quieten her down, told her to leave us in peace because we were doing some business, but she was having none of it. Out came another flood of abuse and then, having got that off her chest – quite a nice one – she threw a drink over me.

How I never hit her then I don't know; certainly not because she was a lady. Instead I just told her, very quietly, that if she didn't behave herself I'd ask Colin, the owner, to throw her out. That really set her off. 'Who did I think I was; blah, blah, blah.' And then she hit me. Not hard; as she said in court, 'I could not have hit him hard because I was wearing a tight blouse and could not have swung my arm'. But it stung and I didn't fancy a repeat dose when she shaped to hit me again. Perhaps my reaction was too fast, yet I don't think

I hit her hard. My hand moved only a couple of inches, and as her friend Julie, flown in from Frankfurt for the trial, said: 'It was a slap like a father would give his daughter.' Unfortunately it was enough to cut the inside of her mouth and give her a hairline fracture of the nose.

They got me a good brief: George Carman, QC, in the days before he became involved in the affairs of the Liberal Party, defending Jeremy Thorpe. I even had to stay at Carman's place the night before the trial, just to make sure I didn't do a runner. Not that I minded; it was a nice house and the bed was warm, even if I didn't sleep much what with worrying about the court hearing and everything. I couldn't deny hitting the girl because I had, and so it all depended on how the magistrate reacted to my plea of provocation. At least I had a good witness in Dougie, and we'd found a lovely old dear from the place Stevie and her friends had been earlier that night. The magistrate was a little less kindly disposed to prim and proper Stevie in her neat brown suit and cream blouse when he heard she'd downed at least eight brandies with Babycham before moving on to the club. That was Brown Bull drinking. All the same I shouldn't have hit her, said Mr Bamber, and despite blaming her for two-thirds of the trouble he found me guilty. I was ordered to pay £75 costs and £25 compensation to the girl, and received a twelve months' suspended sentence. At least I was free, so I celebrated by cracking another girl's skull, on a telephone.

If that had made the court, or the newspapers, there'd have been no trip to Canada, nor the amazing holiday in California and Mexico that followed. Fortunately, if that's the right word, it was an accident, and the girl herself admitted she'd been out of order. But it might have been different.

I'd begun the night, appropriately enough, in Dougie's club, which is where this girl found me. Not hard to do. She was trying to make contact with me for a mutual friend, Noel Cantwell, who at the time was managing Peterborough United. A former Manchester United player, he thought he might be able to persuade me back into the game; whether for Peterborough or for United I don't remember now, because at that time football was the farthest thing from my mind. I wanted to enjoy my drinking. However, the girl stayed around and, when the club closed, moved on with a few of us to one of Manchester's early morning watering-places. Having had little to do with her after initially losing my temper at her for bothering me, I was more than surprised when, about five or six o'clock, she suggested I might take her home; home for her being something like twenty miles away. If she meant mine that was quite out of the question. I was going to Toronto in the morning; except that I failed to get out of bed on time.

Saying no, I wouldn't take her home, produced some mild histrionics, followed by a threat to call the police and tell them we were drinking illegally. No-one took that seriously until she dashed into the hall where the phone was, and then I for one did. I'd had enough trouble with the police for one month; and I was on twelve months' suspended. I grabbed the phone from her while she was dialling, and as I did so she turned away from me and caught her head on the coin box. The scream she made curled the edges of the pot plants and lifted the tiredest heads off the antimacassars. I stood there looking helpless with the phone hanging from my hand and the dial tone buzzing in between her sobs. Someone got her back inside the bar, sat her down and gave her a brandy. I kept telling her how sorry I was and she kept saying it didn't matter. It was really her fault; she shouldn't have lost her temper. One of the people there, meanwhile, called a taxi and we finally sent her home.

What we didn't realise was the extent of her injury. It needed a trip to the hospital the next day for her to discover she'd suffered a hairline fracture of the skull, and that got her father making waves. Now I really did worry. I could imagine what the press would make of it once they got to hear. It was looking as if I spent my spare time going round beating up women. But the girl was great. She let me know that I needn't worry; that everything would be all right. I sent some flowers to the hospital and took myself back out on the town for one last night in Manchester before going into exile in Canada.

This time, despite only three hours sleep, I did get to the airport; somewhat the worse for wear and not at all in the mood for seeing Paddy Crerand, who was waiting to meet someone off an early morning plane. Still, I couldn't ignore him and so, leaving Waggy and Frank Evans to deal with the tickets and the luggage, I sat down and chatted. The next thing I'm aware that the place is crawling with pressmen. The girl, I thought. They've heard about the girl. Her father's gone to the police. He's going to sue me. I looked around again and there, coming across the lounge, is the girl I've hit, her head all bandaged. She's wanting to say sorry for all the trouble she caused. It's just too much. All it needs now is the police and the nightmare would be complete. Instead, who should walk through

131

from Arrivals but Sir Matt. That was it. I couldn't take any more. I picked up my bag, dashed through to the departure lounge, and hoped like hell I was leaving Manchester for ever. In the end it was only for three or four weeks.

For all the money being offered, Canada was a non-starter from the word go. I should have realised that before I left Manchester, but at the time beating tom-toms in a Timbuktu discotheque would have sounded better than another day in Manchester. I needed to be somewhere I could open a newspaper and not find my name in headlines, talk to a girl without it being in the gossip columns, walk down a street without somebody touching my clothing in the hope of a miracle cure. Or a five-pound note!

Toronto was not the place. For a start the press conference was little more than an inquisition into my private life. The only sensible question asked was about my attitude to the fact that, if I played in this six-a-side league, I could be banned throughout the world for playing in a competition that was not affiliated to FIFA. I hadn't thought about it, I said truthfully, but I soon did. I had no intention of ending up like Charlie Mitten and Neil Franklin after the Colombian nonsense. The only question I did find amusing was the one requesting my reaction to the news that Tussaud's waxworks in Blackpool had melted me down to make a model of Rodney Marsh.

'Who's he?' I asked, but the girl had never heard of him either. Pity; it was her only question of the whole press conference.

When it was over and everyone was standing around, wondering what to drink next, a fellow I recognised from England came up to me. Sidney Young I think his name was. Asked if he could come by later when it was quieter and talk to me. Sure, I said, provided it wasn't another interview. He shook his head and said he'd meet me in the bar about six. He did say he'd rather we were on our own, which was the best way of making sure I'd be there. I can't resist a bit of mystery; like redheads and bleached blondes.

Come six o'clock, following an afternoon of rather unsatisfactory negotiations concerning this six-a-side tournament, I sat waiting in a downstairs bar while Waggy and Frank tried to look inconspicuous by cracking jokes in a corner. Right on time the English lad arrived, joined me at my table, and ordered us a couple of drinks. Then he asked me what I knew about Joe Martin, the organiser of this World Indoor Soccer League.

'Not much', I said, 'except that he offered me thirty grand to play a

132

dozen games and I thought it was worth coming over for a look.'

'Well', he advised, 'I'd watch out if I were you. He's a little bit of a tearaway. Been in trouble with the law. In fact, he's still in trouble with the law. You wouldn't be seeing him now except that he's out on bail on appeal. Got three months for showing obscene films.'

It turned out my man was into pornography in a big way: bookshops, strip shows, a place called the Love Cinema on Toronto's Sin Strip. Now he wanted to get into football and I was to be the drawcard. I didn't like it. Waggy and Frank thought it stank, even to a couple of Manchester lads, so that night we decided we'd give Sin Strip the once-over and then quit town the next day. Frank thought he'd probably go back to Manchester; Waggy and I decided we'd fly over to LA and see Ed Peters, an old friend from Spanish holidays who'd often been at us to visit him. That left Joe Martin to sort out, and as Frank was officially there as my business manager I left the job to him. We had until five o'clock the next afternoon to decide whether or not the terms were acceptable, and at four-thirty I was on a plane for New York. Waggy stayed behind to keep Frank company, the arrangement being that he and I would meet up in New York and fly on to the West Coast.

What we didn't anticipate as I waited for Waggy's flight to arrive was that he'd be accompanied by an 'acquaintance' of Joe Martin: a big lad with the right physical qualifications for a minder. He towered over Waggy by a good six inches, which was roughly the height he was going to tower over me once they reached where I was sitting. Sir Matt Busby never went this far, I thought. As it happened the lad was as good as gold. He just wanted to make sure I didn't want to change my mind. I could go on to LA from Toronto if I'd like to go back and sign the papers. But I didn't like, I explained. The set-up wasn't the sort of thing I was looking for and I'd probably end up going back to England. That was okay, he said. If you change your mind you know where we are. And off he went on the return flight.

'Where's the concrete boots then, kid?' I asked Waggy.

'Don't you bloody laugh', he said. 'I saw him first.'

We never could decide if he was there to put the frighteners on me or if he was simply built that way. But it made a good story when we were lying around Ed's pool up the back of Beverly Hills.

Although I'd visited Los Angeles while on tour with United several years earlier, I'd never really had the chance to experience the way of life there. Doing so now was an eye-opener. It was all so easy-going. Like the place in which we stayed. Ed had told us when we called from Toronto that he already had people staying in his house, but a friend of his had an apartment in Laurel Canyon and we could move in there for a week. What he failed to mention was that this friend, Mike O'Hara, shared the apartment with someone else, a former American football quarter-back – I think – called Lance Rentzig. Not that we saw much of him, but I did manage to read his book while we were there. *When the Laughter Turns to Tears*, or something similar. And I thought I had troubles. This guy had apparently exposed himself to a young girl and, because he was a famous football player who was easily recognised, she reported him to the police. For quite some time he had a big problem but, as he explained in his book, he had managed to sort himself out. The one night we did see him we were lying about his place, watching his television, when he walked in with this stunningly beautiful girl; introduced himself and the girl and disappeared into his bedroom. We went out with Mike shortly afterwards and I never did see him again. I've seen her plenty of times since then, though. Pamela Ewing in *Dallas*.

The plan, such as it was, was that we'd lie around LA for a while and then go down to Ed's place in Palm Springs for a change of sunshine. After that, whatever went. Lie around is what you tend to do a lot in LA if you know people like Ed. The pool, a good supply of drink and the right number of pretty girls were just the thing to clear my mind of Manchester United, English winter, stipendiary magistrates and Toronto porn kings. Linda helped too.

I met her at the Candy Store disco in Beverly Hills thanks to Mike O'Hara, though I'm sure he wouldn't appreciate my thanks. He had his eye on her himself when he called out to her to join us, telling us in loud asides how everyone in town was after her and how he'd been trying to date her for so long and she wasn't playing ball. The noise he was making about it I wasn't surprised, but eventually she did come over and join us. We were all introduced, and long before she moved off to go to a party Mike wasn't the only one besotted by her. The only difference was that I had a piece of paper in my hand with her name and telephone number on it. I called her the next day, and until we left Palm Springs that was one side of my holiday which required no help from anyone. Not even Old Blue Eyes' chauffeur.

I never did work out whether he was interested in her for himself or for the man. But we came out of the Candy Store one night and there's the Sinatra motor waiting to whisk Linda off to who knows where. Or whom. Not knowing much about American etiquette in such situations, I did what I'd have done in Manchester. Told him to shove off – in Mancunian, of course. That led to a bit of a scuffle, with Waggy and Linda intervening, and eventually the Sinatra motor went off home alone. The next day the three of us flew down to Palm Springs. Out of bed about ten in the morning, play tennis for an hour or so, cool off with a swim and a beer at the pool, have a sandwich, join up with the girls for the afternoon, go out each night to a different restaurant. In bed by half-past ten or eleven. I hadn't felt so relaxed for years.

But old Scotch and Coke Wagner was getting itchy feet and the time came to resume our wandering. The only thing we had to decide was a place, and we let the airline girl choose that by asking where it was hot. 'Well', she said, 'it's such and such degrees in Hawaii, something else in Bermuda, and it's really hot, they say, in Acapulco at this time of the year.' So Acapulco it was. Ed recommended a hotel, said he'd call them for us, and it was farewell to Palm Springs and lovely Linda Joinett. We didn't know it at the time but we were going to a wedding.

When the airline girl had said it would be hot in Acapulco, she made no mention of the humidity. We stepped from the plane and it was as if someone had smacked us in the face. Quite unbelievable. So was the poverty. I know people think Belfast is bad, but I'd grown up there and become accustomed to it. Here, families were living in Honda motorcycle packing-cases and scavenging in the rubbish bins of the luxury hotels for their daily bread. The contrast was immediate: through your left eye you saw a beautiful hotel with its pools and cocktail bars; through the right eye you saw these hovels.

The other thing that amazed us was the friendliness of the Mexican people, especially when they discovered that the Mr G. Best booked in by Ed Peters from Los Angeles was not one more rich American tourist but Georgie Best, footballer. On arrival we'd been driven in a pink and white service car to our cabin; nothing special, in fact very ordinary for the money we were paying. It was somewhere to put your head down at night, and as we reckoned we'd be spending our days by the pool or out somewhere, it didn't worry me too much. Within an hour or two of our arrival, though, word had got round that Georgie Best was there, and the next thing we know we've our own chalet, our own swimming-pool, and easy access to the main pool which had its own bar in the water. The Mexican lads working at the hotel couldn't do enough for us, especially when I said I'd turn out for the Villa football team on Sunday. Once I'd actually played, albeit for twenty minutes or so, I was king. Nothing was too much trouble for the two little lads from Manchester.

The attendant at the main pool even kept the best sunbeds for us; and there used to be a regular race for them every morning because they were right beside the bar and a moment from the restaurant. As we were up till the early hours at a place called Carlos and Charlie's, there was no way we got anywhere near them on the first few mornings. But then, presto! 'Mr Best, Mr Wagner, I save these sunbeds for you; every morning.' The jet-setters and the millionaires, down from the States for some winter sun, must have wondered who we were. Strolling down to the pool at midday and taking the prime places.

And then there was the wedding. Billy Smart's of circus fame, so we were told. I never had reason to doubt it, just as I could easily believe that his bride was a stewardess on his plane to Acapulco – until he proposed to her. It was that kind of scene. The wedding was down on the beach and the ceremony was conducted by a hippy priest. Most of the guests were stoned, the rest of us were drunk on champagne, and we were all tucking into suckling pig and other delicacies as if we wouldn't eat again for a month. Then someone says I must regret the life I've led, and I can only wonder if they realise what they're saying. You can't regret memories like that; when you really think about it, it doesn't even seem worthwhile regretting the bad times because they're all part of the same life. I might sometimes feel disappointed with myself for prostituting my talent by playing for poor teams simply to make some easy money, but then why do good actors appear in poor films? I was being paid to entertain people and, as in South Africa in 1974, I could have some fun along the way.

The team was called the Jewish Guild, it was run by a fellow who looked all of twenty-five stone and gave the impression that he owned half of Johannesburg, and they were offering me something like £11,000 for four or five games. Manchester was still waiting for summer. Slack Alice was now open and doing a roaring trade, and the former Miss World had had her fill of me, as she so delicately put it. South Africa sounded warm, new and exciting. All I needed was some company, which meant talking Waggy round. He'd just come back from holiday, and with a share in Slack's as well as his hairdressing business he thought his time might be better spent in Manchester. But everyone told him he'd be foolish to miss such an opportunity, and in the end he thought, why not?

For some reason, fog probably, we had trouble getting away from Manchester and had to fly to Paris to make our connecting flight. Then it was a long slog through the night to Johannesburg, most of the time spent drinking and playing cards. Flying, as a rule, never bothered me, but this flight seemed endless and Manchester felt a long way behind when we at last began our descent. Looking at my watch, I tried to work out what I'd be doing if I was still there. Sitting in Phyllis's probably, listening to the gamblers and the grafters tell their tales. 'We're a long way from home, kid' I said to Waggy, and I meant every word of it.

They put me in a suite that had a bathroom the size of a penalty area. Malcolm complained because his suite was some fifty yards smaller; his bathroom was only the size of a goal area. The furniture was unbelievable: a bed which must have been built for a rugby team and big high wicker chairs you could lose yourself in. There was chilled champagne, fresh fruit and chocolates – either they'd heard about me in advance or they didn't know I was supposed to be a footballer.

The games were scheduled for Cape Town, Durban and Johannesburg, but I knew once I'd seen the players in training that I'd have to be ten times better than I was to make any difference. So I settled down to enjoying myself and working on a suntan. The natives thought we were mad, of course; to them it was already winter. After a couple of days, though, the word was going round town that a scene was swinging by the pool at George Best's hotel, and the Jo'burg girls suddenly found there were better ways to fill their days than sitting over their coffee cups. Talk about a shuttle service: I returned to England with two books full of telephone numbers. The press thought it was scandalous and loved every moment of it. They also managed to rake up something I'd written five or six years earlier for a kids' magazine in England about my opposition to racial discrimination, so that got us off to an excellent start. Troublemaker, womaniser, playboy, gambler, hard drinker – they called me the lot. Not that it kept the women away. I was probably the biggest thing to hit Johannesburg since the last All Blacks tour.

Malcolm couldn't believe his eyes some of the time. Or his ears.

There were people phoning for me to model clothes, write articles, attend functions or open shops. All prepared to pay or give me something. By the time we left, Malcolm reckoned he'd paid his way by answering my phone for me. There was one day, a fairly cool 75 degrees so the action at the poolside was a little quieter than usual; not celibate, but quieter. Lunch had come down and we were working our way through this beautifully prepared snack of prawns, oysters and various local seafoods when a call came through from a nearby sports store. Would I go down to their shop and sign fifty footballs? They'd pay expenses. At the time I had a mouth full of oyster, a glass half-full of champagne and an arm full of blonde. 'Tell him £500', I said to Waggy, thinking that would put them off.

'He says that's fine', Waggy gulped back to me.

'And they've got to bring them here', I added. A moment's silence. The guy was probably telling Malcolm to piss off.

'He'll be here in half an hour', he said, putting the phone down. Sure enough, half an hour later, in walks this lad with his boxes of footballs, introduces himself, hands me a pen and a ball, and off we go. As I sign one, he passes me another, and so it goes on until we've finished. Then he hands me an envelope, says thanks very much as only a South African can, and fades. I still haven't moved from my sunbed, but Wagner and the birds have finished the seafood and the champagne.

'That's the last time I do you any favours, kid', I told him.

And then there was Ultra Violet. It wasn't her real name, but Itzy Bloomberg's was. He was a young lawyer we became friendly with, and one of the funniest men I've ever met. With a name like that you'd have to be. Itzy knew Ultra, or vice versa because vice of a mild sort was Ultra's thing. She took her clothes off, and apparently they came in their thousands to see what was left. There might have been a python, too, but I could be getting the story mixed. Life was confusing about that time. Anyway, Ultra phones up one day, quite out of the blue, and says she'd like to come up and see me some time. No mention was made of the python so I thought it sounded like a good idea. And if she did bring the python it would help clear the gallery which, if she had the kind of body Itzy said, might also be a good idea. Only she turns up with some other kind of snake: a newspaper reporter plus his photographer. Ultra wants some publicity.

'Oh no', I said, taking one look at this little entourage and picking up my jacket. 'You'd better get rid of this lot', I growled at Waggy. 'After all the shit they've been giving me since I got here, I'm not going through anything with them.'

On the field the best we did was a 1-1 draw with an outfit called Hellenic, who had Bobby Moore playing for them. The other games we lost, and when I saw the way the people I was playing for treated the black people it didn't worry me too much that I wasn't always giving them their pound of flesh. They say they see it differently, but the millionaires in Acapulco see it differently too. I just see it as a Belfast lad from a council estate who struck lucky because he could kick a ball. At least in Belfast the Catholics and the Protestants could use the same public toilets and travel together in the same bus if they wanted to.

We went to a party one night, very soon after our arrival, where the master of the mansion took great delight in showing us how the black lads should be treated. Nothing physical; just the way he talked down to them. There was one little fellow I particularly remember, sitting turning a spit as regular as clockwork, and this white fellow says to him, 'Tell Mr Best how long you've been doing that for'; as if it was some big deal.

'I've been doing it for ten hours, boss', he replied. Ten hours, I thought, and wondered what the hell I could say to him. Nothing seemed appropriate enough, so I left him there turning his spit and thinking his own thoughts while the white folk laughed and drank and ate and looked each other up and down for the purposes of fornication.

The 'boss' thing bothered me right from the first day when we were introduced to our driver, Patrick, a lovely little lad who took enormous pride in this car with 'George Best – Jewish Guild' plastered along the side.

'You don't have to call us "boss"', I said. 'I'm George and this is Malcolm.'

'Yes, boss', he'd say, and so it went on for a couple of weeks. He wouldn't even call us Mr Best or Mr Wagner. It always had to be 'boss' until finally, not long before we were due to leave South Africa, he came round to using our names.

Playing in Cape Town and Durban upset me too; all those amazingly beautiful coloured women and all the time Itzy's warnings going through my head.

'She might be the most beautiful girl in the world, George, but keep away from her. You'll get yourself into trouble.'

In any other situation I'd have made a joke of it, but it was too serious to take lightly. And yet there were times when you had to laugh to remain in touch with reality. The blacks and the Coloureds manage it, as we discovered one night in Durban. Itzy had told us about this club there, but what he didn't know – or neglected to tell us – was that it had changed hands since he was last there. Understandably then we thought it a bit odd when the girl on the desk told us we mightn't like it inside. That was all right, we said, we'd take a look; and in we went. Two hundred white eyes in a hundred black faces turned to look at us through the gloom, I looked at Waggy and he looked at me. We didn't even need to nod. We just turned around and walked out. The girl at the desk was laughing her head off.

Chapter 11

The disembodied voice called our card numbers and we shuffled through the boarding-gates, across the tarmac and up the steps of the waiting Trident. Waking businessmen and awakened schoolgirls returning from the Easter break, straggling aboard the first shuttle of the morning from London to Edinburgh. No-one fought for the window seats; places were filled at random despite the efforts of the stewardess to move people through the plane. It was too early in the morning for taking orders from people, but then it was also too early for thinking. Just as easy to do as you were told, and so I sat as bid with my back to the bulkhead, pushed my briefcase under the seat, stretched my legs as far as possible without making contact with two nicely turned ankles, and closed my eyes.

I'd been in London only for the night to see Bill Foulkes, now coach of the San José Earthquakes, who was trying to get a team together for the forthcoming North American Soccer League season. He wasn't making any big promises, for which I was grateful; simply laying down the facts and saying he wanted me out there. We'd discussed most of the details on the phone anyway. Late night, early morning calls from California to Edinburgh and from Edinburgh to Florida, where Beau Rogers was arranging to trade me from the Fort Lauderdale Strikers. I knew it couldn't be a wonderful season; you can't take over a franchise at the start of the season, as Milan Mandaric had done, find a team, and win something straight off. We might be lucky if we won some games. But Milan had done well with San José when he owned the franchise originally, seeing the Earthquakes win their Divisional Championship and getting to within two goals of an appearance in the 1976 Soccer Bowl. They had a good little stadium which regularly attracted strong support from around the South Bay area. I remembered thinking that when I played there for the Aztecs. So I signed the contract and had an orange juice to celebrate. Now it was only a question of how much longer I remained in Edinburgh.

Had Hibs made the final of the Scottish Cup I'd have stayed behind, but the previous Saturday we'd gone down 5-0 in the semi-

141

finals to Celtic; a disappointment as we'd played well in the first half and could have turned round at 1-1 instead of a goal down. We missed an easy chance immediately before the interval, and then fell to a sucker punch early in the second half. After that it was a minor massacre. Major finals, it seems, are not my thing. Four semi-finals in the FA Cup, two in the League Cup, one in America and now one in Scotland. It makes me wonder how we managed to reach the final of the European Cup, and when I think what happened afterwards I wonder if it might have been better had we failed there as well. But that's too negative. Like wondering if I'll stay off alcohol when I stop taking the pills. I have to convince myself that the pills are merely a help. I'm the one who has to stop me drinking. That's the challenge.

The engine pitch changes and I half-open my eyes to take in the regulation shoes, the ankles and the long legs beginning to find a woman's shape. There was once a time when I couldn't venture in the street without being pursued by them. I still get asked for autographs, but in days gone by there were many wanting more than that. I even had mothers phoning up and offering it on their daughters' behalf. Poor Mrs Fullaway; she must have wondered what she'd taken on when the girls began climbing through the windows at night. More than once Steve, with whom I shared a room, was shaken awake by some pubescent puss whispering 'Georgie, Georgie' in his ear. There was one morning when Mrs Fullaway came downstairs to find a blonde beauty fast asleep on the sofa.

'What's this then?' she asked, giving the girl a good shaking.

'I came to see Georgie', she said, 'but he wasn't here. So I thought I'd wait for him and I fell asleep.'

'And how did you get in?' Mrs Fullaway was getting suspicious. 'Have you got a key?'

'No, I climbed through the window.'

Mrs Fullaway looked at the girl in her long flowing skirt and her pretty, hippy blouse, and her annoyance turned to amusement. Wickedly so.

'In that case, my girl, you can go right back out of it again.'

'Oh, I can't', protested the girl. 'There are people.'

'You came in this way', said Mrs Fullaway, opening the window, 'you can leave this way'.

And so, much to the amusement of the neighbours, she did. Girlies, Mrs Fullaway used to say, they make such fools of themselves.

The memory of it made me smile, and the schoolgirl opposite,

142

catching my smile, returned it. Oh no, honey, those were other days. I'm a married man now with my assets frozen in a bankrupt Irish bank and the Inland Revenue closing in for the kill. That Georgie Best was left lying between the covers of Mike Parkinson's book, if he existed like that at all. I know he's not me, however much I might have appeared like that to Parky. I was drinking heavily much of the time we worked together on that book and I might well have reached the stage of not realising what a load of crap I was talking. Considering I didn't know what I wanted to do with my life, it wasn't surprising I didn't know what I was saying half the time. I was confused about where I was going to live, whether I wanted to play football or not, what kind of business I might go into. I was messing him around, retiring one minute, coming back the next, and in the end both of us were happy to get the book finished.

The way it was written disappointed me, though. I'd always admired him as one of the good writers on sport in England, and I think he let himself down. He was capable of a much better book than *Best*. Maybe it wasn't objective enough because we were such good friends, more like a couple of drinking pals than co-authors. He was too close to his subject perhaps. However it did upset me that he seemed to get carried away with the sex, as if it was all that mattered. Sure there were girls; you can't be famous in Britain or America and reach thirty without having twice your share. Some women can't keep their hands off celebrities, and who was I to let a good opportunity pass by? But they weren't all five-minute fucks. Some meant something to me, and he got that wrong.

I don't blame him entirely, however. I had the opportunity to say I didn't like what he'd written, the way he put things, but the only person I told was Waggy and it wasn't his place to tell Mike I was unhappy with the book. Nor do I hold any grudge, as people might think. I'm just disappointed because we could have done a lot better, and for the sake of a fast buck we upset a lot of people who were close to me.

The Saab was where I'd left it at the airport, started first time, and cost me a small fortune to get it past the barrier. Rod Stewart was wailing about Georgie as I cruised quietly along the Queensferry Road and the song, plus the neatly turned ankles, got me thinking about another Georgie. She didn't get the chance to attend a public school in Scotland. At sixteen she was already working hard at becoming a model and that's how I met her; back in the days when

I was supposed to be the fifth Beatle and all that. The *Daily Express* had approached me to do a series called 'The Best Set' – anything I wanted to write about, they said. Cars, fashion, music, a bit of football; an open brief. And on the fashion side they were going to launch a new young face, a girl who was also called Georgie. Which tied the whole thing in well. Georgie and I became very friendly, and yet I often felt there was something mysterious about her. She had a sympathy and a wisdom beyond her years. I'm not a particularly inquisitive person, but when you see a lot of someone you learn about her fairly quickly. With Georgie, though, there were parts of her private life of which she never spoke. Nevertheless, for all her reticence, she was one of the few I could talk to when things were getting me down; even years after we'd ceased being close, in any romantic sense, I'd pop round to see her. Sometimes, when the press were giving me a hard time, she'd drop me a note and suggest I call in for a chat. She'd married by then, with a little boy who called me the 'football man'. A good friend, Georgie was. But then she knew what it was like to be afraid of the press and publicity, for it had all come out in the end; that mysterious, unspoken side of her life. Her mother was Ruth Ellis, the last woman in Britain to be hanged.

Before the morning was through I'd had cause to remember another old girlfriend. Pat Booth, so one of the papers said, had written a book called *The Lady and the Champ*. 'I wonder what John Conteh will think of that' flipped across my mind as soon as I saw the article, but reading on I discovered that the book was a novel. At this rate we'll all be at it, I said to Angela.

'How many words have you done today?' she asked, not bothering to look up from the model she was assembling with an engineer's care and precision.

'I've been thinking', I replied.

'Put it on paper', she retorted. So I did.

Cathy McGowan of *Ready Steady Go* fame introduced me to Pat, who at the time had given up modelling and was running the Countdown and Top Gear boutiques in the King's Road, Chelsea. Her father was a boxer in London's East End in his day, so there was no slapping her on the nose if she got out of hand. Not that our relationship was any big thing. If I was in London I'd call her up and maybe see her if we had a few free days. Likewise if she was ever up north. We had some good times together, a few giggles, and then one day, when I called, her friend told me Pat wasn't there. She didn't

144

1968. Hi fans! Pop-star welcome for the 'fifth Beatle' after United's arrival in London for the European Cup final against Benfica. *Central Press*

Top: 1974. Still attracting the fans – a guest appearance for Southern League club Dunstable Town. *Central Press*
Bottom: 1974. Arriving at Marylebone Magistrates Court, with Malcolm Wagner, to be cleared of all charges of trespassing and stealing property from Miss World, Marjorie Wallace. *S & G Press Agency*

1976. Running on easy for Fulham, the ball under close control and my mind working out the options available.
Colorsport

1977. He may have been the greatest but . . . Taking the ball past Pelé and being brought down for my skills during the LA Aztecs' 4-1 win over the NY Cosmos. *Tim Considine*

Top: 1977. Angela Macdonald Janes and the Los Angeles Aztecs. Manchester United would never have allowed it. *Michael Jacobs*
Bottom: 1979. Looking to the future? Commenting on an NASL game for American television. *Browning*

1980. A few drinks after training at Hibs made to look like a one-man orgy. But the reporter's note-pad on the table hints at the truth. *Norsk Presse*

1981. Family man at home in Los Gatos, California, with wife Angela, baby son Calum, and Dallas, our Alsatian. *Eddie Sanderson/Woman Magazine*

know when she'd be back. And that was the end of it. No tears, no broken hearts. A good sixties' relationship that ran its time.

Seventies' relationships, I was soon to discover, were swinging in another direction down the King's Road. I'd gone into Alvaro's for dinner one night and ended up getting in with a group of film and television people. Jane Asher was there, not at all impressed that I'd been the fifth Beatle, and also a well-known television producer to whose house we sloped off around midnight. It wasn't a party, just a few people sitting about smoking, drinking and talking. As the morning drifted on, people would stretch themselves to their feet and make their way home to bed until eventually there was me, the television producer and his valet-chauffeur, a nice-looking lad who looked as if he'd still be there when I could manage to stagger to my feet. For which I was grateful. I'd seen some décor in my time and this was definitely not my scene. Then came the bad news.

'Excuse me, Mr S.', said the valet lad, 'but if there's nothing else I thought I might go home.'

'That's fine', said Mr S. 'I won't be wanting anything else.'

Not half you won't, my darling, I thought. And the moment Mr S. took himself to his violet loo Georgie Best was down the stairs and running, a damn sight more sober than he had a right to be. I hadn't spent a lot of effort avoiding well-brought-up middle-aged men during my racehorse-owning days to go down drunk under some BBC2 intellectual.

The racehorse was owned in partnership with trainer Ian Walker and Alan Ball: we ran it in Everton colours with Manchester United colours as second silks. It was never going to win the Derby, but I thought it might give me something to look for when I watched the ponies on television. I still do watch them; still enjoy a flutter to see how my nose and my luck are holding. Half the fun of winning, though, is telling someone, and the moment I tell Angela she has a go at me for gambling then puts out her hand for my winnings.

'For the house, Bestie', is how she puts it. The amount I put on these days I might eventually win us enough to buy a caravan; horse-drawn of course. But there was a time when I'd sit there in the afternoon, the television on, a form-book in my lap and the telephone at arm's reach. That was a big mistake, having a number to call on credit. I soon lost track of how much I was betting and what I was winning; until the end of the month when the statement came. There was one month I thought maybe I'd had half a dozen bets, perhaps a few more, and I reckoned I'd owe something like three or four hundred pounds. It was £2,500, and that really frightened me. It wasn't so much the amount but the way it could add up without my knowing it. Like the income tax.

Although I'd played around with cards and blackjack in my late teens and early twenties, it wasn't until we opened Slack's that I began gambling in a big way. And then it was mainly to relieve the boredom. In many ways just an extension of Manchester nightlife. Because the city is not too large, people from all the different factions cross paths frequently. The businessmen, the footballers, the show business people, the professional gamblers . . . they all mix and provide the atmosphere for Manchester after dark.

Malcolm wasn't a gambling man, but Colin, the third partner in Slack Alice, had been one for as long as I knew him. He was the same Colin who ran Reuben's at the time I hit the girl Stevie. And it was with him that I grew into the habit of going on to the Casino after we'd closed the club at two. The stakes were low at first, but gradually they got higher and higher. Losing never bothered me, and although winning two or three thousand in a night gave me a lovely feeling, gambling never provided the high I've seen it give other people. But then I've also seen people for whom it's a disease. Owners of clubs would come in, lose what they'd brought with them, and go back to their club to collect more money so that they could gamble on until four o'clock. I never arrived at that stage.

There was one memorable occasion, the year I went to South Africa, that they still reminisce over in Manchester. Just another night playing dice at the Casino. I doubt if either of us had gone in with more than two hundred pounds, and we soon lost that. So we started having call bets; calling the bets even though we didn't have any money. That was disastrous. By quarter past two, between us, we were something like £17,000 down. And the house limit at the time was £100 a bet. Colin had the dice to throw, and we asked the house to raise the limit to £200 to give us a chance to even out before the night was through. They agreed, Colin threw, and from twenty past two until four o'clock we didn't throw a losing roll. Our winnings in that time were something like £26,000 and from being £17,000 down we walked out with £9,000 in our pockets.

It's a typical gambler's good night story, but it has an even lovelier side. Just as we started that lucky roll, an old pal of ours called Melville Davis, a great Manchester character, walked in with just a

146

few quid in his pocket. In the way that gamblers will with friends, he began to follow us and ended up walking out of the place some £500 better off. That was a champagne night. But there'd also be nights when we'd walk away penniless and I'd vow never again. Until the next time. And then I stopped; just like that. If only I could beat the booze as easily I'd have nothing to worry about. But drinking was more than something to pass the time, which is all the gambling was.

Having my own club, I began to lose track of how much alcohol I was consuming, for my drinking was spread over such a long period. No longer was it heavy sessions with the boys and sweating it off in training the next day. Life had turned upside down. Now I was getting up in the late afternoon, having a bath and something to eat, then going off to meet the lads in the pub at six or seven when they were rounding off their working day. I'd stay in the pub till maybe ten, after which I'd go into Slack's where I'd sit with my own bottle of wine, chatting to people and making sure everyone was happy with their food, the service and the music. The club was packed most nights, often with show business people who'd come in for a drink when they'd finished their shows, so I'd always be on edge to make sure everything was right. In the meantime I'm probably putting away four or five bottles of wine, and once we close I want a few drinks to relax, maybe sitting around in Slack's with Yorkshire Mary and the girls or at one of the establishments that cater for the late-night folk. As people went to work, I'd be going home to spend the day in bed.

It sounds a great way of life. Owner of a popular club, a celebrity in your own right, good food being prepared on the premises, plenty to drink, pretty girls who've come for the purpose of seeing whether or not it's true there's a casting couch behind the door marked 'Private'. You've money in your pocket if you want to gamble. The life could be straight out of a Hollywood movie, even down to the point where the hero was a famous athlete who'd thrown it all away and gone from the extreme of highly tuned fitness to that of an indulgence of physical pleasures. The only football I was playing was exhibition matches or five-a-sides for Slack Alice's.

Slack Alice took her name from the imaginary character in Larry Grayson's television act. Before that she'd been an old run-down place called the Club Del Sol, and the state it was in meant we were able to buy it for peanuts. I was playing for Docherty at the time, but every spare moment I had was put into helping the others with the renovations. The place was virtually gutted and then rebuilt in a few months. Having bought it in November 1973 we were open and already flourishing when, one Sunday night in February 1974, I received a phone call there. A lad claiming he was from Mecca, the organisers of the Miss World contest.

'We'd like to bring Marjorie Wallace in to your club tonight', he said. She'd not long been crowned Miss World.

'Sure, but it's usually quiet, being Sunday and all', I warned him. 'We close early 'cause of the licensing hours.'

'Well, we'll still come along.'

'Okay, I'll tell them on the door.'

'Our fee is £150', he said. At least I think that's the amount he said. I was a little flabbergasted at his nerve.

'You've got to be joking', I told him. 'You want me to pay her to come to my club?'

'Think of the publicity', he began explaining.

'Publicity!' I interrupted. 'I need publicity like . . . I'm spending half my life trying to avoid publicity.'

'It'll do your club a lot of good', he argued.

'Look, neither I nor the club need publicity. It's a private members' club and as far as I'm concerned I'm certainly not paying anyone to come here. If she wants to come in as a guest and enjoy herself, that's fine. She's welcome.'

'No', he said, 'that's not the way we operate. Our policy is that we have to be paid.'

I was telling the girls the story when the phone rang again. Same lad. They'd still like to come, and on this occasion they were prepared to forget the fee. Big of you, I thought, and set myself up with another bottle of wine. People started coming in – the little wine bar in the corner was proving popular – and for a Sunday night we were doing a brisk trade. Which goes to show you never can tell. A couple of United players leant on the bar telling me how successfully Docherty was taking them into the Second Division for the first time since the war, and I told them of the club's refusal to allow me to do some publicity shots at Old Trafford. It was only a gimmick: putting all the girls in Manchester United strips and lining them up with me in front of the goalmouth. No way, said the club, and we ended up doing the shots at Maine Road, Manchester City's ground!

The commotion at the door drew my attention to the Miss World entourage. Managers, chaperones, photographers; she had the lot

148

with her. And they'd wanted me to pay for the privilege! Not that she wasn't worth it, and Miss Great Britain was the best I'd managed to date. So we made polite conversation, had our photos taken several times, and somewhere along the way I obtained her phone number in London.

'I sometimes have business down there', I told her. 'Perhaps we can have dinner sometime.'

'My schedule takes me on to Birmingham, I think', she said, 'but if you're in London and I'm in town, sure, let's get together.'

Something in the way she said it made me try the number from time to time, and one night I found her at home. I learnt later that she'd been expecting me to call and, so she said, had put off going to Europe for the weekend with some well-known singing star who, rumour had it, was seeing quite a lot of her. What there was to see was well worth seeing, but I thought we might have had more in common than physical attraction. Well, we did know the same places, much to my embarrassment at the time and my later amusement. There I was, taking her to places like Tramp and San Lorenzo's, thinking they'd be new to her with new faces to meet, and all I was doing was introducing her to people she'd met earlier while with this singer. She enjoyed the Keystone Cops bit, though, when the press got hold of the story that I was taking her about town. The Irish footballer could still draw the column inches.

Come Saturday morning we'd more or less had enough of each other, and the phone call was all it took for the bust-up. I was in the same room, so without disappearing to the bathroom I couldn't help but hear what she was saying, telling whoever it was how much she was missing her boyfriend, racing driver Peter Revson, and how she couldn't wait to get back home. Perhaps I was getting old, perhaps my Presbyterian background was coming through, but this was too much for me. An hour earlier we'd been in bed making love; now here she was coming on all sweet about another guy while I'm sitting there only a yard away. I asked her, when she'd hung up, if she didn't think that was a bit over the limit, she said it was none of my business, and I said I thought it was. Before long we were having a jolly old slanging match, me telling her she was a whore and a cow and she calling me a big-headed so-and-so who was hopeless in bed and that she'd tell the newspapers so. Finally she said she was going shopping with a friend, and I told her that was fine by me and not to expect me there when she got back. Off she stomped, leaving me to revise my plans for the weekend. London had nothing to offer, so I made myself some toast and tea, watched sport on television, and caught an evening train back to Manchester. The time went quickly because I'd brought some interesting reading for the journey: Marjorie's diary. Insurance against the possibility of her going to the newspapers.

The following Thursday morning, just before closing time, I was in Slack's when two lads from the local law came in and asked for a few words in private. Sure, I said, and took them through to the office away from all the noise. I thought they'd received some complaint about the club, or maybe come to ask me to appear in something for them. But no! They tell me I'm to accompany them to Bootle Street station. They've had a call from Marylebone Lane in London, asking them to hold me in custody until two detectives come up to Manchester to take me back to London.

'What's it all about?' I asked, but they weren't prepared to say. Fortunately the Bootle Street nick was just around the corner, so Waggy could bring me in sandwiches and coffee while we waited for the heavy mob from London to arrive. He also got on to Geoff Miller, his solicitor, to explain what had happened. The story was that I'd been accused of trespassing and stealing a fur coat, passport, cheque book and 'other items' from Marjorie Wallace some time between Monday and the previous day. Other items, I was informed, might include jewellery. It was ludicrous, and I told them so. I'd been in Manchester most of the time and could account for my movements from Saturday night onwards. I certainly hadn't gone traipsing back down to London to knock off a piece of Marjorie Wallace's fur, as they were alleging. The charge didn't say breaking and entering: trespassing and stealing was how it read. That meant I'd have had to let myself in, and I didn't have a key. It was something I'd thought of when I left the flat on Saturday afternoon. A good thing I hadn't popped out for a bite to eat because I wouldn't have got back in again.

The local police were great, but they had their instructions and all we could do was wait. There was a slight break in the monotony when they took me back to Mrs Fullaway's to search my car and my room: three of us sneaking about the house quietly so as not to waken Mrs Fullaway. The search was fruitless, as I told them it would be, but there was a moment of high drama when they found a fur coat in my wardrobe: I could see their eyes light up.

'Whose is this?' the constable asked.

'Mrs Fullaway's', I replied; and incredibly they let it go at that. Back we returned to Bootle Street, where they now let me make my phone call.

'Hi Geoff', I said, 'It's George. Did Waggy tell you? Yeah, it's true. No, I'm not joking. There are two detectives on their way up from London for me right now.'

'Do you want me to come down?'

'What I want you to do first', I said, having given it some thought on the way back to the station, 'is call up every newspaper and TV and radio station, tell them I've been arrested, and tell them why. Because', I added loud enough for the police in the room to hear, 'when all this is cleared up someone is going to be in trouble and it's not going to be me. That's the first thing.'

'Right', he said. 'And I'll see you in London in the morning to bring you back, so don't worry.'

'I haven't anything to worry about', I said, and hung up.

Something was worrying me, though. Perhaps as a result of the drinking I'd been doing that night my mind was flashing up all kinds of thoughts, some lucid, others quite unreal. I now began to wonder if the two men on their way from London were indeed policemen. They might be friends of the friend with whom she should have been keeping company in Europe the previous weekend. Perhaps I was being set up. I asked the desk sergeant if he'd mind phoning London to make sure the two detectives coming for me were genuine.

'Why?' he asked. 'What makes you think they're not?'

'I don't know. Just that this whole thing's like a bad dream. It's so unreal I can't believe it's happening.'

He checked, and they were genuine all right; one of them a Detective Chief Inspector. Not very chatty types, though. We drove all the way to London with hardly a word spoken. One stop for petrol and straight on to Marylebone Lane. Into the interview room just after half past ten for four and a quarter hours of questioning. I repeated the story I'd told the Manchester police, then said they may as well wait until my solicitor arrived because I wasn't saying any more. They themselves must have seen how frail their case was because at one time they suggested I might have taken the stuff when I left on Saturday afternoon.

'In that case', I countered, 'how come you've waited till now to arrest me?'

So back we went to where I'd been and who I'd been with from the

151

time of leaving the flat until the time of my arrest. It got so tiresome that I began developing some high-flying theories of my own. Perhaps the fur coat and 'other items' were gifts from the singer man and, having seen what she was up to in her spare time, he thought he'd like them back. For all I knew the flat might have been his. I even entertained paranoiac thoughts about a Rolls Royce I'd seen sitting outside the flat on Saturday afternoon, occupied by two men. In the end all I wanted was sleep. I'd been up for more than twenty-four hours. But it made me realise how the police can sometimes obtain statements. There comes a time when you think anything would be better than going over the same old details for yet one more time.

They charged me at Marylebone Magistrates Court at half past three before a magistrate who adjourned the hearing until the end of March and thought I was a sufficiently dangerous criminal to set my bail at £6,000. Waggy put up five and I was allowed to guarantee the other thousand on my own behalf. 'Thought you were safe, didn't you, kid? Well, I'm off to Spain in the morning' I joked with Waggy as he, Geoff and I walked out of the court building – and hurriedly beat a retreat inside as the mass of reporters, photographers and television cameramen thronged forward. I had all the publicity I wanted, and for once the police seemed quite happy to whisk me away from the press in a Black Maria.

The days that followed were hell; the time was spent brooding at the bar in Slack's and cursing the night I ever set eyes on Marjorie Wallace. I'd call her London number at nights, and if she was in I'd begin effing and blinding at her for what she was doing to me. 'What would I want your bloody fur for?' I'd shout at her. 'I only wanted you in bed and you were no bloody good at that anyway.' It reached the point where Malcolm and a couple of the girls at the club were keeping a guard on the phone to prevent me from getting into trouble for calling her.

On top of all this, both for me and my family, was the worry and concern for my cousin Gary who was lying in a coma in a Belfast hospital after being shot. When they phoned on 26 February to say he'd died the previous night, I began to wonder who was going mad: me or the world. I wanted to scream my pain at someone and Marjorie Wallace seemed the obvious person. In my mind all that had happened came back to her. So obsessive was my anger at her that I grabbed a handful of coins from the till and stood in a Deansgate phonebox shouting abuse at her, blaming her for the trouble I was in and for the death of my cousin. I didn't want her to talk but gradually, through my mad and drunken stupor, I came to realise that she was saying how sorry she was, not just about Gary but about the court case.

'It's nothing to do with me', she said.

'Then who is it?' I yelled. 'What's going on?'

'I can't say. Please don't go on at me. Just forget it. I can't take much more.'

She hung up then, and when I tried to phone her back the number was engaged. I replaced the phone and ran back through the rain to Slack's. Somehow the anger had abated and the whirling in my head was stopping. All I felt now was a sadness.

At the beginning of March, Marjorie's passport and a medallion were returned anonymously to the *Sunday People* newspaper with a note saying that the sender had stolen them and didn't want to see George Best take the rap. A week later her tiara and some cash were found in a telephone kiosk after a man had contacted the paper. To us in Manchester it all looked very odd, and we kept waiting to hear that the police in London were getting somewhere in their hunt for whoever was providing the stuff. Nothing ever happened; I wonder if the police really cared when they saw what fools they were making of themselves by taking me to court. Marjorie Wallace, in the meantime, had flown back to America, and next we heard she'd been stripped of her Miss World crown. Then came the news that Peter Revson had been killed while practising before the South African Grand Prix. What now, we wondered.

The due date, 27 March, arrived but not Marjorie Wallace. Peter Revson's funeral was the forthcoming Friday, the police explained, and the magistrate, looking just a little irritated we felt, adjourned the hearing until 24 April. Another month to wait around, and Waggy was starting to think seriously about his £5,000. By now Geoff was convinced I had nothing to worry about, so I started negotiations with the *Sunday People* to write my account of the story once the hearing was over. The fact that most of it was written before the hearing seemed of little relevance considering I was receiving £12,000 for my troubles. I began to think more favourably about Miss Wallace, especially when she failed to show up on the 24th and the magistrate threw the case out of court. Not that he had any choice. As I heard a police constable whisper to his mate as I entered the dock: 'We won't get far on this one. It's a load of bollocks.' And

153

that's about all it was. Geoff got nicely steamed up complaining of the way we'd been messed about and tried to sue the police for costs, but the old lad on the bench wasn't playing ball. 'Your client may walk out of this court without a stain on his character', the magistrate said in releasing me. And that's exactly how I walked in here, my old love.

Other visitors to Slack Alice were no trouble at all in relation to that episode. That's the way we wanted it, too. All the big names in entertainment would come in after their shows: Leo Sayer, Gilbert O'Sullivan, Jack Jones, Tommy Steele when he was playing at the Palace, Mike and Bernie Winters, Bruce Forsyth, Lonnie Donegan. Dave Allen sat on a bar stool and had us rolling about with laughter while he almost drank us dry. Elton John often dropped in to talk football and would say how great it was to relax somewhere without being mobbed by people. I knew exactly what he meant. That was the sort of atmosphere I'd been aiming to create. A club where the faces could sit at a table or the bar, unwind over a drink or two and enjoy a meal in peace. There was music for those who wanted to dance, but we made sure it was never so loud that you couldn't talk.

Bryan Ferry came in one night bristling with bodyguards to keep the girls away and then couldn't work out why he wasn't being mobbed. Mick Jagger danced through the doors followed by twenty or thirty people, including a coloured dance troupe, and took the place over in one of the most memorable nights ever at Slack Alice. Every available space was filled with people dancing and congo-ing in and around the tables behind Jumping Jack Flash himself. The night David Essex appeared in his white suit Waggy and I thought we'd have to look after the bar and wait on the tables ourselves. Every girl we employed simply stopped whatever she was doing to drool. From time to time Graham Gouldman of 10cc drifted in to recall when he and Waggy drove the Manchester teenies wild in their Whirlwinds days, and, if he was in town, Phil Lynott came along, sometimes with his mother. Which gave me the opportunity, after many years, to repay Phyllis for the many morning hours I'd spent pouring out my heart to her. Thin Lizzy were making waves by then, with Phil writing good hard-driving rock. One of his songs, 'For Those Who Love to Live', might have been written for Georgie Best.

Oh the boy he could boogie,
Oh the boy could kick a ball,
But the boy he got hung up
Making love against the wall.

154

There was a lad named Sean on the door to keep the trouble-makers out, and yet funnily enough he was off the night Eric Clapton accused us of sending in the heavies to sort him out. The heavies were a little Spanish waiter called Eugenio and the barman, Mike McLoughlin, whom you'd lose if you stood him behind a goalpost. Sorting out Eric consisted of asking him to get down from the tables he was dancing on so that the girls could serve dinner. But the lad wasn't seeing things straight that night. 'You're sending in the heavies', he screamed at Waggy. 'You're sending in the heavies.' At which he and half his followers walked out, leaving a dozen or so T-bone steaks uneaten and unpaid for. In the end the matter was sorted out by those who remained to enjoy their meal.

It was just as well they hadn't come in on the night we took all the staff out for their Christmas party. Originally we'd thought of having a party after closing time, but that was no big deal for those who'd been working all night. Then I hit on what seemed a crazy idea but one that got better and crazier the more we thought about it. We'd get some of our regular customers to run Slack's one night – kitchen, bar, tables, disco, the lot. Everyone we approached was full of enthusiasm for the idea, and those who came into the club that night quickly entered into the spirit of it all. Meanwhile, we were living it up in a nearby Italian restaurant, and when we returned to Slack's to be served by our customers you couldn't tell who was having the more fun.

The success of Slack Alice soon prompted us to think of expanding our club interests. The old Waldorf Hotel was up for sale, and with four levels it was ideal for the plans we had in mind. The asking-price for the lease was over £100,000 but we knew we could make arrange-ments to cover that. Where we did over-extend ourselves was in trying to do it all so quickly. What we planned was a Continental-style wine bar for the cellar, a pub which we'd already decided to call Oscars on the ground floor, a disco on the first floor and offices and a banqueting suite on the top floor. On paper it looked great, but getting it done meant spending our own capital to pay builders' bills, bank interest and general running costs. Even with one floor opera-ting, our outgoings far exceeded our income, and so the offers I was getting to make guest appearances for different football teams had a financial attraction as well as providing an opportunity to play again. The longer I was out of the game, the more I found myself missing it, and when, in late 1975, I was approached by the Los Angeles Aztecs

155

to play for them in 1976 the temptation was irresistible. I treated myself to some time at a Surrey health farm in order to reduce my weight and flew to LA to see what they were offering.

It wasn't the first time an American team had approached me. Warner Communications, who owned the New York Cosmos, flew me to New York in January 1975 with the offer of a million-dollar contract over five years. But they wanted to tie me up from first thing in the morning until last thing at night, doing promotions for them as well as playing football, and that wasn't the kind of life I wanted. I let the offer slide and they signed Pelé instead. However, the West Coast, as I'd discovered more than once since my trip there with Waggy, was more my scene and I liked the frankness with which John Chaffetz, the Aztecs' general manager, explained the set-up there. He wasn't promising great things; soccer would never be the major spectator sport in LA and he was still trying to build a side. But he wanted a superstar to match Pelé in New York and ironically I was the man he wanted. He'd like me to advise on players to buy, which I did, we discussed terms, and I agreed. I also suggested a lad I knew in Manchester who might do well for him; not a name but a good, hard-working footballer who could keep the midfield ticking. He said sure, sound him out and let me know. If you think he's okay I'll have the office prepare a contract for him.

Bobby McAlinden was playing in a five-a-side in Stalybridge the night I finally caught up with him. Moving the ball well, sprinting his little legs up and down the gym. You wouldn't have thought he'd not played for eight years, and even then no more than a season or so in South Africa. I'd first met him when I was playing for United's Youth and Junior teams, but as he was playing for City we had little in common then except the day, month and year of our birth. Years must have gone by before we met up again, by which time he was in partnership with a bookmaker and limiting his football to five-a-sides. Even though he'd not made the big time with City I knew he was one of those lads who, had his luck been different, could have gone further. I'd had no hesitation suggesting him to John Chaffetz, and Bobby's record in America proved me right. In three seasons with LA, before things went bad there, he never missed a game, and after being traded to Memphis he played the season through before retiring. Memphis offered him another contract for 1980, but we'd been building up Bestie's bar down on the beach and he wanted to devote more time to that.

156

When I first approached him about going to the States with me he agreed at once but, as he said later, he didn't hold out too many hopes. It all sounded too good. A second chance at a football career, even if it might be for only a season; an apartment on the beach and a car; guaranteed sunshine. What more could a single lad want except a contract? So he pushed the idea to the back of his mind, kept playing his five-a-side and, just in case, worked out at the YMCA to improve his fitness. In January I went back to LA to finalise my own plans, and one afternoon in February I phoned Bobby at work.

'You'd better come and sign your contract', I said. 'We're leaving next week.'

Effectively that was it. Farewell to Manchester. The break I'd wanted to make for four or five years had come to pass and, apart from business and the occasional pleasure, I wouldn't be returning. Fifteen years of possessions went into one tea chest and a suitcase. All that remained were the parties and the farewells. We'd had them once or twice before but this time my plans sounded more definite. I knew where I was going, I wanted to go there, and I had a contract. All the past came flooding back as the old friends called in to say goodbye and ended up drinking the night away as we did in the old days.

Only one of the old crowd was missing. Returning home one night from his restaurant, Malcolm Mooney was killed when his car collided with a lorry at an intersection. He'd achieved those dreams he'd told me of that mixed-up night driving home to Manchester from Sinead's; and then suddenly it didn't matter. His funeral had brought us all together again, making me realise how close our crowd really were. It wasn't that they were hangers-on behind my fame; I was simply one of them, a friend among friends. Now I was leaving them. Danny, Waggy, Big Frank, wheeler-dealer Eddie, Les and Brian, Jimmy the Pill, Coloured Danny and Dollar Danny, George Gent – friends and characters who made my life rich and provided me with great, unforgettable memories.

I've heard it said that the life went out of Manchester the day I left, but that was just the times changing. My presence might have been all that was needed to fill a club or pub inside an hour, but I wanted more for myself than that. I didn't know what, but I knew why. Manchester had closed in on me and I needed air. I was looking for a brand new start.

Chapter 12

LA Aztecs 4, NY Cosmos 1; 2 July 1977

Aztecs at their best to defeat Pelé, Cosmos

by Shav Glick

Jeers that greeted the absence of the Cosmos' Franz Beckenbauer turned to cheers from Aztec fans among the 32,165 who roared their approval as the hometown soccer favorites routed the visitors, 4-1, [Saturday] in the Coliseum.

The highly publicized Beckenbauer, Europe's footballer of the year last season while playing with West Germany's Bayern Munich, allegedly pulled his groin muscle during practice Friday afternoon. Cosmos coach Gordon Bradley elected to rest his $2.8 million talent.

But even with Beckenbauer it is doubtful the Cosmos could have coped with the fired-up Aztecs, who apparently were trying to erase the embarrassment of last Sunday's 5-2 loss at the Meadowlands [Cosmos' stadium] before 57,191 and a West Coast TV audience.

'It was our best game this year', said George Best, whose magnificent talents coupled with those of Charlie Cooke and Steve David, accounted for two Aztec scores. 'The way we played today, I don't think Beckenbauer could have made any difference. We knew we had to take it to them, and that's exactly what we did.'

David stretched his North American Soccer League record for scoring in consecutive games to ten as he upped his League lead to 43 points with two goals. Both were right out of 'How to Play Soccer' playbooks.

The first, which gave the Aztecs a 2-0 lead, came off a close-in pass from Best, who outmaneuvered a Cosmos defender and deftly flicked the ball to David, who stutter-stepped around another defender and gently nudged the ball past the helpless Cosmos goalie.

Los Angeles had taken a 1-0 lead moments earlier on a penalty kick by Phil Beal after David had been tripped in the penalty area by Rildo. It was the first penalty kick given up by the Cosmos this season.

The Cosmos, who were throttled by an Aztec defense that bottled Pelé and Georgio Chinaglia, last year's leading NASL scorer, made their score

Match report reproduced by courtesy of the *Los Angeles Times*.

only on a penalty kick. The Aztecs' Martin Cohen, who had the assignment of marking Pelé, was called for using his hand to stop a ball close to the goal. The Cosmos were awarded a penalty kick and Chinaglia made it.

Terry Mancini, the key in the Aztecs' defense, got a rare chance to score early in the second half and made the most of it. Best was obstructed trying to pass and the Aztecs received a free kick. Cooke rifled a pass cross-field to Mancini and the fullback popped it past goalie Shep Messing, who came to the Cosmos with a degree in zoology from Harvard.

David's final goal was the prettiest of the game. Best, with the ball in midfield, lofted a long pass towards the corner to Cooke. As the Cosmos looked toward Cooke, the 34-year-old Scottish international crossed the ball in front of the goalmouth. David, the fastest man in the League, came flying downfield and leaped toward the air ball at the last second to head it in the corner of the net.

Pelé, making his last appearance before Los Angeles fans, had a frustrating afternoon. On the few occasions he managed to slip away from Cohen's close checking he found Mancini blocking the way. Twice Pelé had the ball, one-on-one with an Aztec in front of the goal, and failed to score. No-one beat the Brazilian King of Soccer one-on-one a few years back, but his 37-year-old legs weren't up to recreating his old talents.

The win was the Aztecs' eighth in nine games at home and upped their NASL-leading points total to 112 and kept them ahead of Dallas in the Southern Division of the Pacific Conference.

LA Aztecs: Rigby; Sibbald, Mancini, Beal, McGrane; Cohen, Cooke, McAlinden; Davies, David, Best.
NY Cosmos: Messing; Morais, Roth, Dillon, Rildo; Garbett, Mifflin, Hunt; Field, Chinaglia, Pelé.

That should have been our season for the Soccer Bowl. Not so much because, on our day, we were the best team in the North American Soccer League, but because we were good for the game. Our football in 1977 was attractive, skilful and above all exciting. We scored goals – more than any other team in the League – and it was goals that the American soccer fans wanted to see. Trinidadian Steve David, despite missing the last two games of the regular season and the play-offs, led the NASL points-scorers with twenty-six goals and six assists for a total of fifty-eight points. I'd missed five games at the beginning of the season, yet still managed to finish third nationally with forty points from eleven goals and eighteen assists. My total of assists – the pass to the goalscorer – tied Pelé's record for one season, and but for the great man himself I might have passed it. I'd picked up the ball in midfield and was, as the Americans say, one-on-one with Pelé as Steve David began a run to my right. Seeing the Cosmos

159

defence go with him, anticipating one of the long, pin-point passes that were a feature of our play together that season, I changed direction left, took the ball around Pelé, and found myself flat on the ground, 'professionally' fouled by the greatest player the game has known. I should have been angry, but in a funny way I took it as a compliment.

Shoddy performances in the last two games allowed Dallas to overtake us for the Southern Division title, but our points tally, boosted by sixty-five goals, had already guaranteed us a place in the play-offs, where we first met San José and needed overtime to beat them 2-1. Dallas Tornados were next, in the two-leg Divisional Championships, and after a comfortable 3-1 win at the Coliseum we annihilated them in Dallas to the tune of 5-1. That answered the critics who thought we lacked firepower without Steve David. But four days later they were vindicated when we slumped 3-1 at home to the Seattle Sounders in the first leg of the Conference Championships. Bobby Mac had put us ahead after a furious onslaught, but then we fell apart as Jimmy Robertson, Steve Buttle and Micky Cave capitalised on defensive errors. However, the NASL home-and-away system determines the result on matches won, not on goal aggregate as in Europe, so we flew up to Seattle knowing that victory there would give us a fifteen-minute sudden-death period which would favour our style of play. A moment of George Best magic in the sudden-death and we'd be Portland-bound to the Soccer Bowl.

There were 56,000 in the Kingdome at Seattle, and when Jocky Scott put the home team a goal up with a header in the fourteenth minute the whole stadium erupted. The scoreboard flashed his and the Sounders' names in lights, the pretty girls danced and pranced in colourful glee, and a fifty-foot-square instant replay screen showed the goal from all angles as we trooped back to the halfway line for the restart. A goal was essential now, but all our attacks foundered as veteran defenders Mel Machin and Mike England organised Seattle's defence superbly. Even when we did get the ball into the goal it was disallowed. Yet it was a goal, and everyone in the Kingdome, including the referee, knew it, thanks to that giant replay screen. The shot, by South African Les Bachos, was reminiscent of Geoff Hurst's for England in the 1966 World Cup final, hitting the underside of the crossbar, bouncing down over the line and then out to be cleared. In the World Cup, the referee had consulted his linesman before awarding the goal. This referee in Seattle had more than just his

160

linesman; he had that replay screen, and as he looked up at it a deathly hush fell over the stadium. Everyone drew breath and waited. Sure enough, the ball appeared to cross the line – and yet, despite this evidence, the referee still disallowed the goal. Dressing-room commiserations from NASL Commissioner Woosnam were no consolation as the Sounders went on to Portland, where the Cosmos beat them 2-1, and I returned to England and Fulham to put in motion the series of events which eventually led to my suspension by FIFA.

In spite of my intentions to quit English football for good, I'd first returned to Fulham at the end of the 1976 American season. Several factors had contributed towards this turn-around, not least being a determination to avoid spending the winter sitting around like a beach bum, getting bored and drunk. Playing and training regularly on the beach every morning had brought down my weight and built up my fitness; equally important, I'd regained my enthusiasm for the game. I now felt I wanted to play out my football days rather than sit in a bar somewhere remembering only the good times of the 1960s. I wanted to entertain again, and America was offering me a stage.

Getting fit had not been easy, and if it hadn't been for Bobby Mac I sometimes wonder whether I'd have made it. When we first moved into our apartment in Hermosa Beach, just a few miles south of Los Angeles International airport, he'd get me down on the beach every morning, working off the effects of four years' heavy drinking and that crazy upside-down life I'd led since opening Slack Alice. There were times during the early days when I thought I'd never be fit again. I couldn't even run half a mile without lying down, but I knew if I was to find any satisfaction in playing football again I'd need to have the legs for it. Training in that Southern Californian sun took some getting used to as well, but it was a sure way of losing weight. In fact, I shed so much one week that the club doctor ordered me to eat more.

The Beach life was good for me in other respects, too. I could walk or cycle down the street without anybody bothering me. I could lie on the sand with a beer and a girl without wondering in which trash drums the *News of the World* and *Daily Mirror* photographers were lurking. No-one cared who I was. More to the point, no-one knew who I was for some time. People talked to me because I was someone to 'rap' with; not because I was Georgie Best. Even later in the season, when the team started winning games and picking up some

161

publicity in the local papers and on television, I was never anyone special; just 'one of those soccer players'.

At the time most of the players were living around the Beach area, for the little stadium we played in was nearby at El Camino College in Torrance. It didn't hold a big crowd, but then we were never likely to attract one. A number of British people in LA would come down, and soccer was popular with the Mexicans, so being in a small stadium helped create an atmosphere. It was nice playing there and I always felt that the move to the larger Coliseum in 1977 was a mistake. An attendance of thirty thousand may have been a record for a local soccer match, but it was nothing in relation to the hundred thousand capacity of the Coliseum. Moreover, we were usually lucky if we attracted ten thousand for most games. The Coliseum, furthermore, was badly situated for many of our regular supporters from 1976, and if the freeways were jammed – a regular occurrence in Los Angeles – many people wouldn't bother attempting to get there. Only the Mexicans, who formed a large section of the population in that part of town, came in any great numbers.

In 1976 we trained mostly on the beach, but the following season we moved our training headquarters up to the Hollywood Racetrack; a move which couldn't have pleased Bobby more. He'd be there first thing in the morning, watching the horses work out and chatting with the jockeys and trainers until the rest of the team reported for training. Then, if there was racing in the afternoon, he'd stay on for that. I enjoyed it every so often, but then horses weren't in my blood the way they were in Bobby's. I'd prefer to return to the Beach and drive the girls wild with my funny accent or sit talking with the guys in the bars. Some afternoons, for variety, we'd drive up to Beverly Hills to see Ed Peters; if Ed wasn't there himself, conducting business with a series of noughts, somebody would be lying by the pool or dropping in for a drink and a chat. I was at Ed's once when a lad called Henry Weinberg was staying in his guesthouse and a lady called Elizabeth Taylor came visiting. James Caan would sometimes call by for a game of pool, and for all I know there were other stars I'd not recognised. But then that's Los Angeles. Celebrities come and go without people taking the slightest notice, unless they're tourists. After England it was so refreshing.

In other ways, too, America offered me a chance to win back my self-respect. Whereas in Britain the sporting hero is of value only while he's at the top of his career, in America he can cash in on his name and fame for many years afterwards. For example, I'd switch on the television and there, in a commercial, might be Jesse Owens, or a footballer or baseball star from twenty or thirty years back. The man still meant something to the people. But how many sporting heroes of the past are seen on British television? Henry Cooper maybe, but that's because he made himself a personality in his own right. What does Bobby Moore advertise on television these days, or Jimmy Greaves or Terry Downes? In America their equivalents would be recognised and respected for their achievements long after they've retired. But in Britain, so it seems, no-one wants to know you once you've had your day.

The lack of hypocrisy was refreshing, too. My lifestyle must have been a newspaperman's delight, and yet, while filling their columns with my exploits, the papers hammered me for not being the blue-eyed boy who wouldn't so much as ask a girl guide the colour of her knickers. The Americans, on the other hand, love their sportsmen to be different. Take Joe Namath, the New York Jets quarter-back who was everything and more that I was in terms of being the jet-setting playboy. His name appeared in every syndicated gossip column across the country; his photo would include a beautiful broad more often than a football. And the ad-men flocked to use him. They knew that, love him or hate him, Broadway Joe was news. He could play a bit, too, even if his legs were virtually tied together with string. Yet when the Georgie Best image turned sour, with all the talk of women and drinking, the advertisers couldn't ditch me quickly enough.

Not having to cope with additional pressures, and feeling so laid-back in myself, I began to concentrate on my football in 1976 in a way that hadn't been possible since the tailend of the sixties. Moreover, it didn't worry me that the team was far from being the best in the League, whereas I had expected Manchester United to be the best. I enjoyed the responsibility of carrying the attack – Steve David did not join until 1977 – and thrived on the challenge of trying to win games on my own if necessary. Losing Charlie Cooke early on with a broken arm was the sort of bad luck that dogs a team struggling to establish itself, but a good team spirit adequately compensated for any setbacks. As John Chaffetz had told me right at the beginning, no-one expected miracles in my first year, and yet by winning a place in the 1976 play-offs as a wildcard we managed to achieve a small one.

That's what's so lovely about the NASL play-off structure. You needn't be out of the running just because you have a bad start to the season. With goals accruing points, as well as a win, a team playing attacking football and scoring goals remains in contention provided it manages to win its share of games. And in the NASL you can only win or lose; there's no such thing as a draw. If the scores are level after ninety minutes, fifteen minutes' sudden-death overtime is played – until one team scores – and if that fails to break the deadlock the game is decided on a shoot-out. This is not penalties, but a one-on-one situation between one attacker and the goalkeeper. The attacker begins with the ball on the 35-yard offside line – another NASL innovation – and has five seconds within which to get the ball in the goal. The goalkeeper may move off his line and is limited only by the laws governing goalkeepers during normal play. Each team nominates five attackers for the shootout – from the team which finished the period of overtime – and a player from each team shoots alternately.

In 1976 we went into our last Divisional game, against Dallas, needing nine points for a wildcard place as the National Conference team with most points, excluding those who qualified as Divisional winners and runners-up. To obtain those nine points, we had to win (six points) and score three goals. (Under the system then operating, one point was awarded for every goal up to three.) The fact that we hadn't scored more than two goals in any one match all season didn't bode well for our chances; nor did a goalless first half. But it was a lovely evening for football, and after a lazy day on the beach I suddenly felt like turning it on for forty-five minutes. If this was to be my last game of the season I might as well give the home fans something to remember me by. I hope they did, because we won 4-1 and I scored two of those goals. So we made the play-offs against all expectations only, in one of those ironies of football, to be drawn against the Tornados in Dallas. This time they beat us by the only goal of the match.

Being eliminated from the play-offs didn't cause me too much heartache. Just getting that far had been a bonus. I was happy enough to be fit and showing people how soccer could be played. Besides, I'd made the NASL All-Star team, as I did again in 1977 when I was also voted 'best midfield player' and the third best player overall behind Pelé and Beckenbauer. And I'd also met the girl who was to exert more influence on my life than anyone could have dreamed possible, including myself. Strangely enough we'd met, if

164

that's the right word, in England some years before, but not in circumstances I'd care to remember. Not long out of school, she was working as a model at an exhibition I attended and, being slim, blonde and very beautiful, she attracted my attention. I didn't attract hers. When I invited her back to Manchester for a few days, she quickly told me to get lost.

We should also have met on Bobby's and my thirtieth birthday, but that was a typical Ed Peters' party. Too many girls and too few guys. Angela Macdonald Janes, invited by Ed because she was English, arrived when the party was in full swing, decided it was not her scene, and took her blonde hair and Californian tan back down the hill in her Jeep. The next time I saw her was at the party Bobby and I threw at Fat-Face Fenners in Hermosa Beach a few weeks later. I'd asked Ed to invite some girls on our behalf, and Angela and her girlfriend thought they'd give us a second try. This time she and I managed to say something to each other; indeed, we spent most of the party together, much to the annoyance of my date who kicked me on the shin and walked off into the night. At the time Angela was working as personal assistant to Cher, the singer, and before coming to the West Coast, she told me, she'd lived in New York, modelling and living with her dog among the famous on Riverside Drive. She rarely saw John Lennon, who was living there at the time with May Pang, but Greta Garbo used to stop and fondle her dog when she was out walking in Central Park. It was fascinating listening to her; she was so full of enthusiasm for life and so in love with what she was doing. I couldn't wait to be with her again.

Because Angela was living with Cher in Beverly Hills, seeing each other regularly meant one of us, often Angela, spending an hour or more on the freeway. And driving down to the Beach in the late afternoon and back to Beverly Hills first thing in the morning was no fun in the peak-hour traffic snarls which are such a feature of freeway life in Los Angeles. Eventually she moved into the house Bobby and I had bought, and for the first time I had someone else to think of but myself. I also came to learn that I was living with a girl who very much had a mind of her own and wasn't at all impressed by the fact that I was George Best, footballer. I was simply a guy with whom she was falling in love, but there was no way she'd become my doormat. Contests of will were a new experience for me and I found myself respecting her for her strength of character. I could see we'd have some fights before the summer was out, but I had the feeling it might be worthwhile.

Being so contented with my way of life, I hadn't given much thought to what I'd do when the American season finished until John Chaffetz told me one day he'd been approached by Fulham. He was prepared to release me for the winter but was stipulating certain conditions, such as a $2,000 penalty for every Aztec NASL game I missed should Fulham want me to stay on during the overlap of the English and American seasons. Whether or not I went was up to me, he said. Angela, never having seen what England did to me, had no objections to coming with me, but my own feelings were mixed. It meant a return to wintry English ground conditions after the firm, reliable surfaces I'd become accustomed to in the States, and moreover I was happy living in LA. On the other hand I had nothing to do all winter, so I thought I'd ask for the world and, if Fulham were agreeable, give them a try. My terms were £500 a week, £10,000 signing-on fee, and an apartment and car for the duration of my stay. No trouble at all, I was told, much to my surprise. 'Sir Eric Miller is one of our directors, there's no worry about the money. He owns the Churchill Hotel, where you can stay until we find a suitable apartment for you. Car? No problem.' The way it turned out, there was nothing but problems.

Fulham doubled their gate the day I made my first appearance at Craven Cottage, against Bristol Rovers. Their average home gate the previous season was 9,740, but there were 21,127 to see me score after just 71 seconds and put Fulham on the way to their first win of the season. A week later the attendance jumped to 25,794, and with an average crowd of 14,589 for the 1976-77 season I reckon Fulham did well out of my presence. Our final League position wasn't marvellous, but for a time early in the season it looked as if we might challenge for promotion to the First Division. Rodney Marsh had come back from Tampa Bay in Florida and Bobby Moore was still good value in defence, but somehow the promise was never realised. For all that, we enjoyed our football and one writer even commented that Rodney and I could be seen laughing during the game – a rare happening in English football. As the attendance figures show, the fans enjoyed our football too.

Off the field, though, it was a different story: one of constant hassle over the signing-on fee, the apartment and the car. The promised Churchill amounted to nothing more than words and the apartment proved to be one small sitting-room, poky bedroom with no more

166

furniture than a bed, and a tiny kitchen. After what we'd both had in America it was totally unacceptable. We were forever getting under each other's feet and it wasn't long before we were bickering and arguing. The failure of any car to materialise meant we were travelling everywhere by taxi or not bothering to go out. Life, which had seemed so simple in America, became complicated again and the inevitable happened. I went back to drinking heavily.

Complaints about our position to Ken Adam, the agent who set up the deal, were met by more promises and little action. Eventually we were moved to a block of so-called luxury apartments near Hyde Park. From what I later gathered, when the affairs of Sir Eric Miller and Peachey Properties were under investigation, these were company flats and should never have been used for accommodating Fulham Football Club players. Not that they were fit for accommodating anyone. We had to fumigate the place twice to make it habitable, and the furniture looked as if it had come off Steptoe's wagon. As Angela's face fell, so my anger rose. Here I was doubling their gates, and they expected me to put up with rubbish. I stormed down the Bayswater Road to Ken's office in Notting Hill Gate, this time threatening to return to America if the club didn't come up with the signing-on fee. This money, I'd now decided, would be a deposit on a flat of our own.

So it dragged on, and the longer it did the more the relationship between Angela and myself deteriorated. Sitting around all day, waiting for me to come back from training, she became bored and frustrated with life in a damp cheerless London. She remembered the excitement of living in Beverly Hills, the satisfaction of working in a show business environment, and the comfort of the California climate. She wanted to work and yet, as I did, she wanted us to spend as much time together as possible. At least I could get out every day and work off my frustration in training; she had nothing to vent her anger on except me. What had once been good old-fashioned get-it-out-of-the-system arguments became blazing rows with both of us remaining bitter for days on end. It was a situation that couldn't go on forever and it didn't. Angela, making use of her connections with the Hefner crowd in LA, went to work at the Playboy Club just down the road in Park Lane and moved into another apartment. Not that we stopped seeing each other; far from it. I made sure of that by banging on her door in the early hours of the morning after a night on the town drinking myself into oblivion. If she wasn't at home I'd slump against the door until she returned. I still wonder sometimes how

I avoided being locked in cells for the night, the disturbances I used to make.

It took an accident to bring Angela and me together again, and even after that we were on and off so often we lost count. The problem, invariably, was my drinking, which is probably what caused the accident. It was late February, by which time I'd at last received some of my signing-on fee and had taken out a lease on a flat in Putney. I also had a car, thanks to Sir Eric Miller who'd lent me his daughter's Fiat when he heard of the trouble I was having getting the promised car from the club. My friendship with Sir Eric had developed at the time I was drinking in a little pub called the Duke of Wellington, just off the King's Road. He came in one night, we got chatting, and after that he'd phone occasionally to ask if he could join me for a drink somewhere. Obviously directors of football clubs enjoy being seen with their star players, but it struck me that this was more than that. He was a troubled man, for all his supposed wealth and beautiful home, and it sometimes seemed that his only relaxation came from meeting up with Bobby, Rodney and me for a couple of beers and a chat about football. It was a sad side of a man who, during the investigations into his business affairs, chose to take his own life.

Driving Sir Eric's daughter's Fiat home from Tramp one night I put it into a lamp-post outside Harrods. No-one else was involved. It was just one of those stupid moments when your eyelids drop for a split second and the next thing you know your head has shattered the windscreen and you've fractured a shoulder-blade. I came round as someone was dragging me from the car, but however hard I tried I couldn't see him properly. I could hear him asking if I was all right, and telling his dog to keep away, but I couldn't see. Panic grabbed me as I thought I'd damaged my eyes; I was blind.

Next thing I knew I was in hospital and I could see again. A doctor, some nurses, and a policeman; the doctor telling me not to worry, I'd be fine. Loose skin from the cuts on my lower forehead had fallen over my eyes. I needed stitches, that was all. What he didn't tell me was that I'd need fifty-seven around my eyes and forehead alone. Then there was talk about being breathalysed and the doctor was asking me if I wanted to talk to the police. No, I muttered, and I could hear him saying that I was in no fit state to see anyone. I drifted off again, only for the doctor to keep me conscious by asking questions. What was my name, my address, my occupation? Where had I been? I tried to answer but half the time I wasn't sure if he was talking to me or someone else. He made some comment to the nurse about brain damage, and through my semi-consciousness I heard myself ask 'How can an Irishman have brain damage?' The nurse giggled, and the doctor said I had nothing to worry about on that score.

When I woke again I was in a ward and it was daylight. My head felt as if it was held together by Sellotape; my skin wouldn't move. I didn't know where I was or if anyone else knew where I was. Angela, it transpired, did know. I'd given her name and address some time during the night, and not long after waking I was told she'd arrived to see me. What I didn't realise was the sight she would see. My face, criss-crossed with stitches and caked with dried blood, was straight out of a horror movie. In she bounced, all smiles and full of life to cheer me up. The moment her eyes saw my face everything drained completely from her own face. She stood there, motionless, as slowly the tears rolled down her cheeks. It was a moment I could never forget; one of those moments when I understood how much she loved me.

Several days later I was discharged from St Stephen's Hospital and, being a quick healer, was back playing for Fulham again at the beginning of April. Having enjoyed such a promising start to the season it was disappointing to struggle through the last games with nothing to achieve, but the Riversiders, the Fulham supporters, provided some consolation by naming me as their player of the year. Basically, though, all I wanted was to get back to Los Angeles. The NASL season had begun – the first games were in April – and with such experienced players as Phil Beal, Terry Mancini, Steve David, Ron Davies and Charlie Cooke, plus myself, in the line-up, the Aztecs had the look of title-contenders.

Success in that 1977 NASL season added a new dimension to my life off the field, for I became a minor celebrity around the Beach area. Not in a heavy way, as it had been in Britain, but in an easy, friendly way. Bobby, myself and two others saw a good business opening in a little beer and wine bar that was up for sale and picked up the lease for a song. Hard Times was the bar's name then and it was aptly named: sawdust floor, few places to sit, mostly bikers drinking there. None the less it had potential. It was only a block back from the beach, on the main drag, and there was room for development. Today, as Bestie's, it's a thriving business with a good mixed clientele that knows how to spend money. There are dartboards – an 'in' game in California – tables and chairs for eating in the bar, and a separate restaurant with a singer at weekends. Getting a liquor licence, which allowed us to sell spirits and cocktails, made the difference, but it also meant that Bobby and I had to sell our house in order to meet the $30,000 required to purchase the licence.

While all this was happening Angela and I were making up, breaking up, or being apart because she was on the road with Cher or I was on the road with the Aztecs. Away games in America involve more than a train journey to London or a coach trip to Leeds for the day. Going to the East Coast from the West might take you away from home for ten days while you play in, say, Fort Lauderdale, Washington DC and Toronto. For a newcomer to the States it's a great way to visit some of the major cities, but after a while one Holiday Inn becomes little different from another Hilton. They all have colour television in the rooms and several bars.

Not that I was drinking night after night. Far from it, even though there were plenty of opportunities with the friends I was making down on Hermosa Beach and Manhattan Beach. It was near-impossible to walk into a bar without meeting someone you knew: he'd buy you a beer and you'd buy him one, and you'd both buy the owner one and he'd set one up on the house, and so it went on. But half an hour on the beach in the morning sun and you'd soon work off the excesses of the night before, so I never really thought I was drinking heavily. However, even if I wasn't conscious of it, my drinking habits were changing. Instead of drinking night after night, as I had in Manchester, I was now going for days, weeks even, with little more than a bottle of beer with the lads after training. Then, without warning, I'd crave alcohol and that would be it. For two or three days I would pour in as much as my system could manage.

Such an irregular pattern made life intolerable for Angela. Days would pass when we'd be deliriously happy, visiting friends, going to movies, eating out, and then one afternoon she'd come in from work and I wouldn't be home. Hoping against hope she'd start preparing a meal. An hour, two hours would pass; still no sign. So she'd get in the Jeep and drive past my known haunts on the chance she'd find me there. Sometimes she would, but other times I'd know better and go to one of the other towns along the beach. Hitching a ride wasn't difficult; all the kids moved about that way. Two or three days later I'd wake up somewhere and it was time to go home, contrite, to find Angela worried out of her mind or packing her suitcases to leave.

170

Not only her friends but mine as well were telling her she was wasting her time with me. And I didn't resent them doing so because I knew it was true. Here was this lovely girl, holding down a high-powered job with one of the highest-paid entertainers in America, a health fanatic who didn't drink, smoke or take drugs, and I was turning her life into a living hell. I made her so frightened one night that she called the local police, which scared the hell out of me. I grabbed the keys of the Jeep so that she couldn't drive up to Beverly Hills to her girlfriend's or Cher's and ran off down the beach. The police had to leave a notice on the windscreen so that the Jeep wouldn't be towed away by the traffic people the next morning. 'Do not remove this vehicle', it stated boldly for all the neighbours to read. 'Owner is the victim of a domestic dispute.'

Another time I came in drunk while she was cutting meat and got abusive when she got stuck into me for drinking. That made her even more beautifully mad, and a fair old slanging match ended with me being extremely vulgar, turning away and suddenly feeling a sharp prick in my right rump. There wasn't much pain, I'd had too much to drink to feel that, but I was wearing shorts and the blood began to trickle down the back of my leg on to the floor. A mad dash to the local hospital and five stitches stopped the bleeding, but the nurse looked very sceptical when I said I'd fallen on the beach and cut myself on a piece of glass.

'Oh yeah?' she said, turning her head in Angela's direction. 'You want to try it from the other side next time, honey.'

American women have this ambivalent attitude towards their men. They want to screw them and at the same time they want to castrate them.

Not that life was all fights; far from it. Indeed, things were so good at one stage that by the time our season ended with defeat by Seattle in the Conference Championships I wasn't looking forward to returning to Fulham to play through the second season of my contract. Nor were the Aztecs over-keen on letting me go back. By playing until the end of the previous season for Fulham I'd missed five NASL and several friendly games for Los Angeles and John Chaffetz wanted the $2,000 per game compensation he'd been promised. Only he was having the same trouble with promises that I'd had. For five months he'd been writing letters, telephoning and sending telegrams without success. He even called in NASL Commissioner Woosnam because Fulham refused to communicate with him. But when

Woosnam informed the Football League and the Football Association, Fulham denied there had been any agreement in the first place. The Football League's attitude to the affair is perhaps best summed up in the words of the then secretary, Alan Hardaker. 'I am not particularly interested in trying to enforce an agreement that we were told never existed. But Best cannot play for Fulham until the American club releases him.' Yet in 1976, when Fulham were trying to register me for that season, the League had stipulated that registration would be allowed only if there was an arrangement between Fulham and Los Angeles that I could complete the season in England.

I meanwhile returned to England, knowing that John himself was flying over later in an attempt to settle matters personally. The Football Association, at Fulham's request, obtained clearance from FIFA for me to play, and the following Saturday I took the field against Blackburn. Yet a week later I was flying back to Los Angeles with John, both of us totally frustrated by Fulham and neither of us sure of my position. Fulham, of course, were screaming blue murder about John kidnapping me and taking me back to the States against my will. Nothing could have been further from the truth.

The way we saw it there were two basic issues in question, and whichever one applied I belonged to the Aztecs. Either, as the Aztecs claimed, there had been an agreement with Fulham and they had reneged, in which case there was a breach of contract by Fulham. Or the Football League, through Hardaker's statement, failed to recognise the existence of any agreement and so, following the argument through to a conclusion, there was no agreement by the Aztecs to release me to Fulham in the first place. My registration as a Fulham player, therefore, was void and I was still one hundred per cent an Aztecs player. Eventually it looked as if things were being sorted out and I went back to Fulham. But not for long. Nine games and two goals later I returned to Los Angeles.

Back in the Southern Californian sunshine I worked in and on the bar, went for runs along the beach, lay on the sand contemplating the surf, and decided to get married. In view of all that had happened before, nothing could have been crazier, except perhaps the wedding itself. We flew to Las Vegas for the day – Angela, her girlfriend Josephine, Bobby and myself – having booked a place called the Candlelight Wedding Chapel for an afternoon ceremony. After that, we thought, dinner and a gamble in one of the casinos before flying back to Los Angeles. A nice quiet day, except that I got it off to a bad start by missing the plane!

Nor did we allow for the newshounds of the British press, who'd got word we were planning to wed. In order to avoid the usual chaos I'd given the exclusive rights to one paper to publish our wedding photo, but this only increased the determination of the others to get in on the act. No sooner had we set off from Vegas airport to the chapel, driven by a representative of our chosen newspaper, than a small convoy of cars swung in behind us. This quite upset our man, who rid us of pre-nuptial nerves with an unconducted tour of Las Vegas at speed in an attempt – successful – to drop off our pursuers. The only problem was that we arrived at the chapel without certain essential documentation from the local registrar's office, which meant another car journey. I didn't dare look at Angela in case she called the whole thing off.

Why we had to bother with the registrar I'll never know. I could have given any names, addresses and ages for Angela and myself. No-one asked for any proof or identification. As it was I gave my own name, at which the little lady behind the counter raised her blue-rinsed curls and smiled at me alarmingly. I was the one who was alarmed; not her.

'Oh, so you're George Best. I've never heard of you myself, but you must be one important guy from the calls we've been having. This phone's been red-hot all morning with people wanting to know when and where you're getting married. Well, dear, now I know I'll just tell them all to get lost, shall I?'

She could have, but it was already too late for that. Sitting outside was another little convoy of pressmen and we were off around Vegas again. Half the time I was sure no-one was following us, but our man had warmed to the task of getting us to the chapel without any hangers-on and he wasn't taking chances.

If getting this far was pure Keystone Cops, the wedding ceremony itself resembled a scene from an Andy Warhol movie. Having paid our $120 or whatever and presented our newly typed documentation, we were ushered into a small room with a table, some chairs, deep velvet furnishings and plastic flowers. An unseen hand pushed a cassette into a tape deck and saccharine sounds filled the room to get us in the mood for marriage. Some chance after what had gone before, and what little chance there was completely evaporated as the minister oozed into the room wearing a lime-green three-piece suit with braid trim. He looked and sounded as bent as a nine-bob note, and it took me all my time not to laugh. Angela wasn't so successful. The moment he opened his mouth she began to giggle.

Dinner afterwards was an equal disaster. No sooner had we sat down than the waiter spilt our drinks over Angela and Josephine, which meant filling in compensation forms for their clothes before we could eat. All in all it was with much relief that we caught the last plane home to Los Angeles. There was no honeymoon; no wedding night to speak of. I went down to the bar, got drunk and finally arrived home at four in the morning, by which time Angela was fast asleep. A couple of weeks later I even wondered if I'd married the right girl anyway. According to a press cutting from an English newspaper, my bride had worn a black skirt and a black and white striped blouse with a blazer. That was Josephine. Angela was wearing a grey skirt, a grey and white shirt and a cream jacket. The most conservative thing she'd worn since her school uniform, she thought – except that she'd looked more sexy in her school uniform.

*   *   *

Only an Irishman could have his money invested in an Irish bank that damned near went bust. And only a Southern Irish bank would use a Northern Irishman's investments as collateral on his business loans so that, in going bust, they ended up owing themselves money. A simplification, perhaps, of a very complicated affair, but if you don't try to see the funny side of it you might feel very sick when you remember there's more than £25,000 of your money involved.

Just as serious, but less amusing, were the events happening in Los Angeles to the franchise of the Aztecs. America being America, football is very much a business, unlike in Britain where many of the directors devote time and money because of an affection for their club, a love of the game generally or a desire for the local importance that comes from being a director of a town's football club. So, although a disappointment to many of us personally, it came as no great surprise when we heard on the grapevine that John Chaffetz and his associates were selling out to a consortium of businessmen in Beverly Hills.

The new owners did three things when they took over. The first was to move the team's home venue from the Coliseum to the Rose Bowl in Pasadena. The second was to call me up to their offices to advise on new players for the coming season, which I did. The third

174

was to ignore every suggestion I made and sign up a busload of Mexicans. The thinking behind this was that Los Angeles had a large Mexican population, Mexicans were soccer crazy, and Mexican players in the team would increase the size of the crowds. What it actually did was make a nonsense of the move from the Coliseum. True, this was not in the most salubrious part of Los Angeles if you happened to be a white European, but Pasadena is not the place you go if you want your support to be Mexican. Pasadena is white middle-class retired – and was miles from anywhere as far as the Aztecs players and regular supporters were concerned.

I tried reasoning with them that the standard of the NASL was now too high for the sort of players they were signing but I was wasting my time. Time would prove me right as it had at United, I knew that, and so I returned to the Beach to look at the waves. The day I looked at our new players all my fears were realised. There was one fellow who didn't look a day under forty, could hardly lift his legs off the ground, and obviously wouldn't last half a game, let alone ninety minutes.

'Came because his buddy wouldn't sign unless he was given a contract too', one of the backroom boys told me. 'Supposed to be twenty-nine and a former international.'

'Twenty-nine pounds overweight and international beer drinker by the look of him', I quipped with hindsight. The player himself confessed, after some prompting, to being thirty-three, but someone later saw his passport and that had him at thirty-six. Not that he had to worry. He was having a ball displaying all his juggling tricks and cashing his cheques at the bank regularly. It was much better than picking grapes up in the valleys.

It was almost a relief when I damaged my toe in training and was given a few days off. But once the season started there was no escaping the fact that it would be disastrous. None of the Mexicans could understand what I was doing with the ball, let alone think ahead what I might do. Long balls were a waste of time. If the ball wasn't placed at their feet they didn't want to know. One loss followed another, with the owners trading players left, right and centre in their search for scapegoats, and there was no satisfaction in being able to say 'I told you so'. I simply didn't want to play any more. In that case, they said, we'll trade you. Which is what happens in American sport when your face no longer fits. You get traded and accept it, or you don't play. One day Detroit, next day Dallas. I got Fort Lauderdale and was lucky. They had a good little stadium with natural grass, an average gate of ten thousand, and experienced internationals in Gordon Banks, Ian Callaghan and Teofilo Cubillas, the Peruvian World Cup star. There was also a lad called Tony Whelan, with whom I'd played at Manchester United, and the place had beaches and sun; plenty of both.

Bobby Mac stayed on in Los Angeles with the Aztecs that season but he was one of the few to survive. Terry Fisher, the young American coach who'd taken us to two consecutive play-offs, was sacked the week I left and replaced by the former Liverpool captain, Tommy Smith. He'd been with the Cosmos when they won the Soccer Bowl the previous season, but for all his experience and aggression he couldn't repair the damage. The Aztecs, only one game away from the Soccer Bowl in 1977, finished 1978 with one of the worst records in the history of the NASL. The next season the franchise changed hands again, and so, in the space of maybe eighteen months, the club had disintegrated. Players and backroom staff were traded or fired, and I doubt whether in mid-1979 there were more than two people still associated with the Aztecs who'd been there at the end of the successful 1977 season. But that's the way it can be in America. Buy a franchise, screw everyone about to show who holds the power, find you don't fancy owning a soccer club after all, and sell out to someone else who thinks he'd like a go. Players? They're there for the hiring and firing.

When I joined Fort Lauderdale in June 1978 they'd won eight games, lost eleven and, apart from a 2-0 win over the Aztecs, were going through a lean spell. My arrival changed all that. A goal with my first touch of the ball in my début match, against the Cosmos, and another later in the match spurred us to a 5-3 win over the NASL champions and avenged an 8-0 defeat the last time the two teams met. It also set us on a winning streak that took us into the play-offs and through to the Conference Championships where we took Tampa Bay to a shoot-out. Moreover we might have won the shoot-out had coach Ron Newman not substituted me and another forward in the sudden-death period that preceded it. It must have been obvious by that stage that we'd end in a shoot-out, and yet he decided to take off two players who would be most effective in that situation.

Not that tactical substitutions were always one of his strong points. He cost us a game against the Cosmos once by making two of the strangest changes I've ever known. We were playing in New York, where the Cosmos were unbeaten that season, before a crowd of

72,000, and with ten-fifteen minutes to go we were winning 2-1; if we'd taken our chances it could have been 4-1. But it didn't matter, because Cubillas, Ray Hudson, formerly with Newcastle United, and I had such control of the midfield that they couldn't get into the game. Up front we had a good strong centre-forward in David Irving, who'd been at Everton, and he was giving their defence such a hard time that they were unable to develop attacks from the back, which they liked to do. It was one of those lovely moments in a game when the scent of victory and the satisfaction of playing well make you ignore your tired legs and you feel like a twelve-year-old again. I was having a ball, I suppose, screaming and shouting instructions, waving my arms and really turning it on for the big crowd. And then, to my disbelief, I saw Ron Newman on the sideline holding up two numbers. He's taking off Hudson and Irving to bring on a young South African of twenty and an American with next to no experience. Bang goes all our control, all our rhythm. These two lads run around like chickens with their heads cut off and New York come back to beat us 3-2.

'Oh, bad luck, lads', he says when he comes into the dressing-room. 'Unfortunate. Looked like we were going to win it.'

'Unfortunate', I yelled at him. 'There was nothing unfortunate about that, just bloody stupidity. You make two substitutions like that, you can't say it was unfortunate. You're just another bloody Alf Ramsey', I said, slinging my shirt at him in disgust. But he knew so little about football, he probably took that as a compliment.

The problem was that on paper there was nothing wrong with the man, and few Americans could understand my attitude to him. According to the record books – on which Americans are big – Ron Newman had produced the goods: ASL and NASL titles as both player and coach, a unique if meaningless achievement, and NASL coach of the year in 1977 when, in his first season at Fort Lauderdale, the Strikers had tied the NASL record for most victories in a season. What the statistics didn't reveal was the strength of the competitions when he coached teams to those titles. His NASL title was won, with Dallas, in 1971 when there were only eight teams in the NASL, and winning the ASL, with the Los Angeles Skyhawks in 1976, was tantamount to winning a non-League title in England. His first-year success at Fort Lauderdale cannot be denied, but he was lucky in going to a club whose owners could and did pay big money for top players. When Gerd Müller joined the Strikers in 1979, Newman had

177

at his disposal one of the strongest goalscoring forward lines in the country.

Which made it even more crazy when he refused to play me. By the end of 1978 I'd become one of his most outspoken critics and there was little love lost between us when the 1979 season began. Yet I'd trained hard in pre-season – despite uncertainty caused by a FIFA ban – and leaving one of your best players on the bench is not the most sure way to success. The fans didn't approve either, writing letters to the local paper in protest, putting up petitions and chanting my name when it became obvious that I wouldn't be in the starting line-up. What he'd do then, of course, was bring me on some time during the second half. This would satisfy the crowd, for to the Americans an appearance, however brief, is playing. I must be old-fashioned; playing to me is being on the field for ninety minutes.

My problems in Florida, however, were by no means confined to Ron Newman. Indeed, I was beginning to feel somewhat like the James Dean character in *Rebel Without a Cause*. I wasn't looking for trouble but it kept catching up with me. The FIFA ban, coming in October 1978 at the same time as my mother's death, was a case in point. I'd thought nothing of it when Ken Adam arranged for me to guest with Detroit Express on their European tour in September. That's what agents are for: to set up deals and save you having to think about everything. So off I went, played a couple of games in Austria, and found all hell breaking loose. Fulham, still in dispute with the Aztecs some eighteen months on, claimed that the terms of my registration allowed me to play outside America only for them. They appealed to FIFA to place a ban on me, preventing me from playing anywhere in the world, including America, and this the world authority did. No request for an explanation, nothing.

The crazy thing was that I wasn't even aware I'd done anything out of order. Contracts were Ken Adam's department, and if anyone should have known my position vis-à-vis Fulham it was Ken. He was the one who set up that little deal. I guess it was just another instance of someone jumping on the George Best gravy train, but I was beginning to learn my lesson. When Angela said she could manage my career as well as, if not better than, others had, I took her at her word and let her get on with it. At least I knew she wasn't in it for the money.

Throughout the crisis with FIFA the Fort Lauderdale owners were wonderful, taking full responsibility for fighting the ban and paying all the legal costs, which included a High Court hearing in London at which Fulham contested any lifting of the ban and the judge found in FIFA's favour. He needn't have bothered, because two days later the ban was lifted so that I could play for the Strikers in the NASL season just commencing. By this time I'd been in Fort Lauderdale for at least a month, training twice a day in the ninety-degree heat without knowing if I'd be allowed to play again, living in a different place every week as I tried to find an apartment, and losing respect by the minute for Ron Newman.

Some of the things he had us doing in training were quite unbelievable; embarrassing really for experienced professionals. I remember one morning he got us in a straight line, about thirty of us, the one behind placing his left arm on the shoulder of the man in front and holding his right leg while the whole line hopped the length of the pitch! Gerd Müller, who according to some accounts had only one leg anyway, walked over to me in amazement to ask, through his interpreter, what the hell was going on. Who was this man? I couldn't truthfully answer him. How do you explain to a World Cup star, a European Footballer of the Year, the mind of a man who considers the length of the grass a vital factor in his match preparations. 'This team we're playing on Saturday', he once said to me in all earnestness, 'they've played their last two matches on Astroturf, so they'll feel at home on short grass. What I'm going to do is not have the grass cut before the game. That'll fool them.'

Towards the end of March Angela flew down to help me find a house, we shipped our furniture over from the West Coast, and when the FIFA ban was lifted life at long last appeared to be coming good. All I wanted now was to get out on the field and play, having missed the pre-season scrimmage games against college teams for fear that it might upset the negotiations with FIFA.

'All I need', I told Newman, 'is a few games to get match-fit, so could you please let me stay on for a full game unless we're struggling and you feel we need some fresh legs.'

He said he understood – he made a big thing of his understanding of players – and as it happened I couldn't have had a better team opposing us for my first game. Like many teams, the New England Tea Men were forced to field a makeshift side until their European players arrived in May and, for all that we didn't play well, we never looked in danger of losing our 1-0 lead. Consequently I had to look twice when, with half an hour still to be played, my number was held up and I was called off. The man didn't understand at all when I said I needed match practice. He didn't even have any consideration for my feelings. Five months I'd been kept out of football and now, in my first game, he was pulling me off. It was too much. All the frustration I'd been holding down for months came flooding to the top as I marched off the field, slung my shirt at him and told him exactly what I thought of him as a coach.

After that there was no way we could work together. He retaliated by putting me on the bench and I reached the point where I no longer wanted to play for him. I drank more and more often and began to miss training. After all, I wasn't playing that often so why bother training? Angela tried to talk sense into me but I didn't want to take any notice. I didn't want to talk to anyone about it any more. To my way of thinking it was simply a repeat of the same old story. Coaches who didn't understand what I was about. It was easier to drink and forget it all. Until one night I returned home and the house was empty. No Angela, no dog. Just a note to say she'd returned to Los Angeles as she'd threatened. You're wasting your life, George, she'd told me several days earlier. You're not going to waste mine as well.

Chapter 13

The water sparkled in the sun and another Californian day warmed under a blue sky perfect except for the occasional feathers of white above the hills. Sounds of waking life disturbed the calm as the sun dug deep into my shoulders: a telephone unanswered, the bronchial coughing of a reluctant Jeep, the sudden enthusiasm of a Mexican gardener and then that barely perceptible hissing of hoses over late-summer lawns. No waking here, as in England, to wonder on the temperament of the weather and so begin the day uncertain. No grey cheerless Manchester, this sky. This is California blue, seemingly never ending like the day that stretched ahead.

The experience wasn't new, for there had been other mornings spent gazing at the water while the sun gained strength over rooftops or down through canyons. Long spells of drinking sometimes ended with my back against a drum, the lengthy solitude of sand preferable to an empty bed or a couch in some beach bum's home. Mornings not so long ago either when, having tired of my dependence on the Antibuse pills, I gave them up only to find myself LA bound on a bender with the boys again. It hadn't happened often of late, but even once was one time too many.

The first was within days of arriving in San José after leaving Edinburgh. I shouldn't have needed to drink: there were no excuses. Angela and I were fine; the publishers were happy with the first chapters of the book. The football in my last few games with Hibs was no better nor any worse than those games that had gone before, even if I had been booked in my last but one game, against Aberdeen, and reported to the Scottish FA. The booking resulted from one of those instantaneous remarks to a referee which get your name in his little black book but never look likely to damage life or limb, as one of the Aberdeen players said to me at the time. Being reported to the Scottish FA followed a post-match flare-up with the Aberdeen captain, Willie Miller, as we were going down the tunnel to the dressing-room. Naturally enough, I suppose, he was upset because we'd held them to a draw, so interfering with their bid to win the Scottish Championship, and he was especially sore at me for protecting our point from the draw by passing the ball back to the goalkeeper rather than risk losing possession. He said something like 'Thought you were supposed to be able to play a bit', to which I retorted 'Yeah, well it's cost you the League', and next thing we're in a bit of a tussle with the other players pulling us apart. The whole thing was over in a moment, but it was enough for the referee to report me and for *The Times* to declare a 'Bad-tempered end to Best's career at Hibs'.

That was mid-week. I played my last game on the Saturday, against Dundee United, and then it was off to San Francisco where I was met and driven the forty or so miles to San José and booked into a hotel. An apartment and car had been promised, but these were still being arranged and would be ready by the time Angela, who was sorting out the Edinburgh and London flats, joined me in America. There were no hassles, I was under no pressure. There was to be a press conference on Thursday, training on Friday, and no game until the following weekend. So what happens? First thing Thursday morning I'm on a flight to Los Angeles to embark on three days' drinking before returning to San José on Sunday.

The next time was even more crazy; about a month later when I'd gone down to Los Angeles ahead of the team for the match against the California Surf at Anaheim. My reasons for doing so were legitimate enough. I had business to attend to, but I also did some drinking while I was there. Not a lot, though, and I was certainly fit to play when I went across to the bar on Sunday morning to meet Bobby, who was to drive me over to Anaheim. A few minutes, he requested, to sort out a few things, and while he was doing them I walked out of the bar and disappeared for several hours. I still don't know why I did it. Again there were no pressures on me, except perhaps those of playing in a mediocre side. I just remember thinking that I didn't want to play, knowing I'd been drinking, and so I sloped off down the beach with a six-pack and found a nice clean drum to lean against. As the sun grew hotter I stripped off my T-shirt, opened another can of beer, and in time remembered another morning when I'd sat on a beach in the sun thinking I'd pay someone twenty dollars for a beer. That was Malibu, in September '79; a very desperate time.

It was three months before then that Angela had walked out of our Fort Lauderdale home to return to work for Cher in Los Angeles. Perhaps I should have followed her, but I hadn't immediately, not knowing within myself whether I wanted to stay on in Florida or not;

182

hoping, too, that the situation with the Strikers might improve. But sober I knew the impasse with Ron Newman could never be overcome and finally I went to the owners to tell them we were all wasting our time. I couldn't play for a coach I didn't respect and he didn't seem to want me in his team. They said how much they respected my views but they retained confidence in the coach. Only till the end of the season, it would have seemed. They had a new coach for 1980 and Ron Newman was back with an ASL club.

By the time I left Fort Lauderdale my football for the season was over. Even if I'd wanted one it was too late for a trade. Life offered nothing better than a return ticket to Hermosa Beach, Bestie's and booze. For a while I thought it was all I wanted, and I didn't miss Angela as I slipped into the old routine of drinking around the bars with the boys till two or three every morning, kipping on couches or wherever I could lay my head, letting one day run into the next. It was Manchester with sunshine and sand. Until the times I wanted Angela and couldn't get near her. Her friends made sure of that, for which I'd abuse them, have a few more beers and go down on the beach. The girls were young, West Coast and willing for anything that relieved the boredom of life. But coke-sniffing twelve-year-olds going on twenty weren't what I wanted. I wanted and needed Angela.

Eventually one evening she came down to Bestie's and asked if we could go somewhere quiet to talk. I didn't want that: I knew what she was going to say. I didn't want her leaving me. Seeing her pale and uncertain I wanted her with me. More to the point I wanted to be with her. But she was no longer sure whether she could live with me. I was making her ill, she said. Building up her hopes and then dashing them as if without reason. I destroyed everything good as soon as we managed to get something going. There was more to life, she told me, than being a punchbag for my mixed-up emotions.

'How about if I go to England for a while?' I pleaded. 'Stay with your parents. At least I'll be somewhere that's close to home life. You know they'll take care of me and I'll get myself straightened out.'

Yet even as I said it I knew I was kidding myself; making a pretence of sorting myself out but never intending to go somewhere for proper help. Why should I? I didn't think I had a problem. I just liked a few drinks with the boys from time to time. Couldn't she understand that?

'All right', she agreed in the end. 'If you do that I'll stay here and come home in a month or so when I know you've sorted yourself out.'

But I couldn't live through the days, being so far away from her. I tried to do some writing, to get out of my head the thoughts that rushed around, but three, four, five times a day I'd be on the phone to her at a pound or more a minute. It was madness, but life without her was hell and life with me was impossible for her. A couple of days in Manchester seeing the old crowd did nothing to ease the need for her. Not that anyone could see it, for on the surface I was the same cool self as the unconcerned kid who made his début for Manchester United one far-away afternoon. Inside I was in torment; fearful of the future, uncertain of the present, not knowing what she was doing or whom she might be with. And when she told me she wouldn't be returning to England after all, that she wasn't sure if she could face the whole situation again, that did it. I told her I'd come back to see her, packed my bag, took the train to London and caught the first available flight to Los Angeles.

Mike McLoughlin, who'd worked for me at Slack's and was now working at Bestie's, met me at the airport and that was bad news, for Angela had promised to. She'd been held up, Mike said; she'd call me later at the bar. But as the afternoon passed into evening the phone calls were never for me. Well, if she wouldn't phone me, I could always phone her. Cher's first, but no, she wasn't there. Nor did they know where she was. She'd left the house at lunchtime and no-one knew when she'd be back. Josephine next; still no luck. Everywhere I tried it was the same old story. Angela had either left town or her friends were playing the old 'protect Angie from that footballer' game.

A trip around the bars took me through the next day, and still no phone call. 'We don't know if she's coming here today' was all I got from Cher's. Angry, frustrated, I now experienced another emotion: jealousy. If she's not down on the beach at Malibu with Cher, and she's not staying with a girlfriend, where is she staying? Has she found another man? Anger becomes fury and by midnight, after an afternoon and evening of drinking, I'm ready to scour LA for her. It didn't matter that I had no car, I'd borrow one. Except that I was so drunk no-one would trust me with his.

Eventually, about one in the morning, a couple of fellows and a girl said they'd drive me up to Malibu. As good a way as any to pass an hour or two, they said. Not that I've any idea how we're going to get into the Colony once we're there. It's one of those exclusive places where the entrance is guarded and you don't get past the guard unless you're known or cleared by a resident. Well to hell with that, I thought. We'd not driven all that way for nothing and so, as the guard came over to us, I stuck my head out the window and shouted 'All right? How's it going tonight?' as if we were big buddies and he'd be thinking himself a fool if he didn't recognise me. It was enough; we were in. I had an address in my pocket and eventually we found it.

'Some place', said the girl, but then so were most of them around there. Barbra Streisand had a place just over the road from Cher's, I'd been told; Neil Diamond lived just up the road and Jimmy Caan had a house somewhere near.

'You can just leave me here', I said to them, but they didn't seem to mind sitting through till dawn, when they had to think about getting back to Hermosa Beach for work. I gave the driver some dollars for the gas, the girl wished me luck, and I stood in the early morning sunshine watching the car disappear. Now that it's light I'm not even sure if I've got the right house or not – for all that there's a car the same colour as one of Cher's in the drive. I can't knock on the door and ask, because if it's the wrong house someone might get suspicious and have a patrol out looking for me. All I can do, I thought, is wait about until Angela shows or until I see someone I recognise.

Soon maids and gardeners began arriving for work and I decided it was time to move about. The Malibu Colony is not the place to sit on the sidewalk, unshaven and wearing the same jeans and jacket you left London in several days earlier; not after the Manson murders it isn't. You could end up as breakfast for a Doberman. Moreover it was getting too hot for staying in one place now that the sun was streaming down the canyons. If I moved about the chances were that anyone seeing me would take me for a Mexican gardener, although curiously I saw few people as I wandered along walkways and across drives before finding myself on the beach. Nor did anyone disturb me as I sat at the water's edge and watched the surf roll in and retreat. Eventually, though, it got too hot, my head was throbbing, and I desperately needed a drink. Anything, but where to find it? I know I can't leave the Colony, which makes the breakfast house further on up the road even more frustrating. A phone, too. Coffee and a phone. My two prime needs, and at last I found a little place that provided both. Several coffees later, and a glance through the sports pages of the *Times,* I phoned Cher's. 'Angela's not here yet', the maid offered. 'She didn't stay here last night.'

185

Every time I hear that it makes me worse; also makes me more convinced than ever that I'm not leaving until I've spoken to her. For now, as well as the jealousy, there's a fear that if she's gone off with someone else I won't be able to get her back.

By eleven I've staked out a place within view of the road but out of sight of anyone approaching. I don't want her driving off the moment she sees me. I don't know what I look like by now but I can imagine. The heat and humidity have made me sweaty, smelly and very much aware that I haven't had a proper night's sleep since leaving England. My eyes close, then my head drops and I jerk awake to see a black Jeep come through the gate and turn off towards the bank several hundred yards away. That's her, I tell myself, and leap to my feet to run like mad to the car park, only to realise then that it's not her Jeep at all. Back I walk to my hiding-place, the sweat pouring off me, my clothes stinking. I'd give anything for a beer and a shower. Anything.

An hour passes, and then, stopping at the gate to talk to the guard, a blonde head leaning from a black Jeep. This must be her. The Jeep moves forward slowly, its paintwork shimmering in a haze of heat, and picks up speed until, when it's no more than ten yards away, I jump out into the middle of the road. God knows what Angela must have thought at that moment: all I could see was the shock and anger on her face as she slammed on the brakes and wrestled the Jeep sideways to avoid me. This was it; the showdown. I stormed towards the Jeep, ready to throw her out, grab the keys and drive off back to the Beach. Who did she think she was, keeping me sitting about all morning waiting in the sun for her? But as I reached the Jeep all the angry words stuck in my throat. I'd never seen someone I loved look so pale and ill. Gone were the California tan and the lively eyes: she looked beaten. I just stood there looking at her while she stared blankly at me.

Then the frustrations, fears and anger overtook the shock and the accusations and demands poured forth, ignoring her pleas for me to listen. I didn't want to listen. I was demanding answers: to know what she was doing, where she was sleeping, who she was living with, what she intended doing about us? And through it all came her answers: what her doctor had said; that I was killing her with my drinking and my moods; that she was staying with a friend of Cher; that yes, she'd talk if only I'd stop screaming at her for a moment. I stopped, until I saw that she wasn't wearing her wedding ring and a

186

fresh torrent of madness broke forth.

'George', she said when I'd calmed down again. 'If you want to talk we've got to talk. Not scream at each other. If you don't stop I'll drive on and have them throw you out. God, just look at you. You don't know what you're doing and saying half the time.'

'Okay', I said, shaking now that I'd spewed out all my anger and had nothing left but fear and self-pity. 'Where do you want to talk?'

'Over there will do', she said, pointing to a stretch of wasteland. 'Just let me turn round and we'll sit and talk.'

I dumbly nodded my agreement and she slowly drove up the road away from me. I watched her go and it suddenly dawned on me. She was driving away. I'd let her go. 'You stupid bastard, Best', I thought to myself. 'You've sat up here all night and now you're no better off. You can't even drive home.' Perhaps she was going to U-turn at the traffic lights, but no. She went straight across and I knew then that was it. I'd lost her. I'd lost my temper and I'd lost her. I'd blown it. I sat down on the curb, rested my head on my hands and looked up the road in the direction she'd taken. A lifetime passed in a minute and there, coming along the other side of the road, was the black Jeep. She'd changed her mind. She was prepared to talk, even though she knew talking would make her take me back again. She also took me back to Cher's to clean up; a beautiful house on the beach I'd never seen before. All the time I'd been waiting outside the wrong house.

Somehow, after that, the good times made the bad times worthwhile. Edinburgh brought us closer together and showed that the crazy drinking bouts could be prevented; that the situation wasn't entirely hopeless. What happened when I moved to San José proved to me that I wasn't yet strong enough to survive without help. I could go for weeks without the pills, sit outside a delicatessen with a few of the Yugoslav boys after training and enjoy a beer; sometimes two but never more. Then, suddenly, something in my head would snap, I'd start feeling depressed, and I'd want to drink. Angela could read the signs now, but even then it wasn't easy to forestall me before I set off on another bout.

However, it wasn't just Angela trying on her own. I wanted life to be different, too. We had so much going for us; life was working out. True, the football with San José in 1980 brought no trophies and very few wins, but no-one had promised immediate success. The future, though, held promise in an area where the people were open and friendly and, having no other professional sport in the town, identified with their soccer team. Not that the Earthquakes received any special treatment; far from it. We shared our stadium with the university football team; we trained at a local junior college at the foothills on one side of the valley in which San José sprawls; a working town for working people. It wasn't a town for superstars but I felt the people there appreciated me – wanted me to belong – and maybe that's why I felt at home there. For it would be home. The offer of a two-year contract in September 1980 ensured there'd be no more split seasons: San José wanted me for the winter indoor season as well as for the NASL summer season. In addition to playing, I'd be able to hold coaching clinics for kids – a rewarding, satisfying occupation in the States – and there were television and business openings to consider. I'd done some television work during the season and found, for someone who has trouble talking to strangers, that the words came naturally when I was discussing football. It wasn't Manchester United, it could never be that, but it was football and I could still give people pleasure through football, whether playing, coaching or broadcasting. America was offering me a new life as it had for generations of wild Irishmen, and if it had taken me thirty-four years to reach some kind of maturity and stability, so what. At least I'd attained it and might still come out on the winning side.

I don't know that I'll never break away and lose myself in drink again. I can promise not to but I'll never be sure. All I can do is go from one day to the next and hope. For those around me it's a strain, I know that. I don't want to hurt any of them: Angela, who has placed so much faith and trust in me; Milan Mandaric, the owner and John Carbray, general manager, of the Earthquakes, who've given me their confidence and a place in their town. The opportunities are there to be taken. We've found a lovely house, Angela is expecting our first child, and for the first time in so many years I'm part of a family again. Like the little lad who sat on the stairs in Donard Street watching the silent television and straining his ears for the first sound of his grandfather stirring. The promises might prove empty, but the hope remains eternal.

A diver's splash breaks the quiet and disturbs the water. The sun is higher now, mid-morning, and I put the pen and pad down to watch the girl drag herself from the pool, shake the water from her sun-bleached hair and throw her bronzed body on to a sun-bed. California brown. My child should grow like that. Loose-limbed, healthy and confident. It's not too much to ask, and I'm asking it only of myself. I pull on my T-shirt, pick up my pen, pad and keys and walk upstairs to the apartment we leave in a week to move into our new house. Angela's there, sitting at the table, surrounded by her vitamin pills, her correspondence and six months of pregnancy.

'How about some tea then?' I ask, dropping the pad on the table.

'Get it yourself, you lazy bugger!' but there's laughter in the way she says it.

'Lazy!' I exclaim, walking through to the kitchen. 'I've only finished my bloody book, haven't I?'

'Bestie!' comes the squeal from the other room. Then, mocking: 'Now all we have to do is sell the film rights.'

'Oh aye, just like that', I say from the doorway. 'Anyway, I've decided who's got your part and it's not you.'

'Don't tell me', she says. 'Brigitte Bardot.'

'Very smart. Well, you'll never guess who's playing me?'

'Surprise me', she says, turning to face me.

'Willie Nelson.'

'Willie Nelson! He's a cowboy singer.'

'That's right', I tell her, turning back into the kitchen. ''Cause that's just what I am. A Belfast cowboy. You know what he is? A loony-man.'

*　　　　*　　　　*

That should have been the end but it wasn't. The Belfast Cowboy blew it. Just when everything was looking so good he went on a bender that carried through days and nights, got himself arrested for driving under the influence and spent what was left of the night in the local sheriff's lock-up. His wife could have gone down to bail him out, but with a two-week-old baby to care for she had enough on her hands. She let him stay there. To think through what he'd done and to realise once and for all that he couldn't do it on his own. He was an alcoholic.

I was an alcoholic. Not in the sense that I needed a drink every day, but in the sense that my life was being governed by alcohol. I'd thought my drinking was something I could regard as a challenge – beating that third defender or walking the ball round the goalkeeper. I got it wrong; it wasn't like that at all. If I thought it was just another game, I had to realise I was playing with my life. Every time I took a drink I was slowly but surely damaging my body and my brain. I didn't just have a drink problem, I had an illness, and that illness was called alcoholism. As I would come to learn, it is something you can rarely overcome on your own. That's a statistical fact.

Through John Carbray and the Earthquakes I was put in touch with an organisation called Starting Point, and in early March 1981 I asked to be admitted to a hospital near San Francisco to begin my rehabilitation. I was going to stand in front of a mirror and learn about myself. Even more important I would have to reveal myself to others – fellow alcoholics; confessing things I had never revealed except in the preceding pages. And even in this book I can see the symptoms of my disease. Looking back to the Manchester United days, for example – or Fulham or Fort Lauderdale – I was using outside influences or situations as self-justification for my drinking. When I couldn't change these situations or 'conditions' – manager's or coach's methods, other players, my own form, business problems – to my own satisfaction, I would resort to drink. It never occurred to me to change myself to meet the conditions. Like so many alcoholics I was too self-centred. Which is not to say my assessment of those situations is wrong. Far from it. What was wrong was using them as an excuse for drinking.

So why drink when everything looked so good? As it did early this year, both professionally and personally. Playing in the toughest division of the North American indoor soccer league we missed the play-offs only on goal difference; a very satisfying achievement after the disappointments of the 1980 outdoor season and, we hoped, a promise of better things for the 1981 NASL season. Equally satisfying was that we drew good crowds, the American public showing great enthusiasm for the non-stop six-a-side game with its mixture of subtle skills and close physical contact. I had also done the first of many planned coaching clinics, with a hundred youngsters over a four-day period, and this was both enjoyable and successful.

On a personal level we had a lovely house which Angela was decorating with taste and flair; we had a car and a Jeep in the garage; we were both looking forward to the birth of the baby. I attended childbirth classes with Angela, and just a few minutes after seven

190

o'clock on the morning of Friday, 6 February – the anniversary of the Munich air disaster – I helped deliver Calum Milan Best, cutting the umbilical cord that tied him to his mother's womb and releasing him into the world. It was the greatest moment in my life.

Back home with Angela and Calum I delighted in doing all those things that fathers are supposed to do to help their wives with new-born babies. And then, with everything so wonderful, I began to drink again. There'd been beers before on nights out at the Hot-Pot, a local beer and wine bar where I went to play darts. But I'd been off the hard stuff and I really did think I had my drinking under control. Talk about a fool's paradise. I was simply going through the dry-drunk syndrome with my system biding time before it needed another shot of alcohol.

They re-ran *The Hustler* on television the other night – for the umpteenth time. But it's one of those movies you can see over and over again. It was a couple of days before my turn in the 'love seat', when you sit before a group of your peers, tell your story and are assessed by them. It's the crunch-point because there's no bull-shitting your way through it. There will be twenty to thirty fellow alcoholics in that room with you and everything you say they've either heard before or they've said themselves. It's the fifth of the Twelve Steps of Alcoholics Anonymous; 'Admitted to God, to ourselves, and to another human being the exact nature of our wrongs.' I was and I wasn't looking forward to it.

Anyway, there was a moment in *The Hustler* when George C. Scott tells Paul Newman that 'Talent isn't enough. You've got to have character too.' I didn't know which way to look. I felt that everyone in the room was looking at me. And then this big, bearded Hell's Angel whose track record made me look like a saint came across and laid his arm around my shoulder.

'You came in here on your own, man', he said. 'You've got character.'

I wanted to cry but I couldn't. Not in front of everybody. I had to wait two more days for that when they got me in the 'love seat'. I knew what I was going to say; so much of it was in my head from doing this book. And then I would be going home. My counsellor was really pleased with the progress I was making and thought two weeks, plus the after-care programme and the weekly AA meetings, would see me through.

So I told my story and they all saw through me. Twenty out of

191

twenty-seven said I appeared to minimise or cover up the effects of my problem; thirteen said I mixed with the group on a superficial level only. Putting up a front with a smile and being everybody's pal but never allowing myself to feel. Eleven said I was too concerned with less important matters, such as getting fit for the season (I'd go jogging daily with a couple of the doctors) and getting my knee to straighten for the first time since my cartilage operation in 1966. (I was thrilled about that, but having a good physio-man working on my knee wasn't why I was in hospital.)

You're not telling the whole story, they said. You're scared of what you're going to do when you stop playing and you won't admit it. You never mentioned your mother. Why? So she's dead. What did she die of? When did she die? You don't know. You've pushed her out of your mind. It's in my book. God damn it, man! No-one's read your book yet. That's just a way out. You haven't admitted it to yourself. You retreat. You're afraid to find the answers why. You pretend these things don't happen and it comes out some other way. Some people get ulcers, some develop high blood pressure and heart trouble. Your illness is alcoholism. You've been trying to con us.

I let the tears roll down my cheeks. They could see me cry, I didn't care. They were my family. They could put their arms around me to comfort me and I wouldn't feel embarrassed. I could hold hands with them at the end of the meeting and say, not just recite, the serenity prayer.

'God grant me the serenity to accept the things I cannot change, courage to change the things I can, and wisdom to know the difference. Thy will, not mine, be done.'

They didn't let me go home. No; they didn't have to let me because they couldn't stop me. It was up to me and I knew I wasn't yet ready to leave. I was still coming to terms with myself and it was going to take many years. Years to get the poison alcohol out of my system; years to learn everything about myself. You can't get rid of guilts, fears and inhibitions you've been hiding for ten or more years in just a few weeks. The time in hospital was only the starting point.

I think, as I try to assess my life, that I'll still come back to 1968, which is why this book begins there. It's where I wanted to start, though at the time it was intuition rather than self-knowledge that made me choose that moment. The end should have come halfway through this chapter but it didn't. Life, as I said at the beginning, rarely works out the way you plan it.

There was, some years ago, a song about me called 'Belfast Boy', sung by country singer Don Fardon. The backing track was called, I think, 'The Echoes of the Cheers', and the lines I remember went something like this. I think they're appropriate.

'With the echoes of the cheers
ringing loudly in my ears,
where do I go from here?'

Los Gatos
1981

The George Best File

Parents: Ann and Dick Best. **Sisters:** Carol, Barbara, Grace and Julia. **Brother:** Ian Busby. **Home:** Burren Way, Cregagh, Belfast. **Schools:** Nettlefield Primary, Grosvenor High and Lisnasharragh Intermediate.

1946
Born in Royal Maternity Hospital, Belfast, on *22 May*.

1961
Joined Manchester United FC as an amateur at fifteen following trials.
    Lived in digs with Mrs Mary Fullaway in Aycliffe Avenue, Chorlton-cum-Hardy.

1963
Signed professional forms on his seventeenth birthday.
Football League début: in 1-0 win over West Bromwich Albion at Old Trafford on *14 September*.
Began friendship with Malcolm Mooney, who was to become his business partner.
Scored first League goal: in 5-1 win over Burnley – his second League game – at Old Trafford on *28 December*. Became a regular member of the first team.

1964
FA Cup début: in 3-2 win over Southampton at The Dell on *4 January* (3rd round).
Scored first FA Cup goal: in 4-0 win over Barnsley at Oakwell Ground on *15 February* (5th round).
European début: in 4-1 win over Sporting Lisbon at Old Trafford on *26 February* (Cup-Winners' Cup quarter-final).
Début for Northern Ireland: in 3-2 win over Wales at Swansea on *15 April*.
Manchester United won FA Youth Cup on *30 April*.
Scored first goal in European club competition: in 6-1 win over Djurgaarden (Sweden) at Old Trafford on *27 October* (Fairs Cup first round).
Scored first goal for Northern Ireland: in 1-2 defeat by Switzerland at Lausanne on *14 November*.

1965
Kidnapped in *February* as part of Manchester College of Commerce students' rag stunt.
Manchester United won 1964-65 League Championship in *April*.

1966

Fined in *March* for speeding.

Hailed as 'El Beatle' following a brilliant display against Benfica in Lisbon on *9 March*.

Opened George Best boutique in *March;* ladies' section opened in *October*.

Third in Footballer of the Year poll in *April* behind team-mate Bobby Charlton and George Cohen of Fulham. Later that month, he entered St Joseph's Hospital, Manchester, for a cartilage operation on his right knee.

1967

Manchester United won 1966-67 League Championship in *May*.

Fined £10 and licence endorsed in *August* for driving without due care and attention, having knocked down a woman who suffered a fractured pelvis.

Opened Edwardia boutique in *September* with Manchester City player Mike Summerbee.

Named in *December* as Irish Footballer of the Year, and as Texaco Sportstar of the Year.

1968

Escaped injury in *January* when his car was involved in an accident.

Signed three-year contract in *February* to model menswear for Great Universal Stores' catalogue – the George Best Collection.

Named in *May* as Footballer of the Year.

Manchester United won the European Cup by beating Benfica 4-1 at Wembley on *29 May*.

Banned from driving for six months and fined £25 in *July* as a result of an early morning accident at Crumpsall in December 1967.

Bought out Mike Summerbee's interest in their boutique in *August*.

Sent off for the first time in his career: on *16 October* in the second leg of the World Club Championship match v Estudiantes (Argentina) at Old Trafford for fighting with Hugo Medina, also sent off. United lost 1-2 on aggregate, having lost the first leg 0-1 and drawing the second 1-1.

Named in *December* as European Footballer of the Year.

1969

Voted third best-looking player in the Football League.

Met Eva Haraldsted while on tour of Denmark with Manchester United in *August*. She asked for his autograph – for her boyfriend – and he traced her through a newspaper appeal for his 'Danish dream girl'. She later joined him in Manchester.

Opened George Best Rogue boutique in *September*.

Reported in *November* that his 'engagement' to Eva Haraldsted is 'off'.

Sued for breach of promise in *December* by Eva Haraldsted.

Bought third share of a race-horse in *December* with trainer Ian Walker and Everton footballer Alan Ball.

Named in *December* as Sportsman of the Year in *The Daily Telegraph* national poll and third in the *Daily Express* poll.

1970

Suspended for four weeks and fined £100 on *2 January* for bringing the game into disrepute – knocking the ball out of referee Jack Taylor's hands after the Manchester City v Manchester United League Cup semi-final at Maine Road in December. Later offered £1,000 per week to appear in cabaret during his term of suspension.

Scored six goals in his first match after suspension: in 8-2 win over Northampton Town in FA Cup 5th round on *7 February*. Described as 'fast, cool, devastating and destroying'.

Guest of Prime Minister Harold Wilson at No. 10 Downing Street on *2 March*.

Sent off for throwing mud and spitting at referee Eric Jennings in the Northern Ireland v Scotland international in Belfast on *18 April*. Later cleared when the International Committee 'could not entirely accept the referee's report' and took the view that Best spat at the ground and 'not at the official'.

Breach of promise writ by Eva Haraldsted settled out of court in *April*.

Defence witness for Paddy Crerand on *23 April* after claims by brothers Todd for damages following an incident outside Blinkers nightclub in January. Crerand was acquitted.

Moved into new £30,000 house in Bramhall, Cheshire, in *November*.

Received third booking of the year on *14 November* for jostling the referee in match v Nottingham Forest at the City Ground.

Scored 100th League goal: in 2-2 draw v Tottenham Hotspur at White Hart Lane on *5 December* before a crowd of 55,693.

Received fourth booking of the year on *12 December* after a tackle in which Manchester City defender Glyn Pardoe suffered a double fracture of the right leg during the local derby at Old Trafford.

Fined £15 and licence endorsed in *December* for three speeding offences; fined £6 for failing to produce driving licence and insurance documents.

Sir Matt Busby resumed as manager of Manchester United on *28 December* after Wilf McGuinness was demoted to Reserves' team manager.

1971

Fined a record £250 and given a six weeks suspended sentence by FA Disciplinary Committee on *4 January* for three bookings. He was ninety minutes late for the hearing.

Dropped from Manchester United team to play Chelsea at Stamford Bridge on *9 January*. Spent weekend with Irish actress Sinead Cusack.

Suspended for two weeks, plus two weeks loss of pay, by Manchester United on *10 January* for missing training and failing to report for a match.

Arthur Lewis, MP for West Ham North, said on *14 January* that he would ask questions in the House of Commons why police and police vehicles were used to assist George Best to 'escape' from the media siege of Sinead Cusack's flat.

George Best Enterprises Ltd taken over by the Lincroft Group on *17 January*.

Cleared on *8 February* of any blame for the injury to Glyn Pardoe after an appeal by Manchester United to the FA Commission.

Set off on *18 August* in match v Chelsea at Stamford Bridge for arguing with team-mate Willie Morgan.

Cleared by FA Disciplinary Committee at a personal hearing on *13 September* for the sending-off in August. Players had not been warned that swearing at each other was a bookable offence.

Named in *October* as the Best-dressed Sportsman in the *Tailor and Cutter* awards.

Withdrew on *1 November* from Northern Ireland's European Championship match v Spain in Belfast on 10 November following threats on his life. The match was postponed until 16 February 1972 and played at Hull.

Subject of *This Is Your Life* television programme on *17 November*.

Named in *December* as Sportsman of the Year in *The Daily Telegraph* poll, and runner-up in BBC television's Sports Personality of the Year poll.

1972

Dropped from Manchester United team to play Wolverhampton Wanderers on *8 January* after missing training all week. United lost 1-3 at Old Trafford.

Ordered to move out of his Bramhall home by United manager Frank O'Farrell on *10 January* and to live in digs at Mrs Fullaway's until the end of the season. Also fined two weeks' wages and ordered to train morning and afternoon, in addition to forfeiting his day off for five weeks.

Scored the equaliser which led to Manchester United's 4-1 extra-time win over Southampton in the FA Cup 3rd round replay at Old Trafford on *19 January*, but in trouble for a televised two-handed V-sign at the press box.

Dropped by Northern Ireland on *19 May* after failing to report for training on 17 May.

Announced retirement from football on *20 May*, two days before his twenty-sixth birthday.

A change of heart. Met O'Farrell on *2 June* and it was agreed that he should play again in the coming season.

Reported three days early, on *10 July*, for pre-season training and agreed to live at Paddy Crerand's for the first four months of the season.

Suspended on *21 July* for two weeks for his failure to join Manchester United in Israel in May and for writing unauthorised newspaper articles.

Reprieved by Northern Ireland on *22 July*.

Broke a finger during training on *7 August* but still played v Ipswich at Old Trafford on 12 August.

Did not play for Manchester United in Bobby Charlton's testimonial match v Celtic on *18 September* before a crowd of 60,538 – the largest-ever for a testimonial.

Sent off on *18 October* five minutes before the end of the Bulgaria v Northern Ireland World Cup match in Sofia for kicking an opponent. He had earlier been booked for dissent.

Returned to live at Mrs Fullaway's in *October*.

Suspended by FIFA on *15 November* for three World Cup matches following the sending-off in Sofia.

Fined by Manchester United on *22 November* for missing training.

198

Fined and dropped from Manchester United team on *29 November* after missing training the previous day.

Incident on *29 November* at Reubens nightclub involving Miss Stefanja (Stevie) Sloniecki, a twenty-year-old waitress. Later accused of causing actual bodily harm.

Took possession of a white Rolls Royce Silver Cloud, valued at £11,000, on *1 December*.

Transfer listed by Manchester United on *5 December* and suspended for two weeks.

Name removed from George Best's Edwardia boutique on *13 December*.

Manchester United chairman Louis Edwards announced on *15 December* that George Best would resume training. It was assumed that he was now off the transfer list.

Announced his retirement in a letter to the United board of directors on *19 December*. At that same meeting, the board dismissed manager Frank O'Farrell, coach Malcolm Musgrove and chief scout John Aston.

Sold his house in Bramhall, in *December*, to Pat O'Dwyer, a former trench-digger.

1973

Blackpool waxworks melted down their figure of Best in *January* to make one of the Manchester City player, Rodney Marsh. Also that month he sold his Rolls Royce after vandals had done damage estimated at £1,000.

Found guilty on *11 January* of causing actual bodily harm to Stevie Sloniecki; ordered to pay £25 damages and £75 costs and given a conditional discharge for twelve months.

Flew to Toronto on *16 January;* offered $30,000 to play in twelve games for the World Indoor Soccer League.

Returned to Manchester on *11 February* after holidaying in Los Angeles, Palm Springs and Acapulco.

Lincroft Group paid Best £6,000 in *March* for his minority interest in the company as compensation for loss of office.

New York Cosmos given permission in *April* by Manchester United to negotiate terms with Best.

Admitted to Ancoats Hospital, Manchester, on *7 May* following a thrombosis in Marbella, Spain.

Carl Boyce, a student, took out a private summons in *June* alleging assault and battery during an altercation with Best in Bridge Street, Manchester. The magistrate refused to serve the summons.

Reported for training at Old Trafford on *10 September*.

Played for 45 minutes in Eusebio's testimonial match in Lisbon on *25 September*.

First game for Manchester United since comeback: in 1-0 win over Birmingham City at Old Trafford on *20 October*.

Recalled for Northern Ireland on *6 November,* after three League games, for the World Cup match v Portugal in Lisbon on *14 November*.

Bought Club del Sol in Bootle Street, Manchester, in *November* with Malcolm Wagner and Colin Burne. Re-opened as Slack Alice.

1974

Final appearance for Manchester United: in 0-3 defeat by Queen's Park Rangers at Loftus Road on *1 January*.

Missed training on *2 January* for the first time since September 1973.

Omitted from Manchester United's team for FA Cup 3rd round match v Plymouth Argyle at Old Trafford on *5 January*.

Suspended by Manchester United on *11 January* for failure to train and transfer listed.

Arrested in Manchester on *21 February:* charged at Marylebone Magistrates Court, London, with trespassing and stealing from Marjorie Wallace, between 18 and 20 February, a fur coat, passport, cheque book and other items. Released on £6,000 bail.

Cousin Gary Reid died on *25 February* eight days after being shot in Belfast.

Marjorie Wallace's passport and a medallion returned on *2 March* to the *Sunday People* newspaper. Cash and a tiara belonging to Miss Wallace were found in a telephone kiosk in London on *9 March*.

Further remanded on bail until 24 April following Marjorie Wallace's failure to appear in court on *27 March*.

Cleared of all charges on *24 April*. Marjorie Wallace again failed to appear in court.

Manchester United relegated to the Second Division on *27 April* after 36 years in the First Division, following a 0-1 defeat by Manchester City at Old Trafford. City's goal was scored by Denis Law and the match was abandoned five minutes before the end after an invasion of the pitch.

A question tabled in the House of Commons on *1 May* about the cost of the court case concerning George Best: £1,606 of public money was spent.

Played in *May* and *June* for the Jewish Guild in South Africa.

Played for Southern League club Dunstable Town in 3-2 win over Manchester United Reserves on *5 August*. Mobbed by fans as he left the field.

Dunstable Town's match on *12 August* delayed by one hour when Best's car broke down. He arrived for his second game with the club with a police escort.

Won on *24 September,* while rolling dice in a Manchester casino, an estimated £26,000 with Colin Burne during a run of one hour forty minutes without throwing a losing roll.

Bought lease of Waldorf Hotel on *25 September* with Malcolm Wagner and Colin Burne.

Malcolm Mooney killed in a road accident on *13 November*.

Played in Manchester City manager Tony Book's testimonial match at Maine Road on *27 November*.

Waxwork of George Best removed from Madame Tussaud's and his fan club disbanded in *December*.

1975

Fined £40 and banned for a year in *March* for driving with excess alcohol and failing to stop at lights in Manchester.

Best: an intimate biography by Michael Parkinson published in *March;* banned in South Africa in *May*.

Suspended on *7 November* from playing in any country under the jurisdiction of FIFA.

Released from contract by Manchester United on *8 November* and the FIFA ban was automatically lifted.

Signed for Fourth Division club Stockport County on *10 November* for a month: 8,000 attended a friendly match between Stockport v Stoke City of the First Division and saw Best score in a 1-1 draw.

Scored twice in Peter Osgood's testimonial match at Stamford Bridge on *24 November*. Also played in Paddy Crerand's testimonial at Old Trafford that month.

Scored twice in his first League game for Stockport County on *28 November*: a 3-2 win over Swansea City. Stockport, 20th in the Fourth Division, attracted a crowd of 9,220 – three times their average gate for the 1975-76 season.

Reported on *4 December* that Chelsea were interested in signing Best on a match-fee basis linked to attendances. Stockport were said to have offered him £300 per game, with no obligation to train or play away matches.

Signed in *December* to play in the North American Soccer League for Los Angeles Aztecs. On *28 December* appeared for Cork Celtic in the League of Ireland Championship.

1976

Dismissed by Cork Celtic on *29 January* for 'lack of enthusiasm' after three games for the club, despite attracting crowds. He was reputed to have received £600 per match.

Arrived in Los Angeles on *20 February* to play for the Aztecs.

Signed contract on *11 August* to play for Fulham. The Second Division club also signed Rodney Marsh from Tampa Bay Rowdies in a bid to improve attendances and win promotion.

Delay over registration for Fulham likely following a statement by Football League secretary Alan Hardaker on *23 August*: 'As far as we are concerned, George Best doesn't exist in this country.' He was eventually registered on *2 September*, the registration to be reviewed on 31 December.

Scored after just 71 seconds in a sensational début for Fulham on *4 September*: in 1-0 win over Bristol Rovers at Craven Cottage before a crowd of 21,127 – double the previous season's average gate. Three days later, 16,467 – almost three times the average gate at the London Road Ground – saw Peterborough United beaten 2-1 by Fulham in a League Cup replay. Best scored one of the goals.

Sent off on *2 October* at Southampton for 'using foul and abusive language' while disputing a free-kick decision.

Played for Northern Ireland on *13 October* in 2-2 draw with The Netherlands in Rotterdam.

Doubts over Best's registration arose on *31 December* when Fulham asked the Football League to sanction it. It appeared that conditions requested by the League would prevent him leaving Fulham before the end of the season.

201

1977

Charged on *4 January* with bringing the game into disrepute by making a 'gesture' at referee John Homewood in the tunnel following the Chelsea v Fulham match at Stamford Bridge on 27 December.

Statement by Alan Hardaker on *6 January* implied that there was 'a secret agreement' between Fulham and 'an American club' for Best to return to the United States before the end of the English season.

Fined £75 on *31 January* for bringing the game into disrepute on 27 December.

Injured in 4.00 a.m. car accident in Knightsbridge, London, on *24 February*. Was out of football until 2 April.

Returned to Los Angeles after playing until the end of the season, *14 May*, for Fulham.

Back in England on *30 August* but could not play for Fulham unless they paid compensation to Los Angeles Aztecs.

Cleared by FIFA on *1 September*, at FA's request, so that he could play for Fulham v Blackburn Rovers on 3 September. John Chaffetz, co-owner of Los Angeles Aztecs, arrived in London to discuss the matter of compensation with Fulham.

Flew back to Los Angeles on *8 September* with Chaffetz. It was alleged that Fulham owed Best £10,000, though the club denied this.

Returned to London on *18 September* and resumed playing for Fulham.

Established a record on *1 October* when he appeared for Fulham v Crystal Palace at Selhurst Park: he had played in all four home countries in ten days – for Northern Ireland v Iceland in Belfast, and v Cardiff (Wales) and St Mirren (Scotland) for Fulham. During the match, Crystal Palace defender Ian Evans's leg was broken in two places following a tackle by Best.

Final Football League appearance: for Fulham in 0-2 defeat by Stoke City at the Victoria Ground on *12 November*.

Suspended by Fulham on *29 November* for not attending training sessions. He had already returned to Los Angeles.

1978

Married Angela Macdonald Janes in Las Vegas on *24 January*.

Suspended by Los Angeles Aztecs in *May* for missing training.

Traded from Los Angeles Aztecs to Fort Lauderdale Strikers in *June*. Scored twice on début for the Strikers v New York Cosmos.

Sent off for fighting in *July* in match v Toronto Metros.

Banned by FIFA on *11 October* – at the request of the FA – from playing anywhere in the world until the dispute with Fulham was settled.

Mrs Ann Best found dead in her Belfast home on *12 October*.

1979

High Court in London endorsed the FIFA ban on *26 March*. Two days later, on *28 March*, FIFA themselves lifted the ban so that Best might play for the Fort Lauderdale Strikers.

Suspended by Fort Lauderdale Strikers in *July* for missing training and matches.

Refused a testimonial by Manchester United in *October*.

Signed for Scottish Premier Division club Hibernian on *16 November*. They were said to have paid Fulham £50,000 and to be paying Best £2,500 per game.

Scored in first game for Hibernian: a 1-2 defeat on *24 November* away to St Mirren, whose usual gate was doubled.

Failed to appear for Hibernian's away match v Morton on *15 December*.

1980

Suspended by Hibernian on *11 February* after failing to appear for the home game v Morton on *9 February*.

Dismissed by Hibernian on *17 February* for failing to be fit for their Scottish Cup 4th round match v Ayr United. Later admitted he had a 'drink problem'.

Re-engaged by Hibernian on *24 February*.

Signed on *13 April* to play for San José Earthquakes in the 1980 NASL season.

Failed to appear for San José Earthquakes' match v California Surf on *1 June*.

Signed two-year contract with San José Earthquakes in *September*.

Bought house in Los Gatos, California, in *November*.

1981

Son, Calum Milan Best, born at Good Samaritan Hospital, San José on *6 February*.

Entered Vesper Hospital, Hayward, on *2 March* to commence treatment for alcoholism; discharged on *20 March*.

International Career

For Northern Ireland

Date	Venue	Opponents	Result	Goals
1964				
15 April	Swansea	Wales	W 3-2	
29 April	Belfast	Uruguay	W 3-0	
3 October	Belfast	England	L 3-4	
14 October	Belfast	Switzerland	W 1-0	
14 November	Lausanne	Switzerland	L 1-2	1
25 November	Glasgow	Scotland	L 2-3	1
1965				
17 March	Belfast	Netherlands	W 2-1	
7 April	Rotterdam	Netherlands	D 0-0	
7 May	Belfast	Albania	W 4-1	1
2 October	Belfast	Scotland	W 3-2	
10 November	Wembley	England	L 1-2	
24 November	Tirana	Albania	D 1-1	
1966				
22 October	Belfast	England	L 0-2	
1967				
21 October	Belfast	Scotland	W 1-0	
1968				
23 October	Belfast	Turkey	W 4-1	1
1969				
3 May	Belfast	England	L 1-3	
6 May	Glasgow	Scotland	D 1-1	
10 May	Belfast	Wales	D 0-0	
10 September	Belfast	USSR	D 0-0	
1970				
18 April	Belfast	Scotland	L 0-1	
21 April	Wembley	England	L 1-3	1
25 April	Swansea	Wales	L 0-1	
11 November	Seville	Spain	L 0-3	

Date	Venue	Opponents	Result	Goals
1971				
3 February	Nicosia	Cyprus	W 3-0	1
21 April	Belfast	Cyprus	W 5-0	3
15 May	Belfast	England	L 0-1	
18 May	Glasgow	Scotland	W 1-0	
22 May	Belfast	Wales	W 1-0	
22 September	Moscow	USSR	L 0-1	
1972				
16 February	Hull	Spain	D 1-1	
18 October	Sofia	Bulgaria	L 0-3	
1973				
14 November	Lisbon	Portugal	D 1-1	
1976				
13 October	Rotterdam	Netherlands	D 2-2	
10 November	Liège	Belgium	L 0-2	
1977				
27 April	Cologne	West Germany	L 0-5	
21 September	Belfast	Iceland	W 2-0	
12 October	Belfast	Netherlands	L 0-1	

Total appearances for Northern Ireland: 37
Goals for Northern Ireland: 9

Other Representative Matches

Date	Venue	Match	Result	Goals
1969				
21 July	Cardiff	Rest of UK v Wales	W 1-0	
1972				
1 May	Hamburg	Rest of Europe v SV Hamburg *(Uwe Seeler's testimonial)*	W 7-3	1
1973				
25 September	Lisbon	Rest of World v Benfica *(Eusebio's testimonial)*	D 2-2	

Club Career

Clubs	Season	*League		*FA Cup		*League Cup		European competitions	
		App	Gls	App	Gls	App	Gls	App	Gls
Manchester	1963-64	17	4	7	2			2	0 CWC
United	1964-65	41	10	7	2			11	2 FC
	1965-66	31	9	5	3			6	4 EC
	1966-67	42	10	2	0				
	1967-68	41	28	2	1			9	3 EC
	1968-69	41	19	6	1			6	2 EC
	1969-70	37	15	7	6	8	2		
	1970-71	40	18	2	1	6	2		
	1971-72	40	18	7	5	6	3		
	1972-73	19	4			4	2		
	1973-74	12	2						
		361	137	45	21	24	9	34	11
Stockport Co.	1975-76	3	2						
Cork Celtic		3	0						
Fulham	1976-77	32	6	2	0	3	2		
	1977-78	10	2						
Hibernian	1979-80	13	3	3	0				
	1980-81	4	0			2	0		
		426	150	50	21	29	11	34	11

North American Soccer League

		App	Gls	Assists	Points
Los Angeles	1976	23	15	7	37
Aztecs	1977	20	11	18	40
	1978	11	1	0	2
Fort Lauder-		10	3	1	7
dale Strikers	1979	19	2	7	11
San José	1980	26	8	11	27
Earthquakes					
		109	40	44	

*Appearances for Hibernian in the Scottish League and Cups; for Cork Celtic in the League of Ireland Championship.
CWC = European Cup-Winners' Cup; FC = Fairs Cup; EC = European Cup